THE CIVIL WAR ERA

VOLUME TWO

A NEW NATION

EDITED BY
HAROLD HOLZER

FOREWORD BY
JAMES M. MCPHERSON

COBBLESTONE PUBLISHING, INC.
7 SCHOOL STREET
PETERBOROUGH, NH 03458

For my daughters, Remy and Meg,
the best examples of family history

Consultant: David Madden, Director, The U.S. Civil War Center

Copyedited by Barbara Jatkola

Design and page layout by C. Porter Designs, Fitzwilliam, New Hampshire

Photo research: Lisa Hill, Melanie Guleserian, Francelle Carapetyan

Interior illustrations by Edith L. Bingham

Printing and binding by D.B. Hess Company

Manufactured in the United States of America

ISBN 0-942389-16-6 (volume 1);

ISBN 0-942389-17-4 (volume 2)

Library of Congress Cataloging-in-Publication Data

The Civil War era / edited by Harold Holzer ; foreword by Ken Burns.
    p.   cm.
    Includes bibliographical references (p.   ) and index.
    Contents: v. 1. A house divided — v. 2. A new nation.
    ISBN 0-942389-16-6 (vol. 1). — ISBN 0-942389-17-4 (vol. 2)
    1. United States—History—Civil War, 1861–1865—Juvenile
literature. 2. United States—History—1849–1877—Juvenile
literature. [1. United States—History—Civil War, 1861–1865.
2. United States—History—1849–1877.] I. Holzer, Harold.
E468.C6244   1996
973.7—dc20
                                                    96-26361
                                                       CIP
                                                        AC

About the Cover

Storming Fort Wagner by Louis Kurz and Alexander Allison (1890) honors Colonel Robert Gould Shaw by capturing the moment when he lost his life on July 18, 1863, after he and the Fifty-fourth Massachusetts Colored Infantry he commanded attacked the fortress. In the end, the Fifty-fourth lost 272 of its 650 men (see page 116). Courtesy The Lincoln Museum, Fort Wayne, Indiana (negative #2183).

PROLOGUE

by Harold Holzer

*By the early nineteenth century, there were really
two different United States of Americas.
One was in the South and the other in the North.
Within a few generations, they were at war with each other.*

The America of the South depended almost totally on agriculture — particularly cotton and tobacco. It relied on a labor force comprising nearly four million human slaves, brought in chains from Africa and then bred here for hard work without pay. By 1860, as many as ten thousand white southerners each owned fifty slaves or more.

The other America, the America of the North, began to turn to manufacturing. More and more people lived in its bustling cities, not just on its farms. New immigrants arrived every week from Europe, bringing new skills and new ideas. Its workers were paid real wages.

Perhaps no one could have prevented these two Americas from one day waging war against each other. As Abraham Lincoln predicted when he ran for the U.S. Senate in 1858, "'A house divided against itself cannot stand.'" The "house" known as the United States was destined to fall.

"Now we are engaged in a great civil war," declared a worried Lincoln, by then president of only half the United States, when he gave his famous address at Gettysburg, Pennsylvania, in 1863. He admitted that he was not even certain that the nation as Americans had known it would "live." But he called for the bloody fight to continue — until America could enjoy "a new birth of freedom."

No war ever fought before or since has cost as many American lives as the Civil War. More than six hundred thousand northerners and southerners died from wounds or disease. And no war more completely changed the country for those men, women, and children who survived.

As one writer put it, before the Civil War people said, "The United States *are.*" After the Civil War, people said, "The United States *is.*" The war finally made America into one country. The two volumes that make up this set explain how this came to be. They explore every aspect of that terrible but fascinating time in U.S. history — a time that first split America in two, then brought it closer together as one.

Volume 1, "A House Divided," offers a picture of the young country created in the name of freedom — but only for some. Here is a land of opportunity for whites but a land of oppression for African Americans. This volume examines the issues that divided America and the leaders who came forward to speak for both the North and the South.

Volume 2, "A New Nation," recalls the bloodiest conflict our nation ever fought. Here are famous generals and ordinary soldiers alike — the warriors and writers, the politicians and people. Here is death on the battlefield and life on the home front. Here are two peoples fighting for the right to plan America's future, each side convinced that its cause is just. And here is a badly wounded nation, trying to put itself together again.

In the powerful words of Oliver Wendell Holmes, Jr., a young soldier who survived several battles and went on to become a justice of the U.S. Supreme Court, the Civil War was a time when all America was "touched with fire." This is the story of how that fire began, how it burned out of control, and how it was finally extinguished. It is the story of how we lived and died to become what we are today.

map by Jack Williams

CONTENTS

FOREWORD

by James M. McPherson

Someone once said that "all history is biography."

I have been a teacher of American history for more than thirty years. From that experience I have learned that the best way to interest students in the American past is to tell it as a story — or, more accurately, as a group of individual stories that fit together to form a grand narrative.

Most important, these must be stories about people — real people, not just names on a page. Someone once said that "all history is biography" — stories of men and women and boys and girls who rose above the concerns of everyday life to lead a nation or an army in war, to fight in the ranks, to save lives in a hospital, to crusade for civil rights, to establish schools for freed slaves, to invent the electric light or the airplane, or to do anything else that affected the lives of other people and shaped the course of history. These are the stories that have made the United States the nation it is today.

Not all history is written this way. Indeed, too often it is presented as a set of facts and figures, of statistical data requiring analysis, of theories about human behavior, of large generalizations about race, class, ethnicity, and gender — as if people could be put in one of these boxes and labeled for delivery. No wonder so many young people are turned off by history.

But this book will turn them on again. It tells the story of the Civil War — a series of dramatic and important events that transformed America, ensuring the survival of the United States as one nation, ending the institution of slavery, which had mocked American ideals of liberty, and creating the constitutional foundations of civil rights. It recounts the tremendous industrial growth of post–Civil War America and the new inventions that shaped our modern world, as well as the wave of settlers who filled up the western frontier at the tragic cost of taking the land and lives of the Native Americans who had lived there for thousands of years. This book weaves together the stories of hundreds of fascinating individuals to make a larger story of the decades from 1860 to 1900. These were among the most exciting years in American history. This book recaptures the excitement, the tragedies and triumphs, the failures and successes. No one who reads it will ever again be bored by history.

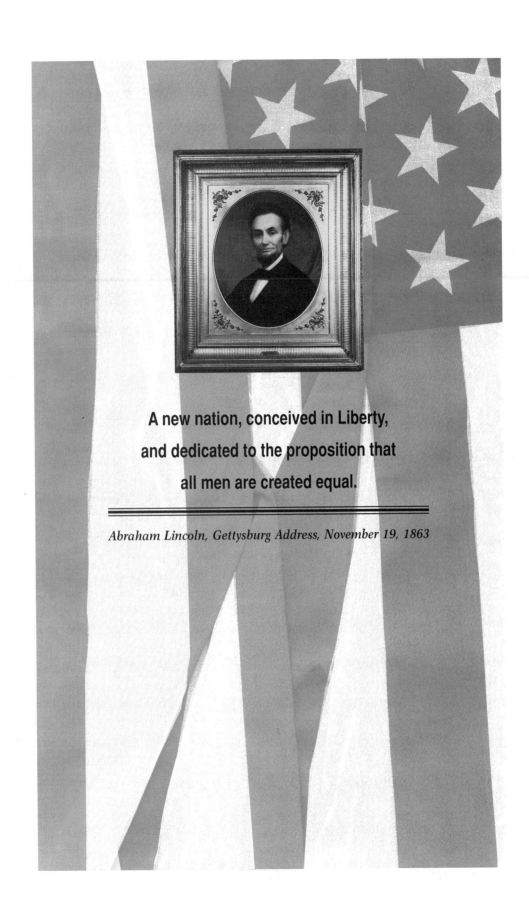

A new nation, conceived in Liberty,

and dedicated to the proposition that

all men are created equal.

Abraham Lincoln, Gettysburg Address, November 19, 1863

INTRODUCTION

by Harold Holzer

On a brutally hot day in July 1863, a nineteen-year-old woman busied herself making bread inside a small brick home in a tiny Pennsylvania town. It might have been an ordinary day in the life of an ordinary young woman. But this was no ordinary day and no ordinary town. This was Gettysburg, where the greatest and bloodiest battle of the Civil War was being fought.

Mary Virginia Wade was the youngster's name, but everyone called her Jennie. Born and raised in Gettysburg, Jennie lived in her sister's house on a quiet lane near the town cemetery, helping take care of her newborn niece. Suddenly, war exploded through the village. After three days of battle, soldiers were still fighting and dying along the town's narrow streets.

The family had sought shelter in their cellar when the battle began. Now, after a few days in hiding, Jennie ventured upstairs to begin baking. The family needed to eat, and if she baked enough bread, she could give some to the Union soldiers outside. They made Jennie feel safer.

From her kitchen, Jennie could hear the sound of gunshots and the constant, earthshaking roar of cannon firing from the hills above town. She heard the fearful cries of the wounded and dying and the mad gallop of horses on the streets outside. Jennie was frightened, but she kept herself busy. She had her bread to bake.

Then one more shot rang out. Jennie probably never heard it. The bullet whizzed through the window and struck Jennie Wade in the back. She fell instantly to the floor, dead.

When the battle outside finally came to a close, more than forty thousand soldiers lay dead or wounded, and another ten thousand were missing. Jennie Wade was the one and only civilian to die at Gettysburg.

But she was not the only young person caught up in the horrors of America's Civil War, nor the only one to sacrifice her life. In fact, there were thousands. And most were not accidental victims like Jennie. They were real fighters, just like adults.

No one knows for sure how many children served in the armies of the Civil War. After the war, the North admitted that at least ten thousand men under the age of eighteen had joined the Union army. More than seven hundred of them were under fifteen. Some were as young as ten years of age. The South had its share of youthful heroes as well. As many as one out of every five men who joined the Confederate army was nineteen or under, and those who enlisted in the navy were usually even younger.

Children had been going off to sea for years, serving as cabin boys and learning to be sailors. So it was not surprising that thousands more young men saw action in the Union and Confederate navies. Many served as "powder monkeys," carrying gunpowder to feed the cannon on board their warships. If their ships were attacked and sank, they often died with their older comrades. Historians do not know exactly how many children died at sea or on land during the four-year Civil War. We do know that many won medals for heroism.

Willie Johnston of Vermont was one of them. Willie was only eleven years old when he joined the Union army to fight alongside his father. Willie was made a drummer boy. This meant that he helped provide music to entertain older soldiers and beat out the rhythms of marches and charges. He also was required to clean campsites and cut soldiers' hair. During actual fighting, drummer boys like Willie stayed behind the lines, caring for the wounded and burying the dead. It was not pleasant work.

In 1862, Willie's regiment was sent to Virginia to capture the Confederate capital of Richmond. The invasion was destined to fail, but Willie bravely drummed through the bloody series of fights known as the Seven Days Battles. He was the only drummer boy in the entire army to bring his precious drum through those fierce battles undamaged. For this, President Abraham Lincoln awarded him the Medal of Honor. No younger man had ever won the decoration. Altogether, more than twenty other Union fighting boys would earn the Medal of Honor during the Civil War.

The Confederacy did not award combat medals of its own, but if it had, one would certainly have gone to thirteen-year-old John Sloan of Texas. He proved so fearless in an 1862 battle that his commanding general wrote an official report commending his bravery. John was severely wounded and, as a result, lost a leg. A Mississippi lad named George Larkin was wounded at the Battle of Shiloh before reaching the age of twelve.

Youngsters who served only as drummer boys also suffered wounds, or even death, during battle. At the Battle of Antietam, one Union drummer boy was struck down by a bullet, only to ask a nearby soldier to lift him to the soldier's shoulders so that he could continue "drumming us through." The story may have been exaggerated, but the tale of the wounded drummer boy of Antietam went on to inspire poets and artists alike.

Perhaps the most famous event of the Civil War involving young people was the Battle of New Market, Virginia, in May 1864. Facing an invasion by northern

HOW THE BATTLES WERE NAMED
by Harold Holzer

Civil War battles usually have two names: one given by the Union, the other by the Confederacy. For some reason, northerners named battles for the body of water nearest the fighting, while southerners named them for the closest town or village. Thus, the Union referred to the first big fight of the war as the Battle of Bull Run (a nearby creek). The Confederates called it the Battle of Manassas (a nearby town). Similarly, the important engagement of September 17, 1862, was the Battle of Antietam (a creek) to the North and the Battle of Sharpsburg (a village) to the South.

On rare occasions, both sides gave the same name to a battle. This is true for Gettysburg, for example, probably because there were no bodies of water nearby. Another example is Fredericksburg. On December 13, 1862, Union forces crossed the Rappahannock River from the town of Fredericksburg, Virginia, beginning a fierce one-day battle. Yet no one ever referred to it as the Battle of Rappahannock. It has always been known as the Battle of Fredericksburg.

Most of today's history books identify Civil War battles by their Union names. That is probably because history is written by those who win wars, not those who lose them.

soldiers, the Confederacy called for as many volunteers as possible to resist the attack. More than two hundred fifty eager young cadets from the nearby Virginia Military Institute quickly answered the call. All of them were between fifteen and eighteen years of age. None had ever carried a rifle into battle before. But when they came face to face with the enemy, they charged fearlessly through thick mud and seized a hill manned by much older Union troops. Nearly fifty of these youngsters were killed or wounded at New Market.

Youngsters who survived battles were emotionally scarred by their ordeal. They were exposed to constant death and saw horrible wounds firsthand. They may have been innocent before the war began, but they grew up all too quickly as the war went on. Not all the youngsters were innocent to begin with. City boys taught farm boys gambling and other bad habits in army camps. One young Pennsylvania drummer boy was even found to be a Confederate spy. No one would ever say whether he was given the same punishment suffered by adult spies — death by firing squad — but such may have been his fate.

Eventually, the war affected the lives of young women as well as young men. Girls accustomed to studying in school or learning homemaking skills from their mothers were asked to do their part for the war. They sewed countless pairs of socks and made clothes for their brothers and fathers in the army and navy. Sometimes they served alongside older women in crowded army hospitals. They, too, saw death and suffering up close. And even those girls not forced to do war work were deprived of the luxuries they had enjoyed before the war.

So it was that the Civil War changed the lives of hundreds of thousands of young northerners and southerners. The war robbed a whole generation of Americans of a prized possession: their childhood.

No one who reads about this time in our history should think of the Civil War as fought only by adults. Today it may be difficult to imagine armies using children in battle, but it was common in the Civil War. No one — no matter how young — was safe until the war ended. If they did not face enemy bullets, they faced the uncontrollable spread of disease, terrible hunger, or the loss of loved ones. That is why many writers have called the Civil War a "children's war."

The stories that fill this second volume of *The Civil War Era* explore the war as it was faced by people of all ages. Some are original material I have written especially for this book. A few are reprinted from a series of books by Discovery Enterprises, Ltd. The remaining are reprinted from various Cobblestone publications, especially *COBBLESTONE* magazine. We rediscover the horrors of the war and its devastating impact on North and South. Then we learn how our nation healed its wounds and formed a new society.

Some have said that the Civil War was America's coming of age. That means that before the war began, we were still a very young nation. When it was over, we had been made more mature by the bloodshed and devastation. We also had come at last to understand that African Americans were part of our society. They were finally free, but they faced years of struggle to achieve equal rights and are still fighting for those rights. Here is how America — and its children — began at last to grow up.

TIME LINE

1619

First African slaves are shipped to the American Colonies.

1700

Twenty thousand Africans a year are sold into slavery.

1776

American independence is declared.

1777

Vermont becomes the first colony to ban slavery.

1787

Founding Fathers draft the Constitution, which officially counts each slave as three-fifths of a human being.

1793

Eli Whitney invents the cotton gin; cotton boom begins.

1808

International slave trade ends.

1820

Missouri Compromise officially divides America in two, allowing slavery in the South but not in the North.

1831

Antislavery leader William Lloyd Garrison starts first abolitionist newspaper, *The Liberator*. In Virginia, slave Nat Turner organizes bloody revolt against local slave owners; he is later captured and executed.

1833

American Anti-Slavery Society is founded.

1841

Escaped slave Frederick Douglass gives speech to the Massachusetts Anti-Slavery Society and becomes leading African American of his age.

1846

Mexican War begins; Americans argue over slavery in newly won land.

1847

Douglass begins the *North Star*, an African American newspaper, in Rochester, New York.

1850

Congress passes the Compromise of 1850, seeking to calm tensions between North and South.

1852

Harriet Beecher Stowe publishes *Uncle Tom's Cabin*, a novel about the evils of slavery; it becomes a bestseller.

1854

Congress passes the Kansas-Nebraska Act, overturning the Missouri Compromise and angering northerners.

1856

Violence erupts in Kansas between proslavery and antislavery groups.

1857

Supreme Court rules in the Dred Scott decision that slaves could never be U.S. citizens and were officially no better than property.

1858

Abraham Lincoln and Stephen Douglas debate slavery throughout Illinois.

1859

John Brown leads a band of followers into Virginia and attacks Harpers Ferry in an effort to free all slaves in the South; he is captured and executed, but his raid infuriates the South.

1860

November 6

Lincoln is elected president of the United States.

December 20

South Carolina secedes from the Union.

1861

January 9

Mississippi secedes.

January 10

Florida secedes.

January 11

Alabama secedes.

January 19

Georgia secedes.

January 26

Louisiana secedes.

February 1

Texas secedes.

February 8

The newly formed Confederate States of America begins drafting a constitution.

February 9

Jefferson Davis is elected president of the Confederate States of America.

February 18

Davis is inaugurated president of the Confederacy at a ceremony in Montgomery, Alabama.

March 4

Lincoln is inaugurated president of the United States in Washington, D.C.

March 6

Davis calls for one hundred thousand troops.

April 12

Secessionists open fire on Fort Sumter in Charleston, South Carolina.

April 14

Fort Sumter is evacuated by federal troops.

April 15

Lincoln calls for seventy-five thousand troops to put down the rebellion.

April 17

Virginia secedes.

April 18

Union abandons arsenal at Harpers Ferry, Virginia, scene of John Brown's raid in 1859.

April 19

Lincoln orders a naval blockade against the Confederate coast.

Mob attacks Massachusetts soldiers as they march through Baltimore, Maryland, en route to defend Washington.

April 20

Robert E. Lee resigns from the U.S. Army to return to Virginia.

May 6

Arkansas secedes.

May 20

North Carolina secedes.

May 24

Lincoln's young friend Colonel E.E. Ellsworth is killed in Alexandria, Virginia, after tearing down the Confederate flag from the Marshall House; first Union officer killed.

June 8

Tennessee secedes.

July 4

Lincoln delivers his "This Is a People's Contest" message to Congress; asks for four hundred thousand more troops.

July 11

General George B. McClellan comes to national attention with a victory at Rich Mountain, Virginia.

July 21

Confederacy defeats Union at the First Battle of Bull Run in Manassas, Virginia.

July 27

Lincoln names McClellan commander of the Union's Army of the Potomac.

August 30

Union general John Charles Frémont "confiscates" all Confederate property in Missouri, including slaves; Lincoln, not ready for emancipation, instructs Frémont to withdraw his order.

October 21

Confederacy defeats Union at Battle of Ball's Bluff, Virginia.

November 1

McClellan is named commander of the entire Union army.

November 7

Union captures Port Royal, South Carolina.

November 8

Union navy seizes Confederate commissioners aboard steamship *Trent;* England threatens to join war against the Union until the Lincoln administration releases the envoys at the end of the year.

1862

January 13

Lincoln names Edwin M. Stanton secretary of war.

February 6

Union, under Admiral Andrew Foote, captures Fort Henry, Tennessee.

February 16

General Ulysses S. Grant demands and wins "unconditional surrender" of Fort Donelson, Tennessee.

February 22

Davis is reinaugurated president of the Confederacy in Richmond, Virginia.

February 25

Union occupies Nashville, Tennessee.

March–August

McClellan launches Peninsular Campaign in Virginia, with the goal of capturing Richmond.

March 8

Worst U.S. naval disaster until Pearl Harbor, as Confederate ironclad *Merrimac* (or *Virginia*) attacks Union's wooden fleet off Hampton Roads, Virginia.

March 9

The *Monitor* battles the *Merrimac* off Hampton Roads, Virginia, beginning the iron age at sea.

March 16

Union abolishes slavery in Washington, D.C., offering to pay compensation to slaveholders.

April 6–7

Union, under General Grant, wins a major victory at Battle of Shiloh (Pittsburg Landing), Tennessee.

April 16

Davis signs a new law allowing the Confederate government to draft able-bodied men into the army.

April 25

Union admiral David Farragut captures New Orleans.

May 3

Confederates abandon Yorktown, Virginia, after Union siege led by General McClellan.

May 5

Battle of Williamsburg, Virginia.

May 8

Confederates win fight at McDowell, Virginia, under General Stonewall Jackson.

May 15

Confederates win naval battle at Drewry's Bluff on the James River, near Richmond.

May 31

Davis names Robert E. Lee commander of the Army of Northern Virginia.

June 6

Union captures Memphis, Tennessee.

June 12–14

General J.E.B. Stuart leads a daring cavalry raid around McClellan's army.

June 19

U.S. Congress abolishes slavery in all federal territories.

June 25

Seven Days Battles begin near Richmond.

June 26

Battle of Mechanicsville (Beaver Dam Creek),* Virginia.

*The North named battles for the closest waterway, the South for geographic location (for example, the nearest town). When both names are used in this book, the northern comes first with the southern in parentheses.

June 27

Battle of Gaines's Mill (First Cold Harbor), Virginia.

June 29

Battle of Savage's Station, Virginia.

June 30

Battle of White Oak Swamp (Glendale), Virginia.

July 1

Battle of Malvern Hill, Virginia; McClellan's army retreats as his Peninsular Campaign ends in failure.

July 22

Lincoln reads to his cabinet a proposed Emancipation Proclamation; he is advised to postpone it until the Union wins a battle.

August 9

General John Pope and General Lee battle at Cedar Mountain, Virginia.

August 29–30

Lee defeats Pope at the Second Battle of Bull Run, Manassas, Virginia.

September 4

Lee's army moves across the Potomac River in the first Confederate invasion of the North.

September 17

Battle of Antietam (Sharpsburg), Maryland; Union forces under McClellan defeat Lee's Confederate troops in the bloodiest single day of the war.

September 22

Lincoln issues the Emancipation Proclamation, ordering slaves free in all states in rebellion after January 1, 1863.

September 23

Sioux uprising ends with their defeat at the Battle of Wood Lake, Minnesota.

October 3–4

Union wins Battle of Corinth, Mississippi.

October 8

Union wins Battle of Perryville, Kentucky.

November 7

Lincoln removes McClellan, names General Ambrose E. Burnside commander of the Army of the Potomac.

December 1

Lincoln proposes paying slave owners to free slaves in Union slave states.

December 13

Confederates defeat Union at Battle of Fredericksburg, Virginia.

December 31

Battle of Murfreesboro (Stone's River), Tennessee, begins; Union victory assured by January 2.

1863

January 1

"Day of Jubilee" as Lincoln issues final Emancipation Proclamation.

January 19–23

Union army bogs down in "mud march" leaving rain-soaked Fredericksburg, Virginia.

January 26

Lincoln names General Joseph Hooker to replace Burnside as commander of the Army of the Potomac.

March 3

Lincoln signs first Federal Conscription Act, calling for the drafting of able-bodied men into the Union army.

April 2

Hungry citizens of Richmond start bread riots.

April 16

Union fleet under Admiral David D. Porter bursts past Confederate guns at Vicksburg, Mississippi.

May 1

Grant captures Port Gibson, Mississippi.

May 1–4

Confederates win Battle of Chancellorsville, Virginia.

May 10

Stonewall Jackson, shot accidentally by his own men at Chancellorsville, dies.

May 14

Grant captures Jackson, Mississippi.

May 16–17

Confederate defenses outside Vicksburg crumble.

May 18

Grant begins six-week siege of Vicksburg.

May 22

Bureau of Colored Troops is established in U.S. War Department to welcome free African Americans into the Union army.

June 14

Confederate victory at Battle of Winchester, Virginia.

June 27

Lincoln names Major General George G. Meade to replace Hooker as commander of the Army of the Potomac.

July 1–3

Battle of Gettysburg, Pennsylvania, largest battle of war and a victory for Union forces; Lee retreats back across the Potomac as his second and final invasion of the North ends in failure.

July 4

Vicksburg surrenders to Grant.

July 8

Union takes Port Hudson, Louisiana.

July 13–16

Draft riots break out in New York City.

July 18

Union troops driven back at Battery Wagner, South Carolina, but heroism of Fifty-fourth Massachusetts Colored Infantry proves that African Americans are capable of fighting for their own freedom.

August 21

Confederate Quantrill's Raiders slaughter one hundred fifty men, women, and children in Lawrence, Kansas.

September 2

Union army under Burnside captures Knoxville, Tennessee.

September 10

Little Rock, Arkansas, falls to Union.

September 19–20

Battle of Chickamauga; major Confederate victory in Georgia.

November 19

Lincoln delivers Gettysburg Address at the dedication of a new national cemetery for soldiers killed in battle there.

November 23–25

Battles of Chattanooga, Lookout Mountain, and Missionary Ridge, Tennessee, end with Union victories.

1864

February 1

Lincoln issues a call for five hundred thousand troops.

February 27

First Union captives arrive at Andersonville Prison, Georgia.

March 10

Lincoln appoints Grant general in chief of U.S. armies.

April 8

U.S. Senate approves a constitutional amendment outlawing slavery.

April 12

Massacre at Fort Pillow, Tennessee, as Confederates under General Nathan Bedford Forrest murder African American troops after they surrender.

May 3

Union begins Wilderness Campaign in Virginia.

May 5–7

Battle of the Wilderness.

May 7

General William T. Sherman attacks Atlanta, Georgia.

May 8

Battles begin around Spotsylvania Court House, Virginia.

May 12

General J.E.B. Stuart dies from wounds suffered the previous day at Yellow Tavern, Virginia.

Fierce fighting around "Bloody Angle," Spotsylvania, Virginia.

May 13

Influential New York editor Horace Greeley demands that Lincoln be replaced as the Republican candidate for the 1864 election.

June 1–3

Battles of Cold Harbor, Virginia.

June 8

Lincoln is renominated to the presidency by the new National Union party.

June 12

Grant crosses the James River to Petersburg, Virginia.

June 15

U.S. House of Representatives defeats a constitutional amendment ending slavery.

June 19

USS *Kearsarge* destroys Confederate ship *Alabama* off the coast of Cherbourg, France.

June 27

Confederates defeat Sherman at Battle of Kenesaw Mountain, Georgia.

July 4

Lincoln refuses to sign Wade-Davis bill, which would have imposed harsh conditions on defeated Confederate states.

July 11–12

Confederates threaten Washington suburbs; Lincoln witnesses attack at Fort Stevens.

July 17

Battles for Atlanta begin.

July 30

Battle of the Crater, Petersburg, Virginia, ends in Union defeat after Union explodes a huge bomb beneath a Confederate position.

August 5

Admiral Farragut inspires his fleet by crying, "Damn the torpedoes — full speed ahead," and takes Mobile Bay.

September 2

Sherman takes Atlanta.

October 19

General Philip Sheridan defeats General Jubal Early for a Union victory at Winchester, Virginia, after inspiring troops with his famous ride to the front.

Shenandoah Valley Campaign ends with a Confederate loss at Cedar Creek.

November 1

Maryland abolishes slavery.

November 8

Lincoln is reelected president of the United States.

November 16

Sherman begins his march from Atlanta to the sea.

November 22

Sherman's troops capture Milledgeville, Georgia.

November 29

Indian massacre at Sand Creek, Colorado.

November 30

Union wins Battle of Franklin, Tennessee.

December 6

Lincoln names Salmon P. Chase chief justice of the Supreme Court.

December 15–16

Union under General George H. Thomas defeats Confederates at Nashville, ending the war in the West.

December 21

Sherman captures Savannah, Georgia.

1865

January 15

Union captures Fort Fisher, North Carolina.

January 31

House of Representatives finally approves a constitutional amendment abolishing slavery.

February 1

Lincoln's home state, Illinois, becomes the first to ratify the Thirteenth Amendment abolishing slavery.

Sherman begins march through the Carolinas.

February 13

Confederacy approves the recruitment of slaves as soldiers, with the approval of owners.

February 17

Union army captures and destroys Columbia, South Carolina.

February 18

Union army marches into Charleston, South Carolina, the city where the Civil War began.

February 22

Tennessee abolishes slavery.

March 4

Lincoln is reinaugurated; Second Inaugural Address blames war on slavery, proposes charity for enemies.

March 11

Sherman captures Fayetteville, North Carolina.

March 27

Lincoln holds final council of war with Grant, Sherman, and Porter aboard the *River Queen,* City Point, Virginia.

March 29

Grant launches Appomattox Campaign.

April 1

Grant defeats Lee at Battle of Five Forks, Virginia.

April 2

Confederate government flees Richmond.

April 3

Grant captures Petersburg and Richmond, Virginia.

April 4

Lincoln visits Richmond.

April 7

Grant urges Lee to surrender the Army of Northern Virginia.

April 9

Lee surrenders to Grant at Appomattox Court House, Virginia.

April 14

Lincoln is shot at Ford's Theatre by actor John Wilkes Booth.

April 15

Lincoln dies.

April 26

Confederate general Joseph Johnston surrenders to Sherman at Greensboro, North Carolina.

May 10

Jefferson Davis is captured by Union troops at Irwinville, Georgia.

May 22

Davis is imprisoned at Fort Monroe, Virginia.

December 18

The Thirteenth Amendment to the Constitution is ratified, and slavery is finally destroyed forever.

1866

President Andrew Johnson officially declares the rebellion to be over, as new governments are formed in the former Confederate states.

Reconstruction begins; Congress and President Johnson battle over how severely the South should be punished and how many rights African Americans should enjoy.

Congress passes the first civil rights bill over President Johnson's opposition.

Congress passes the Fourteenth Amendment to the Constitution, guaranteeing citizenship and "equal protection of the laws" to freed slaves.

The Ku Klux Klan is organized in the South.

President Johnson pardons Jefferson Davis and gives back his U.S. citizenship.

1868

The Fourteenth Amendment is ratified; Ulysses S. Grant is elected president.

1870

The Fifteenth Amendment to the Constitution is ratified, guaranteeing all Americans, "regardless of race, color, or previous condition of servitude," the right to vote.

1877

The last Republican government still existing in a southern state is defeated, and most rights won by African Americans are lost.

1

. . . .

THE GREAT GENERALS

GRANT AND HIS GENERALS

Who were the Civil War's great generals?

Ulysses S. Grant was an unsuccessful businessman before the war. Robert E. Lee had been in the U.S. Army so long that disrespectful younger officers called him "Granny." William T. Sherman had nearly gone bankrupt running a bank. Nathan Bedford Forrest was a slave trader. Until the first guns were fired in 1861, none of these men would have been singled out for future greatness on the battlefield. Yet all of them rose to the occasion and won remarkable victories for the Union and the Confederacy.

The Civil War produced a generation of bril- liant generals. They could inspire men by riding past the ranks, waving their hats like the military heroes of old. And they could successfully maneuver huge armies and plan massive battles, using modern weapons to fight a modern war.

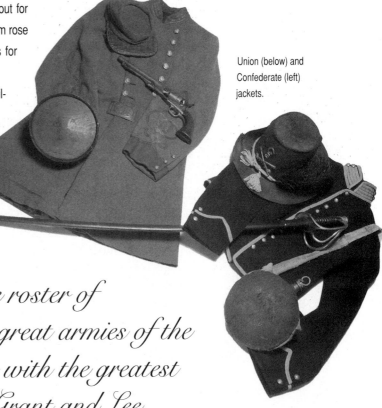

Union (below) and Confederate (left) jackets.

Following is a who's who of the Union and the Confederacy — the roster of generals who led the great armies of the Civil War, ending with the greatest of them all, Grant and Lee.

THE UNION COMMANDERS

by Harold Holzer

Until he chose Ulysses S. Grant to command all Union armies, Abraham Lincoln could not find a general he could depend on to fight and win battles. But the Union military leadership did boast men of true talent and dedication. Following is a roster of leading Union army and navy officers not profiled elsewhere in this set.

Winfield Scott, a Mexican War hero who first served in the military during the War of 1812, was seventy-five years old before the first battle of the Civil War was fought. Known as "Old Fuss and Feathers" because he was so strict and formal, Scott commanded all Union armies when Lincoln took office. He successfully organized troops to protect the new president at his inauguration. Scott asked that General George B. McClellan be made the army's field commander but then grew tired of the brash young commander and retired. It was Scott who proposed the Union naval blockade that eventually starved the South. He lived until 1866, long enough to see the Union victory.

WINFIELD SCOTT

Ambrose E. Burnside is best remembered for his thick side-whiskers, which soon became known by a term we still use today: sideburns. Burnside was only thirty-eight years old when he became commander of the Army of the Potomac in 1862. Lacking confidence, he was certain that he would fail, and he did. At the Battle of Fredericksburg in December 1862, he ordered an ill-fated charge across a river and up a well-defended hill that resulted in the slaughter of thousands of Union troops. Burnside was relieved of his command but went on to fight successfully in the West. He returned to the East in 1864 but was severely criticized for costly mistakes at the Battle of the Crater and was once again relieved of his command. Burnside sent a letter to Lincoln resigning from the army, but his note arrived at the White House hours after Lincoln's death. He later served as governor of Rhode Island and as a U.S. senator.

AMBROSE E. BURNSIDE

JOSEPH HOOKER

Joseph Hooker, born in 1814, became known as "Fighting Joe" for his bravery at the Battle of Williamsburg in 1862. He went on to display more courage at the Battle of White Oak Swamp, Second Bull Run, and Antietam, where he was wounded. Hooker served under Burnside at the Battle of Fredericksburg, then criticized him afterward. When Burnside demanded that Lincoln choose one or the other to lead the army, Lincoln replaced him with Hooker. But in May 1863, Hooker led the army to a huge defeat of his own at the Battle of Chancellorsville. He was quickly replaced. He later fought successfully in the western theater but left active service when General William T. Sherman passed him over for a promotion. He died in 1879.

George G. Meade was the only Union commander to lose his authority after winning a major victory — in his case, the Battle of Gettysburg. Born in Spain to an American naval agent, Meade graduated from West Point in 1835. He fought under McClellan during the Peninsular Campaign of 1862, where he was wounded. He led corps of troops at Second Bull Run, Antietam, Fredericksburg, and Chancellorsville. His aggressiveness at Chancellorsville came to the attention of Lincoln, who named him to replace Hooker. Only days after his promotion, Meade found himself facing Robert E. Lee at Gettysburg. After three days of fighting, the biggest battle of the war ended with Lee retreating back into the South. Lincoln was angered by Meade's refusal to pursue the enemy and soon named Grant to command all Union forces. Meade remained in command of the Army of the Potomac but reported to Grant. After the war, Meade returned to his home in Philadelphia and became a local hero.

GEORGE G. MEADE

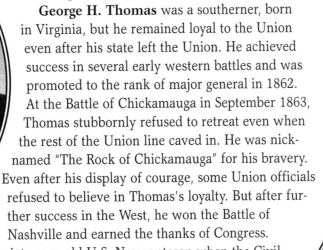

GEORGE H. THOMAS

George H. Thomas was a southerner, born in Virginia, but he remained loyal to the Union even after his state left the Union. He achieved success in several early western battles and was promoted to the rank of major general in 1862. At the Battle of Chickamauga in September 1863, Thomas stubbornly refused to retreat even when the rest of the Union line caved in. He was nicknamed "The Rock of Chickamauga" for his bravery. Even after his display of courage, some Union officials refused to believe in Thomas's loyalty. But after further success in the West, he won the Battle of Nashville and earned the thanks of Congress.

David Farragut was a sixty-year-old U.S. Navy veteran when the Civil War began in 1861. At the age of eleven, he had served as a midshipman in the War of 1812. Farragut was asked to capture New Orleans from the Confederacy. His squadron blasted past two enemy forts on the Mississippi River and captured that city in April 1862. Farragut was promoted to rear admiral. In 1864, he commanded Union naval forces at the Battle of Mobile Bay. When one of his ships struck a mine and sank, some of his officers wanted to retreat. Instead, Farragut shouted his famous order: "Damn the torpedoes — full speed ahead!" He had himself tied to the rope rigging above his ship so that he could command the battle from on high and went on to win the most important victory of his career. After the war, Farragut commanded the American fleet in Europe.

DAVID FARRAGUT

THE CONFEDERATE COMMANDERS

by Harold Holzer

If great generals alone could win battles, the Confederacy would have won the Civil War. Robert E. Lee and "Stonewall" Jackson, for example, are considered by most historians to be the most brilliant commanders of the war.

The South was rich in military talent, but many of its best officers died early, perhaps changing the outcome of the war. Following is a roster of the Confederacy's great generals not profiled elsewhere in this set.

Joseph E. Johnston, born in 1807, commanded one wing of the Confederate army at First Bull Run in 1861. But he feuded with Jefferson Davis, president of the Confederacy, and his military career was never the same again. Johnston served bravely on the Virginia peninsula in 1862 but was severely wounded at the Battle of Seven Pines. He was forced to take a leave of absence to recover, and when he was ready to return, Robert E. Lee had established himself as the leading general of the Confederacy. Johnston was transferred to the West, where he was unable to stop Ulysses S. Grant's early successes. Johnston was then assigned to fight in Tennessee but was reluctant to attack. He failed to stop William T. Sherman at Atlanta and was relieved of his command by President Davis. Johnston never won a great victory, but he never suffered a major defeat either. He surrendered his troops to Sherman in April 1865.

Albert Sidney Johnston was a friend of Confederate president Jefferson Davis, but he earned the opportunity to command because of his great talent and bravery. Johnston nearly defeated Grant at the Battle of Shiloh in early 1862. His daring early-morning charge surprised the Union commander, and it took Grant a full day to recover and turn the tide. As the fighting raged, Johnston was shot in the leg. His men were unable to stop the bleeding, and he died on the battlefield. His death was a great blow to the young Confederate army.

James Ewell Brown Stuart, known as "Jeb," was a dashing young cavalry commander under Lee. He led one of the charges at First Bull Run that turned a certain Confederate loss into a surprising victory. His daring ride around George B. McClellan's entire army in 1862 electrified the South and worried the North. Thereafter, he served as Lee's "eyes," scouting Union forces and conducting daring raids around enemy troops. He participated in all the major battles of the war alongside Lee. But he failed to stay in touch with Lee at Gettysburg, and he did not arrive at the battlefield until the second day of fighting, hurting Confederate chances badly. Stuart was killed in Virginia in May 1864. Lee mourned him deeply, declaring, "He never brought me a piece of false information."

John Singleton Mosby was known as the "Gray Ghost of the Confederacy." He did not serve in the regular army but as a so-called partisan ranger. This meant that he operated in the rear of the army, attacking at will. He kept all the supplies, ammunition, and money that he seized from enemy troops. Even though most military men frowned on such service, Lee liked Mosby and encouraged him. Lee mentioned Mosby in his official reports more often than any other

JOSEPH E. JOHNSTON

JAMES EWELL BROWN STUART

JOHN SINGLETON MOSBY

Confederate commander. But Grant was so furious over Mosby's kind of warfare that he ordered if Mosby was found, he be executed without a trial. Mosby was never caught and returned to the practice of law after the war. He lived another fifty-one years, until 1916.

James Longstreet, who attended West Point along with future enemies Grant and Sherman, attracted attention with brilliant fighting at First Bull Run and Williamsburg. Later, however, he was late in leading his troops onto the field at the Battle of Seven Pines and again at Second Bull Run. In fact, "Old Pete," as his men called him, always seemed to act too slowly when he did not agree with his commanders' plans. He committed the same sin at Gettysburg, delaying his attack on the decisive second day of fighting until 4 P.M. Many historians have blamed Longstreet for the Confederate defeat at Gettysburg. Longstreet also questioned Lee's decision to order the ill-fated Pickett's Charge on the third and final day of fighting at Gettysburg. But Lee liked Longstreet, calling him his "Old War Horse," and admired his dependability and loyalty. After the war, Longstreet shocked southerners by becoming a Republican. He lived until 1904.

Nathan Bedford Forrest was the southerner whom northerners loved to hate. But even his long-time enemy, William T. Sherman, remembered Forrest as "the most remarkable man our Civil War produced on either side." During the war, however, Sherman labeled Forrest a "devil" and ordered him hunted down and killed "if it costs 10,000 men and bankrupts the Treasury." Forrest had been a slave trader before the war, famous for beating slaves at his "Negro Mart." He displayed similar cruelty during the war. Once he slapped one of own men for resisting an order. On another occasion, he ignored a white flag of surrender and continued firing. At one point, he threatened to hang captured preachers. He sometimes sent captured African American soldiers into slavery. Forrest believed that "war means fightin' and fightin' means killin'." As a cavalry commander, he was brilliant. But at Fort Pillow, Tennessee, Forrest outdid himself by slaughtering African American survivors after they surrendered. After the war, he became the first leader of the Ku Klux Klan. Forrest's avowed hatred for African Americans made him one of the cruelest of all Confederate commanders and one of the most feared.

The South was rich in military talent, but many of its best officers died early, perhaps changing the outcome of the war.

GEORGE B. MCCLELLAN: THE 'YOUNG NAPOLEON'

by Harold Holzer

George B. McClellan

· ·

Before serving as a Union general in the Civil War, McClellan attended West Point, fought in the Mexican War, and worked on the survey for the Northern Pacific Railroad route across the Cascade Range. He was a railroad official when the war began.

No Civil War general was ever more popular with his men but less successful in battle than George B. McClellan. The "Young Napoleon," as he became known, was convinced that he was the savior of the Union. He believed no that other commander could train his men as well for battle. He was right about his skill at training soldiers; no one did it better. But McClellan never seemed ready to attack. He postponed, delayed, and made excuses. President Abraham Lincoln repeatedly lost patience with him, and McClellan ended his military career with much less glory than he thought he deserved.

George Brinton McClellan was born in Philadelphia in 1826. He graduated second in his class from West Point and went on to win honors for his service in the Mexican War. Then he helped build forts, taught at West Point, observed the Crimean War in Europe, and even designed a new military saddle that bore his name. In the late 1850s, McClellan left the U.S. Army and became a railroad executive.

When the Civil War broke out, McClellan was quickly appointed a major general and won an early victory at the small Battle of Rich Mountain in western Virginia. He received much praise from a public hungry for heroes and victories. When the Union army was humiliated at the Battle of Bull Run in July 1861, McClellan was named to take over.

McClellan proceeded to train his troops into a well-organized fighting machine, but he seemed reluctant to fight. Lincoln urged him again and again to move against the Confederacy, but McClellan protested that he was not ready. He complained that his critics were trying to destroy his reputation. Yet that November, McClellan won another promotion. He became general in chief after General Winfield Scott retired.

Finally, in March 1862, McClellan led 118,000 troops onto the Virginia coast for a planned march against the Confederate capital of Richmond. He marched inland with unjustified slowness, however, complaining continually — and incorrectly — that the enemy outnumbered him. McClellan won a few battles along the way, but he was unable to conquer Richmond, and he gave up the campaign.

In the meantime, McClellan began making it clear that he opposed the idea of emancipation. In his opinion, the war should be waged only to restore the Union, not to free the slaves. He expressed this view to President Lincoln, even though it was not proper for military leaders to engage in politics. He also feuded with members of Lincoln's cabinet. In July 1862, a disgusted Lincoln relieved McClellan of his command.

That summer, the Union lost the Second Battle of Bull Run, and an embarrassed Lincoln had little choice but to appoint McClellan to command once again. Just as before, McClellan reorganized the army successfully. But also just as before, he fared worse on the battlefield.

When Robert E. Lee's forces invaded Maryland in late 1862, McClellan was able to send him into retreat at the Battle of Antietam. It was the bloodiest single day of the war. But Lincoln was not satisfied with the results, for McClellan refused to chase Lee back into Virginia, and thus lost a chance to end the war once and for all. Lincoln fired McClellan again.

Ironically, the Battle of Antietam was successful enough to allow Lincoln to do just what McClellan so bitterly opposed: issue the Emancipation Proclamation. Two years later, the Democratic party nominated McClellan to run against Lincoln for president. McClellan campaigned for peace, promising to end the war even without complete victory. Many northerners were disappointed that a onetime general now opposed the war. The voters rejected his ideas and chose Lincoln for a second term. Even when the soldiers' votes were counted separately, McClellan won only one out of every five. The men who had once admired him decided that he no longer deserved their support.

McClellan remains one of the great mysteries of the Civil War. He was superbly trained, and he trained others just as superbly. He simply did not want to fight.

Crossing a pontoon bridge was tricky business. Supported by flat-bottomed boats or other structures, these floating bridges were far from sturdy. Here troops prepare for a battle that is taking place in the distance.

WILLIAM T. SHERMAN: THE 'SCOURGE OF THE SOUTH'

by Harold Holzer

William T. Sherman

Of all the generals who fought for the Union, none inflicted greater pain and destruction on the South than William T. Sherman. Sherman may well have been thinking back on his own fierce attack on Atlanta, Georgia, or his devastating "March to the Sea" when he coined the phrase long associated with him: "War is all hell."

Tecumseh Sherman, or "Cump," as he was known in his youth, was left fatherless at the age of ten and sent by his destitute mother to live with a prominent Missouri lawyer named Thomas Ewing. Ewing added the name "William" to Sherman's name and saw to his education. Sherman later attended West Point and fought in the Mexican War. When he was ready to marry, he proposed to his foster sister, Ellen Ewing, but by many accounts their long marriage was not a happy one.

After the Mexican War, Sherman failed miserably as a banker, did somewhat better as a lawyer, and then became the popular and successful superintendent of a military academy in Louisiana. He was so well

BEAUFORT, SOUTH CAROLINA

Photographer Sam A. Cooley of the Tenth Army Corps took this picture of Sherman's men in Beaufort, South Carolina.

Atlanta at war's end.

liked at this school that when Louisiana seceded from the Union in 1861, the new Confederate government asked Sherman to join its army. But Sherman was loyal to the Union and left for St. Louis, where he temporarily served as head of a streetcar company. Not until war actually broke out did he join the Union military as a colonel.

Sherman would go on to become one of the most celebrated heroes of the war, but his path to glory was not an easy one. In late 1861, he suffered what was probably a nervous breakdown and had to be nursed back to health by his wife. Furious when newspapers wrote that he had gone "insane," Sherman fought endlessly with reporters and had several banished from his camps. He was often enraged and frustrated by his critics and won a reputation for toughness.

Sherman very nearly ruined his first great opportunity in battle, at Shiloh, Tennessee, in 1862, but his commander, General Ulysses S. Grant, defended him against criticism and made him an important leader of his western armies. Sherman helped Grant conquer Vicksburg, Mississippi, on July 4, 1863, and later that year joined Grant in the attack on Chattanooga, Tennessee, becoming commander of the Army of the Tennessee. Then in 1864, when Grant was made general in chief of all U.S. armies and headed to Virginia to take up his new post, he named Sherman commander of all western forces.

Sherman set his sights on the city of Atlanta, moving against that stronghold with one hundred thousand men. After a brutal siege and a series of fierce land battles, Atlanta surrendered. The city was left in ruins, its population homeless. Sherman ordered the city evacuated so that what remained could be destroyed. When its mayor protested, Sherman replied, "You might as well appeal against the thunderstorm as against these terrible hardships of war."

Next Sherman proposed one of the most daring campaigns of the war. He would cut his army off from its own supply line and march it from Atlanta across the entire state of Georgia, living off the land and "smashing things" in his way, as he put it. In so doing, Sherman promised to cut the Confederacy in half, destroy southern morale, and then join Grant on the coast to conquer the capital city of Richmond.

Sherman's "March to the Sea," as it became known, proved as ruthless as it was bold. The general vowed to make "Georgia howl," and he did — by destroying railroads, factories, government buildings, and any opposing army that dared to challenge him. When his twenty-six-day march was done, Sherman's army had done $100 million worth of damage and reduced the midsection of Georgia to ruins.

Sherman ended his eastern advance by seizing the city of Savannah, which he presented as a Christmas gift to President Lincoln in a famous letter that December. Lincoln acknowledged Sherman's triumph by admitting that he had been wrong to doubt that Sherman could conduct such a long march so successfully.

In early 1865, Sherman turned his army north toward the Carolinas and inflicted additional destruction as he headed toward Richmond. Before he could get there, however, Lee surrendered to Grant at Appomattox Court House, Virginia. Two weeks later, Sherman forced his long-time foe, Confederate general Joseph Johnston, to surrender in a North Carolina farmhouse.

Ironically, the man southerners accused of brutality was criticized in the North for being too generous to the army that surrendered to him. Sherman took it upon himself to agree to return all property to southern citizens. Worse, he did not exclude emancipated slaves from these terms. Even Grant, his strongest defender, realized that Sherman had gone too far. The new president, Andrew Johnson, had no choice but to disapprove the surrender. Sherman was infuriated but obeyed orders. Johnston meekly surrendered to Sherman yet again.

This unusual ending to Sherman's military career did not hurt his reputation for long. He became one of the most popular veterans in the postwar years, writing his memoirs and giving many speeches. Americans also admired him because he refused to enter politics, even though he could easily have won nomination for the presidency.

"My aim," Sherman recalled, "was to whip the rebels, to humble their pride, to follow them to their inmost recesses, and make them fear and dread us." Sherman did precisely that, in the process earning the nickname, the "Scourge of the South." The man who burned Atlanta and destroyed central Georgia on his March to the Sea had done more than any other Civil War general to inflict the cruel realities of modern warfare on his enemy.

Thure de Thulstrup's *Sherman at the Siege of Atlanta.* In this painting, Thulstrup captures an artillery officer reporting the early results of the Siege of Atlanta to Sherman and his aide (with field glasses).

Thomas Jonathan "Stonewall" Jackson

This is one of the few photographs taken of Jackson during the war. It shows him with the full beard he grew while serving in the Confederate army.

Opposite: Painter Everett Julio rendered this interpretation of the last meeting between Lee and Jackson before the Battle of Chancellorsville.

'STONEWALL' JACKSON

by Harold Holzer

If Thomas Jonathan "Stonewall" Jackson had not died in 1863, it is entirely possible that the outcome of the Civil War might have been quite different. Had he lived, Robert E. Lee's most feared and talented lieutenant might well have changed the course of history.

Jackson was born to a poor family in Virginia in 1824 and orphaned as a child. Like many future Civil War generals on both sides, he was educated at West Point and saw military service in the Mexican War. Jackson later served at forts in Florida and New York and then became a professor at the Virginia Military Institute (VMI) in Lexington. He taught courses in artillery and natural philosophy.

Although Jackson resigned from the U.S. Army soon after joining the faculty at the institute, he did command the VMI cadets who journeyed to Charles Town, Virginia, to witness the hanging of John Brown in 1859. He wrote home to express admiration for Brown's courage facing death. In future years, Jackson would seldom show any sort of sympathy with those opposed to Virginia or the southern way of life. There was never any doubt that his sympathies lay with his native state and, when it seceded, the Confederacy.

Jackson became a colonel in the new Confederate army in April 1861 and quickly advanced to brigadier general, the rank he held when he fought at Bull Run that July. During the battle, another Confederate general tried to rally his retreating troops by pointing to his fearless colleague and shouting, "There stands Jackson like a stone wall!" Jackson's bravery at Bull Run earned him another promotion, this time to major general, and a nickname. Thereafter, he was known as "Stonewall" Jackson.

Jackson went on to fight with his usual fierceness and boldness, but without earning similar success or attention, throughout the rest of 1861 and on into the early months of 1862. Then he conducted a brilliant campaign in the Shenandoah Valley of Virginia in May and June. Jackson earned the respect of both his own army and his enemies for his toughness and determination.

In the spring of 1862, Jackson worked side by side for the first time with an older general who had been serving without much notice in western Virginia: Robert E. Lee. In the months to come, Lee would emerge as the leading commander in the Confederacy, and Jackson would rise in fame alongside him.

Lee took command of the Army of Northern Virginia in May 1862, and Jackson's forces were ordered to Lee's side. They went on to fight together on the Virginia peninsula that summer to block Union general George B. McClellan's march toward the Confederate capital of Richmond. Although Jackson's performances on the peninsula were surprisingly poor, McClellan was turned back and Richmond spared.

That August, Jackson played a huge part in the defeat of Union forces at the Second Battle of Bull Run, one of the most decisive Confederate triumphs of the war. In September, he fought impressively once again at the Battle of Antietam, although the Confederate army lost. Then in December, Jackson was an important

24

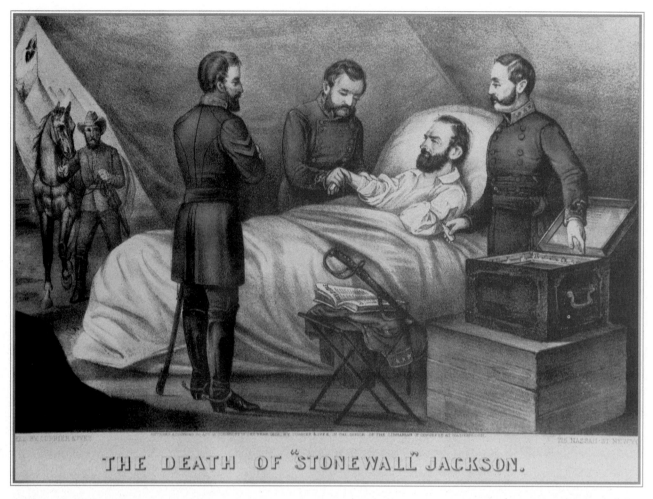

THE DEATH OF "STONEWALL" JACKSON.

Jackson was wounded in both arms on May 2, 1863, by friendly fire from a South Carolina regiment who thought Jackson's escort was Federal cavalry. Jackson's left arm was amputated. He died of pneumonia on May 10 — not in a tent, but in a house.

factor in yet another great Confederate victory at the Battle of Fredericksburg.

Jackson returned home for a long-awaited visit with his family in the spring of 1863, when he saw his new baby daughter for the first time. Shortly after beginning his vacation, he learned that the Union army was preparing yet another attack into Virginia. Displaying his usual sense of duty, he left immediately to return to his army.

Jackson fought brilliantly to repel Union troops and proved especially successful at the climax of the fighting, the Battle of Chancellorsville on May 2, 1863. To challenge Union general Joseph Hooker's larger army, Lee daringly ordered Jackson to take his men and circle around Hooker's force until he could attack it from the rear. Together, Lee and Jackson sandwiched the unsuspecting Union army and crushed it. It was perhaps the greatest Confederate victory of the war.

Just as southerners were learning of the triumph, a tragedy occurred that made the battle seem unimportant. Shortly after sunset that night, Jackson was returning on horseback to his camp when his own men mistook him for an enemy spy and shot him. Jackson fell from his horse, his left arm shattered and bleeding heavily.

Jackson was taken to a nearby house, where his arm was amputated. For a time, doctors were sure that he would recover. But he developed pneumonia and died on May 10. "I know not how to replace him," a sorrowful Lee admitted.

The entire Confederacy joined Lee in mourning the loss of Jackson. In South Carolina, one admirer exclaimed, "How I loved him! He was my hero.... There was mourning deep and true throughout the land when that news came." A southern newspaper declared him the "idol of the people." And even in the North, one newspaper expressed respect for the fallen general in predicting that the Union's chances for victory had improved greatly because of his death.

Jackson was a highly unusual personality. He wore a battered old hat, was sometimes seen sucking lemons, and was passionately secretive. A deeply religious man, he never smoked, drank, or played cards, and he often held prayer meetings for his men in camp. The only thing he liked better than listening to a Sunday sermon, one southern lady declared, was using his Sabbath to defeat the enemy.

"Old Jack," as his men often called him, was sometimes as tough on his own men as he was on his opponents. He was known to punish his soldiers severely if they did not live up to his standards of discipline or bravery. He had little sympathy for the wounded, thinking them weak.

Many critics thought Jackson odd, and some believed him demented. But no one ever questioned his skills as a military commander. Certainly no one could question the fact that after his death, the Confederate army never again equaled the success it achieved while "Stonewall" Jackson lived.

A PASSION FOR HORSES

by Mary Morton Cowan

Georgetown, Ohio, was full of excitement. A traveling circus was in town. In the ring, a trick pony threw off one rider after another. Then came young 'Lyss Grant's turn. The pony bucked and kicked, but 'Lyss hung on. A circus clown tossed a monkey onto the pony's back, but nothing could distract the boy. He clung on and won the prize.

Grant's boyhood home and tannery in Georgetown, Ohio.

Throughout his life, Ulysses S. Grant had a passion for horses. His father, Jesse Grant, owned and operated a successful tannery. As a toddler, Ulysses crawled among the teams of horses at the tannery, sometimes swinging from their tails.

Jesse and Hannah Simpson Grant's first child was born on April 27, 1822, in a two-room house overlooking the Ohio River. Named Hiram Ulysses, the boy was called Ulysses, or 'Lyss, even though he wrote Hiram in his books.

In school, he solved math problems easily but did not care much for other subjects. No one knew what he did care for, because he was very quiet. A short, stocky boy, 'Lyss was not athletic and was painfully shy like his mother, causing townspeople to pick on him. Some folks nicknamed him "Useless."

Shy as he seemed among people, he was confident with horses. By age five, he could stand on the back of a horse while it trotted. Two or three years later, he harnessed and drove teams by himself. By the time he was eleven, he did all the cultivating and harvesting on the farm and hauled wood for the family and the tannery. 'Lyss was so skillful at breaking a feisty colt to saddle or harness that men paid him to break their new horses.

Once 'Lyss was determined to have a certain horse. His father agreed to pay twenty-five dollars for it, and he gave his son some bargaining advice. Eight-year-old Ulysses said to the owner, "Papa says I may offer you twenty dollars for the colt, but if you won't take that, I am to offer twenty-two fifty, and if you won't take that, I am to give you twenty-five." He may not have been a respectable horse trader at age eight, but he was undeniably honest. And he got what he wanted.

He also got what he did not want — wisecracks. Folks teased "Useless" about the horse trade for a long time.

'Lyss preferred activities he could do alone or with a few friends, such as fishing or swimming in the creek. He refused to hunt, for he did not enjoy killing animals. Perhaps that is why he detested his father's tannery. Killing animals and tanning their hides horrified him. The tannery also smelled awful. Whenever his father needed extra help, 'Lyss paid schoolmates to work in his place.

By chance, Jesse Grant learned of an opening for an Ohio man at the U.S. Military Academy at West Point, New York, and he arranged to have his son appointed. Military life did not appeal to Ulysses, and he feared he would fail the entrance exam, but rather than argue with his father, he consented. So at seventeen, Hiram Ulysses Grant headed for West Point. He barely qualified physically, for he was only one inch taller than the minimum height of five feet.

A Union cavalry "hardy hat."

When Grant arrived at West Point in May 1839, he discovered that he had not been registered under his given name. Unknown to him, his congressman had made an error in his appointment papers, assuming Grant's first name to be Ulysses and his middle name Simpson (his mother's maiden name). Either he was Ulysses S. Grant or he could go home. Having never liked the way his initials spelled "HUG," he settled for "U.S." "U.S." sparked another nickname, "Uncle Sam," soon shortened to "Sam."

Sam did not like drill practice and could not keep step in the marching band, but mostly he stayed out of trouble. Like every cadet, he received demerits (marks against his record), but his were mostly for minor infractions — perhaps leaving a button undone on his uniform or reporting late for duty. In the history of West Point, only one man had graduated with no demerits — Robert E. Lee.

Grant was known for his daring horsemanship at West Point. While there, he set a school jumping record that stood for years. But he did not set any academic records. His grades in mathematics were excellent, but his other grades pulled his rank down to twenty-first in a class of thirty-nine. Upon graduation in 1843, Second Lieutenant Ulysses S. Grant requested a cavalry appointment but was instead assigned to the Fourth Infantry, stationed in St. Louis, Missouri. He planned to complete his required military service, then teach mathematics. He did not yet know how much circumstances beyond his control would change his plans.

CROSSING RAPPAHANNOCK RIVER BELOW
FREDERICKSBURG, VIRGINIA

FIRST IN WAR

by Harold Holzer

Grant's army on the move during the spring of 1864.

When the Civil War began, thirty-eight-year-old Ulysses S. Grant's fortunes had fallen so far that the veteran could not even get himself assigned to a small command. By the time the war was over, he was the most celebrated military hero in the nation. No American officer ever rose higher or faster than Grant.

Not until a sympathetic Illinois governor came to his aid in the spring of 1861 did the frustrated Grant win appointment as a colonel in the Twenty-first Illinois Infantry. Within two months, he had transformed a group of unruly, inexperienced men into a polished fighting force and was promoted to brigadier general.

Grant's path to glory was not smooth. His first battle as commander — an attack on a Confederate camp in Belmont, Missouri, in November 1861 — ended without significant success. Grant lost more than one-fifth of his men. But his aggressiveness in the field won the attention of his superiors, who were frustrated by the caution so many other Union generals were showing at the time. He also earned the respect of his men by the calm way in which he organized the Union retreat.

Grant came into his own in February 1862, when he captured two crucial Confederate river strongholds, Fort Henry and Fort Donelson in Tennessee. In the midst of his ferocious attack on Fort Donelson, its commander, Confederate general Simon Bolivar Buckner, sent Grant a message asking his terms for a cease-fire. Grant quickly replied that he would accept nothing less than "unconditional and immediate surrender." His strong words in battle coincided with his initials. In the North, U.S. Grant became known to an adoring public as "Unconditional Surrender" Grant. President Abraham Lincoln immediately promoted him to major general of volunteers.

Grant nearly lost his first great battle two months later. His army was on the verge of defeat after an initial day of bloody fighting at Shiloh,

Ulysses S. Grant

A relaxed-looking General Grant poses in a photographer's studio in the midst of the Civil War. In truth, Grant spent little time in the large cities that boasted photo galleries. Once he was named to command the Union army, he stayed at army headquarters.

Tennessee, on April 6, 1862. But Grant refused to retreat and with bulldog determination rallied his troops to triumph by attacking ferociously the next morning. Some critics labeled Grant a butcher, a charge that would hound him for the rest of the war. Other critics whispered that Grant drank too much. The general simply began to consider his next battle.

Grant proved that he could not only win lightning-fast battlefield victories but also triumph in long, drawn-out sieges. In the winter of 1862–63, his first attack on the city of Vicksburg, Mississippi, the last major Confederate position on the Mississippi River, failed from the north. So Grant joined forces with Admiral David Dixon Porter of the Union navy. Porter's ships carried the Union army and its supplies downriver past Vicksburg. Grant decided to attack and surround the city from the south and east instead. When Grant's daring attempt to seize Vicksburg still failed to produce immediate success, he cut off the city's supplies and patiently ordered a bombardment. For more than six weeks, citizens of the city lived in caves to escape Grant's relentless shelling. When Vicksburg surrendered on July 4, 1863 (just one day after the famous Battle of Gettysburg), the Union took control of the river.

General Grant continued his dogged drive on Confederate strongholds. He broke the siege of Chattanooga, Tennessee, in the fall of 1863 and proceeded to win impressive victories at the Battles of Lookout Mountain and Missionary Ridge. By November, Grant was universally recognized as the most successful — and the most feared — Union general. Lincoln promoted him to general in chief of all Union armies in March 1864 and awarded him the rank of lieutenant general.

Grant then took personal command of fighting in the East, while masterminding a coordinated plan to fight the war on other fronts. It was Grant, for example, who helped design and then ordered General William Tecumseh Sherman's attack on Atlanta and later the famous march through Georgia, which split the Confederacy. By the end of 1864, Grant was so admired that he probably could have seized the Republican presidential nomination from Lincoln himself. But he refused suggestions that he run for the presidency, preferring instead to win the war in the field. "I propose to fight it out on this line," he declared, "if it takes all summer."

It did — and more. For the first time, the Army of the Potomac, under Grant's leadership, continued south instead of retreating north after each battle. In battle after bloody battle, at places like the Wilderness, Spotsylvania, and Cold Harbor, the Union lost thousands of men to the Army of Northern Virginia, led by Grant's Confederate counterpart, the great Robert E. Lee. But Grant's forces outnumbered

Lee's, and he could replace wounded or killed soldiers more easily. Slowly but surely, Grant forced the Confederate army to be stretched dangerously thin. In the spring of 1865, Grant took the city of Petersburg, Virginia, which had been besieged for nearly a year, and then captured Richmond, the capital of the Confederacy. In the final campaign of the war, Grant outmaneuvered Lee and forced him to surrender at Appomattox Court House, Virginia, on April 9, 1865.

On that day, Lee arrived in brilliant dress uniform, a gleaming sword at his side. Grant met him in what he described as a "rough traveling suit, the uniform of a private with the straps of a lieutenant-general." The contrast between the two great figures of the war could not have been more dramatic. Grant, who had failed so often before the war, had become one of the most famous Americans of his time. Even Lee's admirers appreciated that Grant allowed the defeated Confederates to return home to their farms with the horses they had used in battle. Ulysses S. Grant proved as generous in victory as he had been ferocious in battle.

Grant's headquarters at Vicksburg, Mississippi.

WHEN GENERAL GRANT LOST HIS COOL

by Lloyd Linford

General Ulysses S. Grant was known for his quiet, reflective personality when he commanded Union forces during the Civil War. His calm composure, even under the most trying battlefield conditions, was a source of wonderment to his associates, as was his aversion to the use of profanity and the inhumane treatment of animals — two frailties that were all too common among fighting soldiers.

The nearest Grant came to losing his temper in the presence of his close associate and aide Colonel Horace Porter was once during an especially critical engagement late in the war. The general's party happened upon the scene of a Union teamster, utterly beside himself with fury, trying in vain to persuade a team of horses to pull an army wagon out of a mud hole. The agitated teamster was whipping and flogging the horses and reviling them in the most abusive terms when Grant rode up.

Leaping from his saddle and clenching his fists as he ran, Grant charged up to the offending soldier and demanded, "What does this conduct mean? Stop beating those horses!" The enraged teamster finally calmed down when he saw that the general meant business, but not before taking another healthy swing at the reluctant horses.

Grant ordered the man seized and disciplined on the spot. But the incident continued to rankle him, as he mentioned it several times to Porter, even as bullets were flying around them in the heated battle that followed.

By nightfall, Grant was still upset. Over supper, he was moved to say, "If people only knew how much more they could get out of a horse by gentleness than harshness, they would save a great deal of trouble for both the horse and the man. A horse is a particularly intelligent animal; he can be made to do almost anything if his master has the intelligence to let him know what is required."

Grant's confrontation with the teamster, wrote Porter in his memoirs, "was the one exhibition of temper manifested by Grant during the entire campaign, and the only one I ever witnessed during my many years of service with him," which included the postwar period when Grant was president.

Later, while sitting quietly around the campfire one night, Porter asked the leader of Union armies how it happened that, through all the rough-and-tumble of army service and frontier life, he had never been provoked into swearing. Grant replied thoughtfully, "Well, somehow or other, I never learned to swear. When a boy, I seemed to have an aversion to it, and when I became a man I saw the folly of it. I have always noticed, too, that swearing helps to rouse a man's anger. And when a man flies into a passion, his adversary who keeps cool always gets the better of him.

"In fact, I could never see the use of swearing. I think it is the case with many people who swear excessively that it is a mere habit, and that they do not mean to be profane. But, to say the least, it is a great waste of time."

AT THE BATTLE OF SHILOH

by John Y. Simon

While Major General Ulysses S. Grant ate breakfast on April 6, 1862, he heard the roar of cannon seven miles away. He suddenly realized that he had made a terrible mistake. A great battle had begun!

Grant had brought his army up the Tennessee River to attack Confederate forces at Corinth, Mississippi. But while Grant prepared his army and waited for Brigadier General Don Carlos Buell and his twenty thousand troops to arrive, the Confederates had unexpectedly attacked the Union army encamped at Shiloh. Some of Grant's troops were still asleep when the Confederates charged at five in the morning. Many Union soldiers fled in panic.

Grant boarded a steamboat to join his army. He ordered reinforcements to assemble at Pittsburgh Landing, a steamboat docking site on the Tennessee River and the gathering point for his army. When Grant reached the battlefield, he found that his army had been forced back. There was danger of the Confederate army trapping the Union forces against the swollen Tennessee River. Already many soldiers huddled in panic at the riverbank, hoping to be evacuated.

Fortunately for Grant, steadfast troops under Brigadier General Benjamin M. Prentiss delayed the Confederate advance until late afternoon. After hours of fighting, Prentiss and his men became isolated and surrounded, and they surrendered. But they had given the rest of the army time to form a line of defense along the bluff overlooking the river. After dark, Buell's reinforcements arrived. Grant's army had been mauled that day, but he told General William Tecumseh Sherman that he would whip the enemy the next day.

Grant attacked the next morning. This time, the Confederates were surprised. They had attacked so successfully the day before that they had expected to win easily. The Confederate commander, Albert Sidney Johnston, had been killed during the first day of fighting, and his replacement, General Pierre G.T. Beauregard, now had fewer men than Grant's reinforced army. Grant hammered the Confederates with all his troops. After a second day of hard fighting, Beauregard withdrew toward Corinth. The Union army was left in possession of the battlefield and could claim a bloody victory. Casualties on both sides were enormous. The North had lost more than thirteen thousand men, the South more than eleven thousand. No previous battle fought in the United States had left so many dead and wounded.

After the battle, some northern newspapers criticized Grant for not preparing for a Confederate attack. They blamed him for the many casualties and called for his removal. President Abraham Lincoln, however, admired Grant for his attack on the second day. Lincoln knew that generals afraid to fight battles would never win the war to save the Union. He decided that Grant was a fighting general and insisted, "I can't spare this man: he fights."

At Shiloh, Grant showed what kind of general he was. He kept cool in the midst of battle. As he rallied his men to avoid defeat on the first day of fighting, he planned his strategy for a successful counterattack, and his calm self-confidence encouraged teenage boys to fight like veterans. He learned valuable lessons in each battle. The Battle of Shiloh taught him not to underestimate the enemy. Three years later, by the time he began the final campaign against Confederate general Robert E. Lee, Grant had mastered the strategy that eventually brought an end to the war.

ULYSSES AND JULIA

by Kathiann M. Kowalski

From poverty to fame and back again, Ulysses S. Grant and his wife, Julia Dent Grant, stood by each other for almost thirty-seven years of marriage.

Ulysses met Julia when he was a young lieutenant at Jefferson Barracks, Missouri. The family of his West Point classmate Frederick Dent lived nearby, and Ulysses began to spend a lot of time at their home, White Haven. Ulysses learned that he and Frederick's sister, Julia, shared a love for horses, and the two often went riding together.

One day when the couple were traveling to a friend's wedding, they had to cross a rickety bridge over a racing river. Ulysses promised to protect Julia, and she clung fast to him. When they reached the other side, Ulysses asked her, "How would you like to cling to me for the rest of your life?"

Julia said yes to the proposal, but the couple had to wait four years, until the Mexican War was over, before they could marry. Their first son, Frederick Dent, was born on May 30, 1850. They were expecting their second son, Ulysses, Jr. (nicknamed "Buck"), when Ulysses was transferred to the West Coast in the summer of 1852.

"You do not know how forsaken I feel here!" he wrote to Julia from Fort Humboldt, California. Desperately missing his wife and children, and unable to raise enough money for his family's trip west, Ulysses resigned from the Army in April 1854 and returned to White Haven.

Civilian life was a constant struggle for Ulysses. He worked hard but had bad luck as a farmer. He also was unable to support his family with a job in real estate. Unemployed, he turned to his father for help. He became the accountant for his father's leather business in Galena, Illinois, at a salary of six hundred dollars a year.

Despite their financial problems, the Grants were happy. In 1855, their daughter, Ellen (nicknamed "Nellie"), was born. Their fourth child, Jesse, arrived in 1858. Ulysses loved spending time with his children.

When the Civil War broke out in 1861, Ulysses rejoined the Army. Once again, he was separated from his family. He wrote home often, sending Julia

Julia and Ulysses Grant

In 1864, Grant's wife, Julia, and son Jesse joined him in camp.

A DIFFICULT PROBLEM

by Kathiann M. Kowalski

Ulysses Grant and his wife, Julia, looked at slavery in very different ways. Julia's family had owned slaves for many years, and she kept slaves even after she married Ulysses. In contrast, Ulysses's father, Jesse, was bitterly opposed to slavery. Jesse had once worked at a tannery owned by Owen Brown, whose son John later led the famous raid at Harpers Ferry, Virginia, in 1859. Probably one of the reasons Jesse and his wife, Hannah, did not attend their son's wedding at the Dent home was because the Dents owned slaves.

Ulysses did not publicly challenge the Dents' position on slavery. While struggling as a poor farmer in 1859, however, he freed William Jones, a slave given to him by Julia's father. And in 1862, when his wife's slave Black Julia ran away in Mississippi, he refused to pursue her.

love and "kisses for you and the children."

Whenever possible, his family visited him at camp. Julia and some or all of the children joined him in Cairo, Illinois; Corinth, Mississippi; and at least a dozen other places. The children loved visiting their father at army camp. "To the small boy it was 'father's army,'" recalled his youngest son, Jesse. Often the soldiers would carve toys or make molasses candy over the campfire. Jesse especially loved riding with his father to inspect the troops, either mounted on his own Shetland pony, Rebbie, or perched behind his father on a big buckskin horse named Mankiller.

The Grants' oldest son, Fred, then twelve years old, stayed with his father throughout the long Vicksburg Campaign in 1863. Fred carried a sword at his belt and bore the everyday hardships of army life. The following year, Fred went with his father to Washington when President Abraham Lincoln put Ulysses in charge of all Union forces. Ulysses's love for his family made him sensitive to the families of all soldiers. After victory in battle, he acted compassionately, seeing that everyone got food and medical attention. "This will all come out right in good time," he once assured Julia, "and you must not forget that each and every one of my soldiers has a mother, wife, or sweetheart, whose lives are as dear to them as mine is to you."

HOME FROM THE WAR

by Lori A. Gordon

After the end of the Civil War, Ulysses S. Grant began a new career — as national hero. Crowds gathered to see "the gallant hero who symbolized the valiant struggle to maintain the Union." Individuals, towns, and cities showered him with gifts. He received lavishly furnished homes in Philadelphia, Pennsylvania, and Galena, Illinois; cash in New York City; a collection of leather-bound, gilt-edged books in Boston; and more. It was quite a change for a man who had been largely unknown before the war.

Eventually, Grant purchased a house in Washington, D.C., and settled in with his family. In 1866, he was promoted to four-star general — the first ever in the U.S. Army. His task was to oversee the Reconstruction of the South.

The political climate in Washington was unsettled at this time. When President Abraham Lincoln was assassinated in 1865, Andrew Johnson had become president. A fierce battle over Reconstruction raged between Johnson and the Radical Republicans in Congress. The Republicans felt that Johnson was too lenient, too ready to forgive and forget. Grant was drawn into the battle. He served briefly as acting secretary of war under Johnson but found himself more and more in agreement with the Radicals.

In 1868, Grant became the Republican presidential candidate because he feared "the loss...of the results of the costly war...we have gone through" and felt he could prevent that from happening. He was not exactly enthusiastic, later saying, "I was forced into it in spite of myself," and did not campaign. But his immense popularity brought victory in 1868 and again in 1872. Not everyone was pleased. Former secretary of the Navy Gideon Welles said, "It pained me to see how little he understood of the fundamental principles and structure of our government."

Grant saw the job as a "gift of the people," and his agenda was simple: "A purely administrative officer should always...execute the will of the people.... Let us have peace." It was a hard time to be president. Relations with Great Britain were strained due to its support of the South during the Civil War. A bloody revolution was under way in Cuba. At home, the nation was still divided. The price of gold and the national debt were sky-high. Grant had his work cut out for him.

Throughout both his terms, Grant's presidency was mired in scandal after scandal. An attempt by Jay Gould and Jim Fisk (financiers and friends of Grant) to corner the gold market resulted in a stock market crash on Friday, September 24, 1869. Banks failed, stock brokerages closed, and the country panicked. President Grant ended the crisis by releasing government gold reserves, but the scandal of "Black Friday" lingered. Grant's vice president and some members of Congress were entangled in the Crédit Mobilier scandal, which involved insider

"Let us have peace."

Ulysses S. Grant as he looked as president. Grant was the first president since Andrew Jackson to serve two full terms in office.

dealing and bribery during the construction of the Union Pacific Railroad.

Though innocent of any wrongdoing, Grant was guilty of misjudgment. He was a man of honor and loyalty, unable or unwilling to see dishonor and disloyalty in those he trusted. The savvy military leader seemed a poor judge of character in civilian life.

Grant did have some successes. His secretary of state, Hamilton Fish, was an able foreign policy advisor. Advances were made in the more humane treatment of Indians. Taxes were reduced. Grant made gold the money standard, promising that all U.S. debts would be paid back in gold. This helped to curb inflation and stabilize the economy. All of the southern states were readmitted to the Union, and territorial disputes in the Northwest were settled. The healing of the nation began.

Personally, the Grants were happy in the White House. They traveled and entertained. After two terms, however, Grant was voted out of office. In December 1876, he addressed Congress: "It was my fortune, or misfortune, to be called to the office of Chief Executive without any previous training.... I have acted...from a conscientious desire to do what was right...and for the...best interests of the...people.... Failures have been errors of judgment, not...intent." In the end, Grant left office "amid general goodwill."

Civilians again, the Grants decided to travel until their money ran out. In

May 1877, they departed for England, where Grant was greeted as a hero. Their world tour lasted more than two years. They met many world leaders, including Queen Victoria and Prime Minister Benjamin Disraeli in England, Otto von Bismarck in Germany, and General Li Hung Chang in China.

When the Grants returned to the United States, Americans greeted their former president with affection, his past "sins" apparently forgiven. There was a suggestion of a third presidential term in 1880, but that effort failed. It was time for Grant to look ahead.

'TO WITNESS THESE THINGS'

by Meg Greene

On a summer day in 1884, Ulysses S. Grant sat down to lunch at his vacation home in Long Branch, New Jersey. While eating a peach, he complained of a terrible pain in his throat.

At first, he shrugged it off. But the pain was more than a minor annoyance. When he returned to New York City in the fall, Grant visited a local specialist. The diagnosis was not good. Grant was suffering from the early stages of throat cancer. Immediately, he set about looking after the financial security of his family.

Earlier that year, the editor of *Century Magazine* had approached Grant about writing a

Bankrupt and suffering from throat cancer, Grant moved with his family to Mount McGregor, New York, in June 1885. He spent his last days working on his memoirs there. He is shown here three days before his death.

series of essays on his Civil War campaigns. Grant reluctantly agreed and produced accounts of the Battles of Shiloh and Vicksburg. The articles were so successful that *Century* asked Grant to consider writing his memoirs. "Do you really think," Grant asked, "anyone would be interested in a book by me?"

Despite pain and fatigue, Grant worked every day. He sat at a large, square table in his study on the second floor of his New York home, interrupted only by his doctors and visits from his children and grandchildren.

When Grant's friend Samuel Clemens (better known as Mark Twain) learned that Grant was writing a book, he also found out that *Century* was not paying Grant any advance money. Clemens, who had met Grant five years earlier at a dinner in Chicago, believed that the magazine probably would not pay Grant very well for his work either. So he called on Grant at his home.

After two days of hard negotiations, Clemens offered Grant a ten-thousand-dollar advance and seventy percent of the book's net profits. Clemens's own publishing firm, Charles L. Webster & Company, would publish the book.

By June 1885, Grant's condition was worse. The family decided to spend the summer at Mount McGregor, in the Adirondack Mountains of upstate New York. As their train rolled through the Hudson Valley, crowds gathered to cheer the great general on what would be his final journey.

Upon arriving at Mount McGregor, Grant set to work. When he was not writ-

GRANT'S TOMB

by Glennette Tilley Turner

Richard Theodore Greener was a senior at Phillips Academy in Andover, Massachusetts, when the Civil War ended. He and his classmates idolized General Ulysses S. Grant. In 1870, Greener became the first African American graduate of Harvard University and went on to earn a law degree. When Greener was appointed secretary of the Grant Monument Association after Grant's death in 1885, he regarded it as a great personal honor. He believed that "like Washington and Lincoln, Grant was risen up by God to lead the Nation in a time of need."

The monument was to be built in New York City with private donations. Greener was instrumental in involving individuals and organizations in the fund drive. After the association raised more than six hundred thousand dollars, an imposing white granite structure in Riverside Park was built high above the Hudson River. Both General and Mrs. Grant are buried there. A display at the memorial tells of Greener's role in making it possible. Grant's famous words "Let us have peace" are carved over the entrance.

ing, he received visitors and well-wishers, many of them former Union and Confederate officers. Despite these distractions, Grant kept writing, often sitting on the porch bundled in a blanket or settled in a chair in the house, pencil in hand, scribbling furiously. He wrote that he was grateful "to witness these things," having lived long enough to see former enemies become friends.

Meanwhile, Clemens sent an army of salesmen throughout the country to sell subscriptions (prepublication orders) to the book. The publisher was working around the clock to make sure the book would be ready on time. Delays arose in part from Grant's insistence on revising the manuscript himself. He wanted his book to be perfect. Finally, on July 16, 1885, Grant laid down his pencil. "There is nothing more I should do to it now," he said. A week later, on July 23, he died.

Personal Memoirs of U.S. Grant proved to be a great critical and commercial success, selling more than three hundred thousand copies. The two-volume work was proudly displayed in many American parlors, evidence of Grant's enormous popularity. The book's success also ensured his family's financial security. Clemens presented Julia Grant with the largest royalty check ever written at the time — $200,000. In the years to come, Grant's memoirs earned between $420,000 and $450,000 for his family.

With its clear, direct prose, *Personal Memoirs of U.S. Grant* remains one of the greatest military narratives ever written. Every page of this Civil War classic reflects the quiet dignity of its author.

FALLEN FAMILY: ROBERT E. LEE'S EARLY YEARS

by Brandon Marie Miller

On June 18, 1793, at her family's red-brick plantation house overlooking the James River, Ann Hill Carter married Revolutionary War hero Henry "Light-Horse Harry" Lee. Although the Lees were one of Virginia's first families, Harry's money problems were well-known, and the Carters did not approve of twenty-year-old Ann's decision to marry him. Their concern was warranted.

By 1802, despite a sparkling political and military career, Harry was tens of thousands of dollars in debt because of bad investments. He was forced to sell most of the family lands under his control. Ann's father was so concerned about Harry's behavior that he rewrote his will so that Ann and her children's inheritance would be safe from the "possession or molestation from her husband, General Lee."

By 1806, despite the family's dire financial circumstances, Ann and Harry had four children, Algernon Sydney (who died in childhood), Charles Carter, Ann Kinloch, and Sydney Smith. Their fifth child was born on January 19, 1807, shortly after the death of Ann's beloved father. The boy was named Robert Edward after two of her brothers.

When Robert was two, his father was arrested and sent to prison for not paying his debts. Harry spent his time in prison writing his memoirs of the Revolutionary War. Ann's family encouraged her to leave him, but she refused. "Mr. Lee," she wrote, "constantly assures me his intention is to live with his family after his release from his present situation."

This 1795 painting by an unknown artist (bottom) is of Ann Hill Carter Lee, wife of Henry "Lighthorse Harry" Lee (below), a hero of the American Revolution. Ann and Harry were the parents of Robert E. Lee.

Shortly after Harry's release from prison in 1810, the Lees moved to the Potomac River city of Alexandria, just outside the new capital of Washington, D.C. There the children could go to school, and Ann could be closer to Lee and Carter relatives.

With Ann's income from her father and the generosity of relatives, Ann and Harry began a new life in Alexandria. But Harry hated living so close to people who looked at him with pity or disdain. He blamed others for his lack of success and in July 1812 traveled to Baltimore to help a journalist friend who opposed America's new war with Britain. An angry prowar mob attacked a group of Federalists (including Harry and his friend) defending the presses. Harry barely escaped with his life. In May 1813, still suffering from health problems stemming from his wounds, he went into exile in the Caribbean. Occasionally, he sent his family letters and gifts.

In one letter, he asked Carter to "hug my dear Robert for me and kiss little Mildred," Ann's last child, although he barely knew his two youngest children. Harry did try to return to Virginia in 1818, but he died making the trip.

A Lee relative arranged for Ann and the children to move into a large home at 607 Oronoco Street. By 1816, Ann was feeling the pinch of an economic depression. Her brother helped by sending Carter to Harvard. Ann wrote Carter urging him to economize as his mother, brothers, and sisters did each evening when they decided how to spend their few cents for the next day's food.

Little is known about Robert E. Lee's childhood. His half-brother, Henry Lee IV (from Harry's first marriage), recalled Robert greeting him looking "sheepish and shame-faced," trying to hide a lost tooth with a bone replacement that would not stay in place. He was accomplished at skating, was an excellent dancer, and enjoyed riding in the country.

Ann Hill Carter Lee

Even as a child, Robert worked hard at being good. He excelled in school, studying Latin, Greek, and math. In early 1824, seventeen-year-old Robert applied to the U.S. Military Academy at West Point, New York. The academy provided a free education and a career. Ann was now suffering from tuberculosis and spent time at a relative's house in the country. She wrote her son Smith, who was away in the U.S. Navy, "Alas, alas, I wish I had my little boys Smith and Robert living with me again." She lived long enough to know that Robert graduated second in his class at West Point. He was home when she died in 1829.

As an adult, Lee wrote, "A child learns all that it has of good from its mother." He fretted over his own children's upbringing and preached duty, self-denial, and discipline. From a troubled childhood, he emerged to rescue the tarnished Lee name, becoming the most famous son of a famous American family.

Artist William Edward West captured Lee as a lieutenant in the U.S. Army Corps of Engineers in 1838.

SOLDIER OF HONOR: LEE'S EARLY MILITARY CAREER

by Shari Lyn Zuber

The summer sun shone brightly as eighteen-year-old Robert Edward Lee disembarked from the steamship that had brought him up New York State's Hudson River to the U.S. Military Academy at West Point. The academy's beautiful but Spartan grounds were but a foreshadowing of the harsh lifestyle that awaited the young Virginian. Yet his difficult youth had prepared him well for what lay ahead.

Of the eighty-seven young men who began their education with Lee in 1825, only forty-five others would graduate with him in 1829. Lee graduated second in his class, and he was the first student to graduate from West Point without a single demerit (a mark against a cadet because of a rule violation).

Because of his standing, Lee was appointed to the elite U.S. Army Corps of Engineers. His first assignment was to aid in the construction of Fort Pulaski on Cockspur Island, near Savannah, Georgia. In poor health, the project's commander passed most of his responsibilities to the twenty-two-year-old Lee, who learned how to exercise authority.

The War of 1812 had shown that the United States needed a strong Atlantic coastal defense. Lee served most of the next sixteen years upgrading coastal fortifications, from Fort Monroe at the entrance to the Chesapeake Bay to Fort Hamilton in Brooklyn, New York.

By 1835, Lee was assigned to survey the Ohio-Michigan border. In the summer of 1836, he was given the monumental task of rerouting the Mississippi River to prevent the destruction of the city of St. Louis, Missouri. Lee devised a series of dikes that deflected the river's currents and stopped the formation of sandbars, which would have isolated the city from river traffic. For his success, he was promoted to captain.

With the annexation of Texas by the United States in 1845, Lee experienced his first combat. Reporting to San Antonio, Texas, in September 1846, he began serv-

WEST POINT

West Point started out as a military post but became the U.S. Military Academy in 1802.

ing under General John E. Wool. For the next three months, Lee led engineers in building bridges, improving roads, and removing the obstacles to Mexico.

Wool's inability to locate Mexican general Santa Anna's forces led to Lee's acting as scout. With just a young Mexican as a guide, Lee pinpointed the enemy and then rode forty miles back to camp. With only a three-hour rest, he led the U.S. troops to the enemy campsite, which ensured General Zachary Taylor's success at Buena Vista.

At the special request of General Winfield Scott, Lee joined his command and supervised the construction of the gun batteries that assisted in the capture of Veracruz, Mexico. Further distinguishing himself at Cerro Gordo, Lee made it possible for American troops and equipment to scale the mountain fortress village and surprise Santa Anna attacking from the rear.

He also found a route through a supposedly impassable lava bed, clearing the way to Mexico City. For his service at the Battle of Chapultepec (the fortified steep hill protecting the Mexican capital), Lee was promoted to brevet colonel.

With the war's end, Lee once again returned to fort construction duty, until his appointment as superintendent of West Point in 1852. Lee tightened the school's budget, modernized the curriculum, and improved cadet uniforms and living quarters. Although he was a strong leader, he did his best to err on the side of the student and always regretted having to give a demerit or dismiss a cadet.

The development of new regiments to police the expanding western frontier resulted in Lee's reassignment to Texas in 1855 as a lieutenant colonel in the Second Cavalry. However, the death of his wife's father in 1857 required that Lee take a two-year leave of absence to settle estate problems at Arlington, the family home in Virginia.

Confederate battery at Harpers Ferry, Virginia.

In October 1859, Lee commanded a force of U.S. marines to the site of the U.S. military garrison at Harpers Ferry, Virginia, where he suppressed an uprising led by abolitionist John Brown, who with his followers had seized the armory for weapons to incite a slave revolt. Lee then returned to duty in San Antonio to command the headquarters of the Department of Texas.

In February 1861, General Scott ordered him back to Washington. Since Abraham Lincoln's election, southern states had been seceding from the Union. Lee was offered the command of Union forces. For the first time in his career, he was forced to decide where his greater loyalty lay — with the country he had served for thirty-two years or with his ancestral state. Lee's father, Light-Horse Harry Lee, had once said, "Virginia is my country; her I will obey, however lamentable the fate to which it may subject me." So was the choice made by the son.

THE CIVIL WAR YEARS

by Harold Holzer

As hard as it is to imagine, Robert E. Lee spent the first year of the Civil War in obscurity. He did nothing heroic, nothing dramatic. He was merely in charge of the defense of western Virginia, and he even proved unable to prevent Union forces from seizing that territory.

Many in the Confederacy concluded that Lee had grown too old for important command. His critics called him "Evacuating Lee" and "Granny Lee." Few southerners in 1861 would have guessed that he would soon emerge as the greatest Confederate military hero of the war.

Ironically, northerners seemed to appreciate Lee before southerners did. Abraham Lincoln offered him command of all Union forces in early 1861, but Lee declined. He said that he would never raise his sword against his native state, and by then Virginia had seceded to join the Confederacy. Lee returned home,

Wounded soldiers receive medical attention in the field near Fredericksburg, Virginia, on May 2, 1863, after the Battle of Chancellorsville.

believing that he would fight no more.

But Confederate president Jefferson Davis had faith in Lee and made him his personal military advisor after the general's early failures in western Virginia. Then, in the spring of 1862, Confederate general Joseph E. Johnston was gravely wounded in action, and Lee was named to take his place as commander of Confederate forces throughout the state.

It was a moment of crisis. Union troops seemed poised to take the Confederate capital of Richmond and win the war. Now in command of the Army of Northern Virginia, Lee reorganized his force and summoned the legendary general Thomas "Stonewall" Jackson to join him. In the Seven Days Battles that followed, Lee turned back the much larger Union invasion force and sent it into retreat toward Washington.

That August, Lee again met Federal forces in battle at Bull Run, in Manassas, Virginia, site of the war's first Confederate victory the year before. This time, with Lee in command, the Confederate triumph was even greater.

Confident that he could now invade the North and force Lincoln to end the fighting and recognize the Confederacy, Lee marched into Maryland. There he met Union forces at the fierce Battle of Antietam on September 17, 1862. It was the bloodiest day of the war. Some twenty-three thousand soldiers were killed or wounded in the fighting. Although Lee commanded brilliantly, he was unable to defeat the enemy and was forced to retreat back into Virginia. Lee's defeat encouraged Lincoln to issue the Emancipation Proclamation a few days after the battle.

Three months later, Union forces marched on the Confederacy. On December 13, the two armies met at the Battle of Fredericksburg, where Lee dealt the North a crushing defeat. Cleverly positioned in the heights overlooking town, the Confederates were able to pick off Union troops as they crossed the Rappahannock River and attempted to scale the hills.

Lee's masterpiece, however, was the Battle of Chancellorsville in May 1863. There, a brilliant strategy produced a great victory for the South and a humiliating defeat for the North. But it was Lee who suffered the greatest loss that day. His chief lieutenant, "Stonewall" Jackson, was shot by his own men, who mistook him for a Union soldier, and died a few days later.

Lee won almost all his battles against much larger opposing armies, earning him a reputation as one of the greatest military leaders America has ever produced

From left to right: Major General G.W. Custis Lee (Robert E. Lee's eldest son), General Robert E. Lee, and Colonel Walter H. Taylor at Richmond, Virginia, April 1865.

FREDERICKSBURG — 1863

This view of Fredericksburg, Virginia, seen from across the Rappahannock River, was captured by photographer Timothy H. O'Sullivan in February 1863.

Rather than wait for the enemy to take advantage of this tragedy, Lee went on the offensive. He launched his second, and last, invasion of the North, reaching what became known as the "High Tide" of the Confederacy in July 1863 at the biggest and most famous encounter of the war: the Battle of Gettysburg in Pennsylvania. On the second day of furious fighting outside the sleepy village, Confederate forces failed to win the decisive high ground from the Union. Lee might have retreated that afternoon, but he decided to gamble by ordering a massive attack the following day.

It was the most controversial decision of Lee's career. Pickett's Charge, as the assault became known, ended in a huge death toll and defeat, and Lee marched his beaten army south, never again to regain the glory of early 1863. The fact that he was able to save his army and bring it back to the South, however, was itself a triumph for Lee. Had Union troops pursued him, he would have been trapped by the floodwaters of the Potomac River. Forced to fight yet again, Lee might have been crushed, ending the war. But Union forces stayed put in Gettysburg, and Lee was able to escape.

By this time, although Lee had become a beloved hero in the South, he had been slowed by advancing age and crippling heart disease. Still, there was never any thought of replacing or even resting him. Somehow, he went on to face a Union army twice the size of his own when Ulysses S. Grant marched against Richmond in 1864. At the Wilderness, Spotsylvania, and Cold Harbor, Lee held Grant at bay, while fifty thousand Union soldiers fell in action. But with supplies dwindling, his soldiers beginning to desert, and northern reinforcements vastly outpacing his own troops, Lee knew he would be unable to survive.

Now the commander of all Confederate armies, he convinced his government to allow him to recruit slaves to fight for the South. Although this plan was never put into action, it would have been a cruel blow to African Americans, asking them to fight to save the system that held them in bondage. Although Lee did believe that slaves who served in the Confederate army should be freed, this proposal was not his finest moment.

In the spring of 1865, Lee was finally forced to surrender Richmond to the Union. He was no longer able to protect the capital. As Jefferson Davis and his government fled farther south, Lee made one final attempt to link up with Confederate forces in North Carolina. But Grant's troops surrounded and trapped Lee's men. The general had no choice but to surrender his army, which now numbered only twenty-eight thousand exhausted, hungry, badly equipped men. Lee himself, though only fifty-eight years old, had aged beyond his years. In just four years, he had changed from a robust middle-aged man to an elderly-looking veteran with a thick white beard.

Although many historians believe that Lee erred twice by marching north on invasions doomed to failure, no one has ever questioned Lee's genius at command or his extraordinary ability to devise masterful battle strategies and inspire his men. He outguessed his opponents; knew precisely when to attack, wait, and counterattack; and chose brilliant and devoted field generals. Most remarkable of all, Lee won almost all his battles against much larger opposing armies, earning him a reputation as one of the greatest military leaders America has ever produced.

DIGNITY IN DEFEAT

by Harold Holzer

Robert E. Lee had become famous for the way he waged war. But he became even more famous — and more beloved — for the way he waged peace. Even though he was "vanquished," wrote his military aide, he seemed somehow "a victor."

By 1865, the Civil War had been raging for four years. Poorly clothed, inadequately armed, and ill fed, Confederate soldiers began deserting in great numbers. Those who remained from Lee's once-fearful Army of Northern Virginia were soon surrounded by superior Union forces under General Ulysses S. Grant. In early April, Lee reluctantly came to the conclusion that he must surrender to Grant before more lives were sacrificed to a cause now hopelessly lost.

Appomattox Court House, Virginia, a town about one hundred twenty miles from the place where the first battle of the war had been fought four years earlier.

Timothy O'Sullivan's photograph of the McLean house at Appomattox Court House, April 1865.

At first, Lee proposed that Grant meet him to discuss peace terms, but the Union commander refused. There could be no discussion, only surrender. Lee might simply have sent word that he was giving up and returned home to his family. But he probably remembered that the famous British general Lord Cornwallis had been much criticized for refusing to attend the ceremony of his surrender to George Washington during the Revolutionary War. Lee decided that he would personally surrender his army, just as Grant desired.

On April 9, Lee donned a glorious new full-dress uniform, placed a gleaming sword at his side, and rode slowly to the place that had been chosen for the ceremony: the home of a man named Wilmer McLean in the town of Appomattox Court House, Virginia. The town was about one hundred twenty miles from the place where the first battle of the war had been fought four years earlier.

Lee's appearance shocked some of the onlookers who gathered outside the McLean home to await his arrival. He seemed older and balder than wartime photographs showed him. But one eyewitness noted that he "never appeared more grandly heroic than on this occasion." He gave no hint of the sorrow or anger that undoubtedly filled his heart. "Those who watched his face to catch a glimpse of what was passing in his mind," another observer reported, could detect "no trace of his inner sentiments."

Grant's appearance was in marked contrast to his opponent's. His own dress uniforms had failed to arrive at his headquarters, so he had no choice but to wear a plain and dusty field uniform. The two great figures of the war greeted each other solemnly, taking seats near the fireplace as Grant reminded Lee that they had met before — during the Mexican War, when both men were ambitious young officers.

Finally, they got down to business. As they agreed to peace terms, Grant's aide, Lieutenant Colonel Ely S. Parker, wrote them down. Lee inquired about his soldiers' horses and pistols, and Grant generously agreed to permit the men to keep them. Lee thanked Grant, saying that it would mean a great deal to them as they returned home to work their farms.

Then both men sat in silence, the scratch of pen on paper the only sound in the room. Grant later recalled that Lee's expression had given no hint as to whether he was "glad that the end had finally come, or felt sad and was too manly to show it." There was "no theatrical display," said one of the officers who crowded into the McLean parlor to witness the historic event. Another asked, "What man could have laid down his sword at the feet of a victorious general with greater dignity?"

When the papers were signed, Lee rose, shook Grant's hand, and walked slowly to the front porch, looking to one eyewitness suddenly "older, grayer...very tired." Lee betrayed his emotions only then, clapping his hands together and calling loudly for an orderly when he could not find his horse, Traveller. He then rode slowly back to camp as his men surrounded him and offered their last tearful cheers and salutes. The war was finally over.

"What man could have laid down his sword at the feet of a victorious general with greater dignity?"

The surrender at Appomattox.

A National Cemetery:
The Fate of Lee's Arlington Plantation

by Mark Travis

Union quartermaster general Montgomery Meigs was angry when Robert E. Lee quit the Union army and later led a Confederate army in the Civil War. His anger grew deeper as time passed and thousands of Union soldiers died in battles with Lee's army.

Meigs wanted revenge. He saw his chance in the war's fourth year, when he was told to find a new place to bury the dead from the latest campaign against Lee. He picked the Lee family home, a Virginia plantation near Washington, D.C., called Arlington.

Meigs knew his choice meant Lee could never live there again. But he could not have known where his decision would lead. In the years to come, Lee's home would become the nation's greatest monument to its war dead: Arlington National Cemetery.

Lee loved Arlington. As a young soldier, whenever Lee returned to Arlington for vacations from far-off posts, he liked to lie in bed and read to his children. He would order them to tickle his feet. "No tickling, no story," he would say.

When his father-in-law died in 1857, Lee came home again. Arlington had fallen into a sad state of disrepair. The roof leaked; fences were down; the lawns were overgrown with bushes and weeds.

Montgomery Meigs

Above: U.S. quartermaster general Montgomery C. Meigs (1816–1892) was responsible for creating Arlington National Cemetery.
Below: Arlington, the Lee family home.

Mary Custis Lee

William Edward West painted Mary Randolph Custis Lee, wife of Robert E. Lee and great-granddaughter of Martha Washington, in 1838.

Lee's slaves at Arlington brought new life to the fields by planting corn and other grains under his direction. Lee and the Irish laborers he hired worked hard, too, fixing the roof and repairing fences. He managed money with care, renting land he could not use to others. And he began bringing Arlington back.

The house, with its front entrance framed by eight thick pillars, looked more like a monument than a home. In fact, it was a monument. Lee's wife, Mary Custis, whose family actually owned Arlington, was a descendant of Martha Washington, and Arlington had been built as a museum honoring her husband, George. It was filled with the Washingtons' belongings. Lee's father-in-law would sometimes reward visitors by digging out a paper Washington had signed, tearing off his signature, and giving it away.

Arlington sat on the Virginia border. It was a beautiful spot atop a hill just across the Potomac River from the nation's capital. Standing at the front entrance, Lee could see the Capitol Building in the distance.

When the Civil War came, Lee had divided loyalties. After a night of pacing in his second-floor room, he made his choice: He would fight for his home state.

Lee left Arlington on April 22, 1861. The next month, Union troops moved in, making Arlington the headquarters for the defense of Washington. Many of the Lees' possessions disappeared, including much of their George Washington collection. Several forts were built on the property.

In 1863, as the war raged on, freed slaves streamed into Washington. The government built a town at Arlington to house thousands of them. It was called Freedmen's Village, and it included schools, homes, churches, and a hospital.

The first Union soldier was buried on the property on May 13, 1864. By the end of the year, more than seven thousand soldiers had been buried near him, an average of more than thirty a day.

When the war ended in 1865, Lee wanted to contribute to peace. He did not try to reclaim Arlington, knowing that doing so would make northerners angry. He saw Arlington only two more times, from a distance, on visits to Washington.

Freedmen's Village closed after thirty years, leaving Arlington to be what it remains today: a cemetery. As the years passed, more soldiers served in more wars, and many of them were buried there. With time, the neat rows of simple markers began to seem very special. Arlington now honors the thousands of men and women who have served the nation Lee helped create. Each year, about four million people come to visit.

Among the two hundred thousand people buried at Arlington is Montgomery Meigs, the quartermaster general responsible for making it a graveyard. His body lies not far from Mary Lee's old rose garden.

Lee is not buried at Arlington, but the house there has been restored as a memorial to him. For that reason — and even more for what Arlington represents — it seems certain that Lee would still feel very much at home.

A SCHOOL FOR GENTLEMEN

by Virginia Calkins

On a chilly morning in early October 1865, Robert E. Lee began a new job and a new life in a new home. On that morning, the former Confederate general took the oath of office as president of Washington College, a small school in Lexington, Virginia. For the brief ceremony, Lee wore one of his gray army uniforms with the insignia removed; he had no other clothes.

Washington College was in poor financial condition. It had only a handful of students and a faculty of but five professors. Its buildings and equipment were in bad shape. The year before, Union soldiers under General David Hunter had looted its library, destroyed its scientific equipment, and damaged its buildings.

School opened that autumn with fifty students, but thanks to Lee's reputation, the number increased until the enrollment reached four hundred. Many who applied did not even know the name of the school and sent letters to "Lexington College," "Washington Institute," "Virginia University," or "General Lee's College."

Students today (inset) walk along the Colonnade (below) at Washington and Lee University in Lexington, Virginia.

Lee worked hard at his new job. As he wrote to his son Rooney, he wanted to "be of service to the country and the rising generation." Lee believed that the students should learn practical skills to help rebuild the South. Under his administration, the school started new fields of study, including departments of mechanical and civil engineering, practical mechanics, practical chemistry, and modern languages.

These new programs would require more professors, classrooms, and equip-

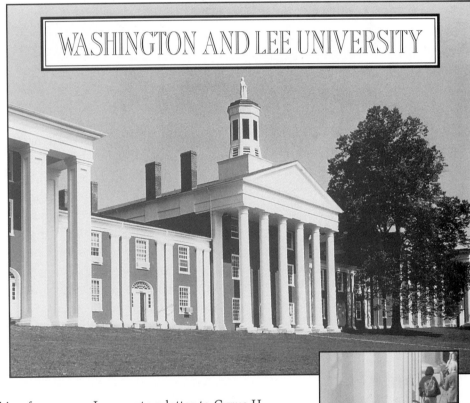

WASHINGTON AND LEE UNIVERSITY

ment. Although he disliked asking for money, Lee wrote a letter to Cyrus H. McCormick, the inventor of the reaper. McCormick, a native of Lexington, had moved to Chicago and become very wealthy. He responded with a check for ten thousand dollars for a new classroom building and later sent additional contributions. Other northern businessmen, impressed by Lee's ideas, donated money and books to the school.

In the impoverished South, parents had to make great sacrifices to send their children to college. One boy, Harvey Butler Fergusson, walked all the way from Alabama carrying a gold watch and three hundred dollars, all that his family

After Lee's death, Richmond sculptor Edward Valentine was commissioned to create a recumbent (reclining) statue of the general. He sculpted Lee as if he were asleep on a battlefield cot. In 1883, a special chamber to house the sculpture was added to the Lee Chapel at Washington and Lee University. The Lee family mausoleum (tomb) is located in the area beneath the statue.

Lee poses on the porch of his Richmond home a few days after he surrendered to Grant. He is still in uniform.

could scrape together for his four years of college. The boy spent summers in the Lexington area working as a field hand to help pay his expenses.

Lee knew each student at Washington by name. Many were veterans who had served with him during the war. Such men often had a steadying influence on the younger boys. Lee received weekly reports on each student's classwork. If a boy had a problem, he was called into the president's office, where Lee gave him helpful advice. Though usually kind and gentle, Lee did not hesitate to expel any student who behaved badly and brought disgrace to the school. Lee did not believe in too many rules. Once, when asked by a couple of students for a copy of the school regulations, Lee told them, "We have no written rules. Each student is expected to act like a gentleman."

Students from many northern states also came to Washington College.

As enrollment increased, the college chapel became too small to hold all the students. So Lee suggested that a new chapel be built. It was approved in July 1866. Lee's son Custis, who headed the engineering department at the nearby Virginia Military Institute, selected the design of the chapel, and Lee chose the site and supervised the construction. When it was finished, he moved his office to the basement of the chapel.

The years of war had put a strain on Lee's heart, and his responsibilities as college president took a further toll. His health gradually declined, and on October 12, 1870, he died of a stroke. He was entombed in a vault in the basement of the college chapel, a few feet from the room that had been his office. In his honor, the name of the school was changed to Washington and Lee University. To many people, however, it would always be "General Lee's College."

TRAVELLER

by Brenda Brammer

During the fall of 1861, in the mountains of western Virginia, Robert E. Lee purchased a five-year-old gray horse first named Jeff Davis and later Greenbrier. Renamed Traveller, this gallant animal unfailingly served Lee through the terrible years of the Civil War.

Lee had four other horses in his entourage (Richmond, Ajax, Brown Roan, and Lucy Long), but the "Confederate Gray" soon became the general's favorite. Traveller stood sixteen hands high (sixty-four inches at the point of his shoulder). He was dark iron gray and had a black mane and tail. Even under the poorest conditions, when snow and mud were knee-deep and the only food was corncobs, this noble horse seemed untiring and always responsive to his master's commands.

Lee once wrote lovingly about how a painting of Traveller should look: "Such a picture would inspire a poet, whose genius could then depict his worth or describe his endurance of toil, hunger, thirst, heat and cold, and the dangers and sufferings through which he has passed."

Eventually, the calm gray warhorse became as well-known and recognizable to the Army of Northern Virginia as the general himself. Traveller accompanied Lee from Virginia to Georgia and north to Pennsylvania. In one letter home, Lee wrote that at Richmond, the "Gray" had carried him through seven days of battle, and in the campaign of 1864, the saddle was seldom off his back.

It was Traveller whom Lee rode to Appomattox Court House on April 9, 1865. After accepting the surrender conditions of General Ulysses S. Grant, Lee rode Traveller back to his troops. As their valiant commander passed by, many of the soldiers lovingly patted the flanks of the gray horse they knew so well.

When Lee accepted the presidency of Washington College in Lexington, Virginia, Traveller continued to serve him. Before his family arrived in Lexington, he wrote, "Traveller is my only companion, I may also say my pleasure." Lee often took long rides, sometimes accompanied by his daughter on Lucy Long, who also had survived the war.

Lee would sometimes allow Traveller to graze on the lush green grass of his front lawn, believing that the horse deserved some pampering after the ordeal of the war. Lee's horse had become so famous that he was sent sets of saddles and bridles from England, Baltimore, and Richmond. His favorite was thought to be an American saddle from St. Louis. During a holiday trip, Lee wrote to his clerk, "How is Traveller? Tell him I miss him dreadfully, and have repented of our separation but once — and this the whole time since we parted."

Traveller performed his final act of service for his master on October 15, 1870. The celebrated warhorse, with empty saddle and bridle draped in black crape, was led by two Confederate veterans following Lee's hearse to the college chapel.

Traveller survived his master by only two years. He contracted tetanus (lockjaw) from a nail that had penetrated his hoof and could not be saved. For years, Traveller's skeleton was displayed in the museum at Washington and Lee University. Now the warhorse is interred at the university near the tomb of the master he served so well.

WAR AND MEDICINE

The Civil War was a **new kind of war**,
*fought with new kinds of weapons that
inflicted new kinds of wounds.
It called for a new kind of medicine.*

But medical care in the Civil War remained hopelessly primitive. Soldiers shot in the arm or leg faced only one kind of treatment: amputation. Wounds to the chest or head were almost always fatal. Seriously wounded soldiers died quickly if they were fortunate. The unlucky ones usually lingered in pain until they, too, died.

Soldiers faced an even greater foe than enemy bullets: disease. Doctors had little idea how to fight infection. Drugs were usually ineffective. Malaria, measles, pneumonia, diarrhea, consumption, and other illnesses killed more Civil War soldiers than bullets. Diarrhea alone claimed 44,000 lives. Altogether, the Union lost 360,000 men during the Civil War — but only 67,000 died in battle. Many of the rest died of illness or starved in Confederate prisons. More than 300 died just from sunstroke!

Easing the suffering were dedicated nurses who tended the sick and wounded with great tenderness. Their efforts were criticized by those who thought it improper for women to care for men.

*But had they been forbidden to nurse soldiers,
the suffering brought on by war would
have been far greater.*

FRONTIER PHYSICIANS

by Mary Gores

With a bottle of whiskey to make his patient insensible to pain and a bowie knife as his surgical tool, Kit Carson must have performed some memorable operations. Although Carson's surgery might be considered crude and unsanitary by today's standards, many frontiersmen owed their lives to similar hunting-knife surgeries performed by whoever was available and able. And if no one else was around, a frontiersman would do his own surgery. On the unpopulated western frontier of the early 1800s, doctors were rare and arrow, gunshot, and

In 1862, ambulance bearers of the Army of the Potomac were photographed as they took part in a drill for removing the wounded from the battlefield.

other wounds were common problems.

The few doctors who came to the West in those early days came with expeditions. They were usually better educated than others on the expedition, so they used their education for many things besides medicine. Expedition doctors kept the daily journals, acted as peacemakers with the Indians, and kept records of geology and animal and plant life.

Because of their contributions to science and the development of the West, some of the expedition doctors were honored by having their names given to the plants, animals, or landmarks they observed and recorded. The Steller's jay got its name from Dr. George Steller, the doctor on the Vitas Bering Expedition to Alaska. James Peak, a mountain in the Rocky Mountains of Colorado, is named after Dr. Edwin James, who accompanied Major Stephen Long's expedition surveying the Platte River.

Toward the middle of the 1800s, military forts and encampments were established to aid exploration and settlement of the West. These military posts brought the first professional medical men to the western frontier — the military doctors.

Conditions in the military outposts were usually poor. The barracks were filthy, damp, and stuffy. Food for the soldiers consisted mainly of wild game, white bread, and soda biscuits. Everything was cooked with plenty of lard and

served up with strong, black coffee. Because of the shortage of fresh fruits and vegetables, many of the men suffered from scurvy, a lack of vitamin C. Military doctors searched the countryside for wild fruits or grew cabbages and tomatoes in nearby garden plots to make sure the soldiers' diets were better balanced.

Scurvy was not the only problem. Common ailments treated by the doctors included arrow and gunshot wounds, broken bones, frozen hands and feet, snakebite, and diseases such as pneumonia, typhoid, and smallpox.

Many of the military doctors had practiced during the Civil War, when harsh living conditions, limited medical supplies, and many severe injuries made amputation the best cure for many problems. If a soldier's broken leg did not heal properly or an arm wound became infected, military doctors in the forts would often cut it off. At that time, doctors in both the East and the West did not know what else to do to stop infection from spreading. They did not realize that infection might be caused by a dirty knife or bandage.

When the doctors at the outposts were not busy treating patients, they performed other tasks. By order of the U.S. secretary of war, military doctors studied the weather, plants, geology, and Indian customs of the area. Military surgeon Dr. Albert Myer became so fascinated with Indian smoke signals that he invented his own system of signaling using flags by day and torches by night. Myer became the chief signal officer of the U.S. Army, set up the Signal Corps, and helped extend the military telegraph throughout the West.

As the West became more settled, many military doctors stayed on to start private practices. In the late 1800s, these ex-military physicians, along with other doctors recently settled in the West, became known as "horse-and-buggy doctors."

But conditions on the frontier were slow to improve. Settlers lived in musty, damp sod houses or drafty log huts. They got their drinking water from the same ditch in which their neighbors washed laundry. An injured person was often put on a horse — a dirty rag covering his or her wound — and galloped miles across the prairie to the nearest doctor. And even though ether came into use in 1846 and chloroform in 1872, whiskey was still a commonly used painkiller. Epi-

In 1861, Edwin Forbes covered the Army of the Potomac as a staff artist for *Frank Leslie's Illustrated Newspaper*. He concentrated mostly on the Union soldiers' daily life. In 1863, he captured a soldier eating his Christmas dinner after being relieved of picket duty for two hours. Soon the soldier will retreat to his shelter to escape the cold.

An amputation being performed in a hospital tent at Gettysburg, July 1863.

demics of typhoid, diphtheria, and smallpox were frequent. Although a smallpox vaccine was available, many westerners were more afraid of the vaccine than the disease.

Drugs of that era did not come in packaged, ready-to-swallow pills but in bulk shipments from the East as roots, leaves, herbs, or bark. The doctor then mashed, pounded, and mixed them. Powders were put into little squares of newspaper and liquids into small hand-blown bottles. Bottles of leeches for bloodletting were available into the late 1800s.

Frontier medicine was not a profitable business for the hard-working doctor. Payment — when there was any at all — was usually made in chickens, cows, or labor. When money was paid, charges for a house visit might be two dollars, a leg amputation fifty dollars, and setting a broken arm twenty dollars.

Few laws specified what requirements a doctor should meet. A man did not even have to have a college degree to practice medicine. Many fake doctors, called quacks, traveled about the countryside, taking advantage of the ignorant.

But even honest, educated doctors often failed to cure or even understand their patients' ailments. Internal problems especially stumped frontier physicians, who did not yet have the benefit of x-rays and other technology. In addition, physicians often lacked the opportunity to study the human body because autopsies were considered disrespectful.

By the early 1900s, the quality of medical care in the West was, in general, as good as that in the rest of the country, although in rural areas there was less access to the best available care. With the coming of the automobile, both the open frontier and the horse-and-buggy doctor gradually disappeared. But the practice of frontier medicine remains a fascinating chapter in the history of American medicine.

VICTORY OVER PAIN

by Laurel Sherman

Before the discovery of anesthesia, patients who underwent surgery entered their operations fully awake and sensitive to pain. The patients were strapped onto tables and held down by doctors' assistants so that they would not move during the operation, and their screams could be heard all over the hospital. Doctors who could listen to these cries and continue their surgery must have been very hard men indeed. Many patients died from the shock of surgery regardless of the skill of the surgeon. Others killed themselves rather than submit to the agony. Naturally, the dream that someday there would be surgery without pain was popular with surgeons and patients alike.

But such a dream was far from the minds of the crowds of people who flocked to see the demonstrations put on by traveling medicine shows in the 1840s. Among the hilarious acts was one in which a person from the audience would inhale nitrous oxide (laughing gas) or ether until he acted mildly drunk and silly. The friends of the poor man would laugh at his crazy antics, brought on by the odd effects of the gas. Gradually, ether and laughing gas parties became a common entertainment among young people.

About this same time, a Boston dentist was looking for a painless way to fix teeth. William Thomas Green Morton had a dental practice in Boston that was only moderately successful. But he had an idea for making new crowns for decaying teeth. He knew that if he could make this crowning process painless, he would have more business than he had ever had before.

Morton knew of the experiments of Horace Wells, his friend and fellow dentist. Wells had discovered that under the influence of laughing gas, people frequently injured themselves without feeling it. Wells had used the gas on himself and a few others to perform painless operations. But before he had perfected his use of the gas, he attempted a demonstration before the medical students at Harvard University. The demonstration was a miserable failure. Wells had neglected to experiment with the gas enough to understand fully its effects on all patients, and as soon as the operation started, his patient screamed. The students jeered and laughed at Wells, who fled from the demonstration hall in humiliation. Wells never fully recovered from this experience. Later in life, he began to drink heavily and finally committed suicide.

But William Morton was a more patient man than Wells. He used Wells's experience and the advice of a scientist friend named Charles Thomas Jackson to conduct experiments. Jackson had suggested the use of ether instead of laughing gas. Only after months of trials was Morton confident that he had found a way to put people to sleep safely. He used Jackson's sulfuric ether and Wells's technique of having the patient breathe the vapor. He experimented on his dog and on himself. He worked on the family goldfish and on trout he caught in a nearby stream. Not even the beetles in the woods were safe!

Soon Morton was ready to try his experiments on people. He went to work to perfect the device for giving the gas to patients. He had to regulate the amount of ether taken in so that the effect would always be the same. Too little and the patient would become wild and uncontrollable. Too much and the patient might die from it.

He tried using the device on himself first. After he had inhaled enough gas, Morton had one of his teeth taken out by his friend Dr. Hayden. As they expected, Morton felt no pain; the experiment was a success. So when a man came to Morton in pain a few days later needing a tooth extracted, Morton did not hesitate to use the ether again. Again the procedure worked.

Now Morton felt that he was ready to make his discovery known, and in only two weeks he was preparing to demonstrate his ether device before the students and staff at Massachusetts General Hospital in Boston. Dr. Warren, the surgeon who had permitted Horace Wells to demonstrate at Harvard, was convinced by Morton's confidence to let him try the demonstration.

The patient, Gilbert Abbott, was to have a tumor on his neck removed. By nine o'clock on October 16, 1846, everything was ready — except Morton. He was still with the instrument maker having the last few adjustments made on his inhaler. Just before ten

William Thomas Green Morton

Morton (1819–1868), a dentist and physician from Massachusetts, was a pioneer in the use of surgical anesthesia.

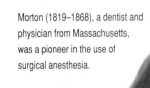

o'clock, Dr. Warren said that he could wait no longer and was about to cut into the patient when Morton rushed in.

The demonstration began. Morton gave Abbott the gas, and Abbott began to drift into a deep ether sleep. Before beginning the operation, the surgeon pinched him and asked whether it hurt. "No," Abbott answered, as he grew drowsier and drowsier. Finally, the surgeon went to work, cutting out the tumor and stitching the wound. When the patient began to rouse, they asked what he had felt. After a rough sensation on his neck, he said, all he could remember were wonderful dreams. The audience was electrified. The surgeon declared, "Gentlemen, this is no humbug."

The next day, the newspapers carried the story. Many medical people immediately accepted Morton's discovery. But there was opposition to anesthesia as well. Some religious people proclaimed that God had intended for people to suffer pain. Other people were afraid of the painless sleep and wondered whether they would ever wake from it. Some cities even advertised that anesthesia was not used in their hospitals.

Morton had dreamed of growing wealthy and famous from his discovery, but this did not happen. He named his gas Letheon and refused to tell others that its only working ingredient was ether, a substance available to any doctor. He tried to sell the mysterious Letheon, but doctors and hospitals refused to buy it without knowing its ingredients.

Meanwhile, challenges arose to Morton's claim to the discovery of anesthesia. Morton's scientist friend Charles Jackson said that he deserved credit for the discovery because he had suggested that Morton use ether. And later it was learned that a Georgia physician named Crawford Long had performed painless operations using ether in 1842, several years before the Morton demonstration.

None of these men ever benefited from the discovery of anesthesia. Morton died penniless. Jackson ended his days in an insane asylum. Long became a lost figure in history. But the breakthrough in which they all took part provided tremendous benefits to people everywhere.

ANGELS OF THE BATTLEFIELD: CIVIL WAR NURSES

by Harold Holzer

Before the Civil War, it was not considered proper for women to nurse sick men, no matter how desperately they needed medical attention. Such barriers began to come down during the war. For one thing, most able-bodied men, North and South, volunteered or were required to serve in the military. They could not be spared for nursing. More important, the war's huge battles produced so many casualties that there were simply not enough people to care for them.

Before long, female nurses were playing an important role in the Civil War. Grateful soldiers called them the "angels of the battlefield." But many Americans continued to feel that women should not nurse men and criticized the women who did so, no matter

Harriet Douglas Whetten served as an army nurse from 1862 to 1865 on hospital ships out of New York and Philadelphia.

how dedicated they were.

The best-known Civil War nurse was Clara Barton, a Massachusetts-born former schoolteacher. She had worked from the age of fifteen but had no real experience as a nurse except for the care she had given her sick brother for two years in the 1830s.

In 1855, Barton journeyed to Washington, D.C., in search of a warmer climate. Eventually, she landed a government clerking job, working for the U.S. Patent Office. Such jobs were usually held by men, but during the Civil War many were held by women because so many men had joined the army.

Barton became involved in the care and comfort of Union soldiers even before a battle was fought. Citizens of Baltimore rioted against Massachusetts soldiers when they passed through the city on their way to defend Washington. Barton helped the soldiers replace their lost belongings when they arrived in the capital.

After the Battle of Bull Run, she was alarmed to learn that wounded troops had not had access to medical supplies. Barton advertised in newspapers for donations, and she began supplying bandages and medicine to the army. In 1862, the U.S. Surgeon General gave her a special pass to travel with the army and distribute "comforts for the sick and wounded." At last, she would work as a nurse herself.

Over the next three years, Barton nursed and brought supplies, food and water to Union soldiers on battlefields from Maryland to South Carolina. At one point, she served briefly as supervisor of nurses under General Benjamin F. Butler's command. Otherwise, she never held an official post during the war.

There was never any doubt about her bravery or her devotion to the soldiers.

"I went in while the battle raged."

Clara Barton

Above: Barton (1821–1912) was the organizer of the American Red Cross. Before she served as a nurse in the Civil War, she was a teacher and worked in the U.S. Patent Office. Left: Barton's home from 1897 to 1912 in Glen Echo, Maryland, is now a national historic site.

She did her work without asking for public credit. "I did not wait for reporters and journalists to tell us that a battle had been fought," she said. "I went in while the battle raged." At the Battle of Antietam, she was the only "Woman Kind" in sight, but that did not stop her from riding into the fray on an ox cart laden with many supplies. That day, she removed a bullet from a wounded soldier for the first time in her life.

To those who complained that battlefield nursing was "rough and unseemly" for women, Barton countered

"ready to rush into the Florence Nightingale business." But it proved to be a difficult business indeed. One worried Confederate soldier advised his wife never to volunteer as a nurse. "You cannot imagine the labor you would have to undergo," he warned, "and disgusting much of it is."

Nevertheless, an astounding number of dedicated women served soldiers both North and South during the long and bloody war. "God knows what we should have done without them," one appreciative Union official recalled after the fighting had ended. "I have never seen one of them flinch for a moment."

'CYCLONE IN CALICO'

by Cynthia Butler

When the Civil War broke out, few people appreciated the terrible years that lay ahead. It was not until the wounded and sick were carried from the battlefields that civilians realized how poor the conditions actually were. Many tried to help in any way they could, and some, like Harriet Tubman, Elizabeth Blackwell, Clara Barton, and Mary Ann Bickerdyke, are well remembered for their efforts.

In 1888, a group of Civil War veterans were at a meeting in Topeka, Kansas. Suddenly, near the door, a great cheer went up. The chairman could not restore order, although he rapped loudly with his gavel. "Gentlemen!" he shouted. "It is impossible to conduct business in this confusion!"

"Mother Bickerdyke is here!" was the excited reply. "The meeting can wait!"

"I knew her at once," said one veteran, "though her hair has turned to white."

"I knew her by the tender eyes and the kind mouth," said another. "I shall never forget how good they looked to me after the battle of Resaca, where I lost my foot, and gave myself up to die, I was in such pain. I tell you, it seemed as if my own mother was doing for me, she was so gentle." He wiped his wet eyes with the back of his hand.

The men pressed forward to greet her. Many of them remembered her personally, for Mary Ann Bickerdyke had tended thousands of sick and wounded during the Civil War.

When the war began, the Union army was totally unprepared to care for casualties. Makeshift hospitals soon sprang up, but they were dirty and poorly supplied, and they lacked proper nurses.

Soldiers sometimes wrote letters about hospital conditions. The following letter was sent from Camp Griffen, near Washington, D.C., on November 12, 1861.

"I suppose you would like to hear what we are doing in Virginia in the way of bringing the rebels to subjection. As yet we have done little fighting, but have lost a large number of men. They are dying daily in the camps and hospitals from pneumonia, dysentery, and camp diseases, caused by severe colds, exposure, and lack of proper food when ill. We have taken very heavy colds lying on our arms in line of battle, long frosty nights. For two days and nights there was a

Mary Ann "Mother" Bickerdyke

Bickerdyke (1817–1901), a Union nurse, was a friend to soldiers and Generals Grant and Sherman.

very severe storm, to which we were exposed all the time, wearing shoddy uniforms and protected only by shoddy blankets, and the result was a frightful amount of sickness. We have about thirty in our regimental hospital who will never again be good for anything, if they live.

"Our hospitals are so bad that the men fight against being sent to them. They will not go until they are compelled, and many brave it out and die in camp. I really believe they are more comfortable and better cared for in camp, with their comrades, than in the hospital. The food is the same in both places, and the medical treatment the same when there is any. In the hospital the sick men lie on rotten straw; in the camp we provide clean hemlock or pine boughs, with the stems cut out, or husks, when we can 'jerk' them from a 'secesh' cornfield.

The Sanitary Commission was established to make sure that sanitary conditions were kept in camp. Here, at Fredericksburg, Virginia, in May 1864, nurses and officers of the commission take time out from their duties to pose for the camera.

"In the hospital the nurses are 'convalescent soldiers,' so nearly sick themselves that they ought to be in the wards, and from their very feebleness they are selfish and sometimes inhuman in their treatment of the patients. In the camp we stout hearty fellows take care of the sick, rough in our management, I doubt not, but we do not fail for lack of strength or interest. If we could be sure of being halfway well cared for when we get sick or wounded, it would take immensely from the horrors of army life.

"We need beds and bedding, hospital clothing and sick-diet, proper medicines, surgical instruments, and good nurses, and then a decent building or a good hospital tent for the accommodation of our sick. I suppose we shall have them when the government can get around to it, and in the meantime we try to be patient."

Mother Bickerdyke was not patient. When the war broke out, she was a forty-four-year-old widow living in Galesburg, Illinois. Boys from her town were dying, just like those in the letter. They had not yet left Illinois, much less seen battle. It was more than she could bear.

With money raised by the town, she went to their aid in Cairo, Illinois, with food, clothing, and disinfectant. She took the supplies and stayed, against all rules. The army could not do without her. By hook or by crook, she kept her patients clean, warm, and fed. If that meant breaking rules or cutting red tape, it was nothing to her. It was with good reason that she was called a "cyclone in calico." As she told one meddling doctor, "I guess you hadn't better get into a row with me, for whenever anybody does, one of us two always goes to the wall, and 'tain't never me!"

"We have about thirty in our regimental hospital who will never again be good for anything, if they live."

Above: Wounded soldiers from the Battle of the Wilderness, Fredericksburg, Virginia, May 1864.
Inset: After the war, Mary Ann Bickerdyke went to Washington, D.C., where she worked hard to secure pensions for nurses and veterans.

Mother Bickerdyke's work in Cairo established her reputation. She was loved by the patients, trusted by the generals, feared and respected by those in between. A certain surgeon, given to drunkenness, ordered her out of his hospital. She replied, "I shall stay as long as the people need me. If you put me out of one door, I shall come in at another. If you bar all the doors against me, I shall come in at the windows, and the patients will help me in! When anyone leaves, it will be you, not me!"

General Ulysses S. Grant saw the good results of her straightforward, no-nonsense methods. He took her side in such disputes, as did General Benjamin M. Prentiss. She was left alone to do her work, but her supplies were not safe from theft.

The sick-diet kitchen Mother Bickerdyke set up had barely enough basic foods such as beef broth, tea, and bread. Special items were rare. One time, some folks from Illinois sent a case of dried peaches. She warned the cook, "These are for sick men, not well ones. Keep your hands off 'em!" She stewed up the lot, with plenty of brown sugar and cinnamon, and left them to cool. "Just you remember, now. Not a soul touches these peaches. They's for my sick boys."

As she watched from another room, the usual parade of staff members invaded the kitchen for a drink of water. Strange sounds began to seep through its closed door. She flung it open to let her patients enjoy the sight. All over the kitchen floor, retching men cursed and groaned in pain, clutching their stomachs.

Mother Bickerdyke was not ready with sympathy this time. "What's the matter, fellows?" she asked cheerfully. "Peaches don't agree with you, huh? Well, let me tell you, you're lucky. All you got was a little emetic to make you vomit. Next time it'll be rat poison, and then you will have something to groan about. When I tell you to leave the patients' food alone, I *mean* it!"

Some system and order began to be seen at the Cairo hospitals. Battles were fought, and the sick were joined by the wounded. After the Battle of Fort Donelson, Mother Bickerdyke helped in the transportation of injured soldiers. Cries of "Mother! Mother!" were heard as she went among them. When all the wounded had at last been removed from the field, rescue parties returned to Cairo for badly needed rest. Darkness fell. Looking from his tent at midnight, an officer saw a faint light flitting back and forth on the abandoned battlefield. It was Mother Bickerdyke with a lantern, searching among the dead lest some poor soul lay there, still alive.

From the hospitals established at Cairo, Mother Bickerdyke moved on to field hospitals hurriedly set up near battle lines. After Shiloh, Tennessee, she was in a dozen places at once, tending kettles of soup for the wounded and dressing their wounds as well. A surgeon, newly arrived, marveled at her skill but felt compelled to question her. "Madam," he said, "you seem to combine in yourself a sick-diet kitchen and a medical staff. May I inquire under whose authority you are working?"

Without pausing in her work, she answered, "I have received my authority from the Lord God Almighty; have you anything that ranks higher than that?"

The truth of the matter was that she was under nobody's authority but her own. Eventually, she received government permission to serve the troops, but it was a mere formality. She had always taken matters into her own hands and always would.

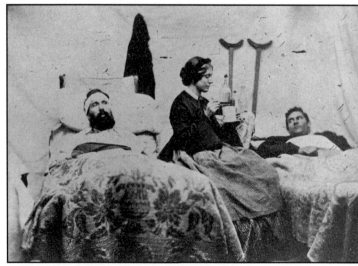

Nurse Anne Bell cared for wounded soldiers during the Civil War.

One time, she finagled some bath water. Cleanliness was next to godliness; it also saved lives. After the battle at Corinth, Mississippi, the well at Academy Hospital ran dry. When General Stephen A. Hurlbut was brought in on a stretcher with a severe chill, Mother Bickerdyke insisted that several men carry water from a spring in barrels and heat it on the kitchen stove. After the general had a good soak, that very same water bathed sixteen men right off the battlefield. They needed it a lot worse than the general, but it would never have been hauled and heated just to wash enlisted men.

Another time, near Chattanooga, Tennessee, on New Year's Day, hundreds of men were in danger of freezing to death in hospital tents. Mother Bickerdyke promised a crock of toddy to any able-bodied soldier who would risk court-martial to save the wounded. She proposed to tear out the logs from a fortification. She did not have authorization, but the enemy no longer threatened, and fires were sorely needed for her patients. When the commanding officer accused her the next day, Mother Bickerdyke said, "All right, Major! I'm arrested! Only don't meddle with me till the weather moderates; for my men will freeze to death, if you do!"

HOSPITAL #7, BEAUFORT, SOUTH CAROLINA — 1864 —

Supplying the hospitals with food was serious business, but once Mother Bickerdyke had a bit of fun with it. She applied for thirty days' leave to go to the North and fetch fresh eggs and milk. Dr. Irwin in Memphis said he knew she was pigheaded, but he had not thought she was daft. Didn't she know they would spoil? No, she did not think so. She would just go get her leave approved by General Hurlbut.

Back she came a month later with a hundred cows and a thousand hens. Spoil indeed! She had put that doctor in his place!

Generals knew not to underestimate Mother Bickerdyke. General Grant himself gave her a pass through the lines. General William T. Sherman trusted her with his military plans for the Atlanta Campaign so that she would know where to expect casualties. Finally, on the morning of May 24, 1865, in Washington, D.C., the boom of a cannon signaled not battle but the start of a parade. The war was over! At General John A. Logan's personal request, Mother Bickerdyke rode next to him at the head of the Fifteenth Corps.

Her boys had spent the night grooming her horse, Whitey, and covering his blanket with forget-me-nots. On his back, they placed a brand-new lady's sidesaddle. She had long wanted one, considering "riding a-straddle" on an army saddle neither seemly nor comfortable. In her excitement over the gift, she had no time to change into the fine riding skirt given her by friends in New York. Instead, she took her place next to General Logan in her everyday calico dress and sunbonnet. They nodded to Generals Grant and Sherman in the reviewing stand, and General Logan said, "Come on, Mother. They're expecting us."

"Me? Land sakes, General, they don't want me up there."

"Yes, they do. General Sherman told me to be sure and bring you."

"Well, that's real nice of them I must say. But I can't do it. You get along up there. I got work to do."

All day, the parade surged on. In Mother Bickerdyke's first-aid tent, she refreshed her boys with lemonade and sandwiches. She applied cracked ice for sunstroke and dressings for blistered feet. The casualties were minor and the occasion joyous. She could have been reviewing the parade in style, but as always her soldiers came first.

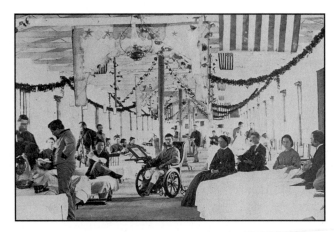

A ward in Armory Square Hospital, Washington, D.C.

HOSPITAL SKETCHES
by Louisa May Alcott

Nursing the wounded and administering aid and supplies contributed greatly to military success and troop morale during the civil War. Thousands of women served as volunteer nurses in both the North and South. They were faced with overwhelming casualties, crowded and unclean conditions, and widespread disease. For most, it was an unforgettable experience.

Author Louisa May Alcott worked at the Union Hospital in the Georgetown area of Washington in January and February of 1863. She was at the hospital for six weeks when a "severe attack of fever" forced her to return to her home in Concord, Massachusetts. Louisa's letters to her family, detailing her experiences as a volunteer nurse, were first printed in the "Commonwealth" magazine and later in book form.*

The first thing I met was a regiment of the vilest odors that ever assaulted the human nose...and the worst of this affliction was, everyone had assured me that it was a chronic weakness of all hospitals, and I must bear it. I did, armed with lavender water, with which I so besprinkled myself and premises, that, like my friend, Sairy, I was soon known among my patients as "the nurse with the bottle." ...I progressed by slow stages up stairs and down, till the main hall was reached, and I paused to take breath and a survey. There they were! "our brave boys," as the papers justly call them, for cowards could hardly have been so riddled with shot and shell, so torn and shattered, nor have borne suffering for which we have no name, with an uncomplaining fortitude, which made one glad to cherish each as a brother. In they came, some on stretchers, some in men's arms, some feebly staggering along propped on rude crutches, and one lay stark and still with covered face, as a comrade gave his name to be recorded before they carried him away to the dead house. All was hurry and confusion; the hall was full of these wrecks of humanity, for the

From Phyllis Raybin Emert, ed., *Women in the Civil War: Warriors, Patriots, Nurses, and Spies,* Perspectives on History Series, pp. 40–43. Copyright © 1995 Discovery Enterprises, Ltd., Lowell, Massachusetts.

*From *Hospital Sketches* edited by Bessie Z. Jones. Copyright © 1960 by the President and Fellows of Harvard College. Reprinted by permission of Harvard University Press.

most exhausted could not reach a bed till duly ticketed and registered; the walls were lined with rows of such as could sit, the floor covered with the more disabled, the steps and doorways filled with helpers and lookers on; the sound of many feet and voices made that usually quiet hour as noisy as noon; and, in the midst of it all, the matron's motherly face brought more comfort to many a poor soul, than the cordial draughts she administered, or the cheery words that welcomed all, making of the hospital a home.

The sight of several stretchers, each with its legless, armless, or desperately wounded occupant, entering my ward, admonished me that I was there to work, not to wonder or weep; so I corked up my feelings, and returned to the path of duty, which was rather "a hard road to travel" just then. The house had been a hotel before hospitals were needed, and many of the doors still bore their old names; some not so inappropriate as might be imaged, for my ward was in truth a *ball-room*, if gunshot wounds could christen it. Forty beds were prepared, many already tenanted by tired men who fell down anywhere, and drowsed till the smell of food roused them. Round the great stove was gathered the dreariest group I ever saw — ragged, gaunt and pale, mud to the knees, with bloody bandages untouched since put on days before; many bundled up in blankets, coats being lost or useless; and all wearing that disheartened look which proclaimed defeat.... I pitied them so much, I dared not speak to them, though, remembering all they had been through since the rout at Fredericksburg, I yearned to serve the dreariest of them all. Presently, Miss Blank tore me from my refuge behind piles of one-sleeved shirts, odd socks, bandages and lint; put basin, sponge, towels and a block of brown soap into my hands, with these appalling directions:

"Come, my dear, begin to wash as fast you can. Tell them to take off socks, coats, and shirts, scrub them well, put on clean shirts, and the attendants will finish them off, and lay them in bed."

Hospital tents at Gettysburg.

★ ★ ★ ★ ★ ★ ★ ★ ★

IN HOSPITAL AND CAMP
by Sophronia E. Bucklin

Women of all ages from various walks of life volunteered during the war as military nurses. Many kept diaries and journals of their experiences, and a number of them were published in book form years later. Sophronia Bucklin, a young schoolteacher from New York,...[was an eyewitness] to the horror and sufferings of battle.

Our duties here were to distribute food to the patients, when brought up from the kitchen; wash the faces and hands, and comb the heads of the wounded; see that their bedding and clothing was kept clean and whole, bring pocket handkerchiefs, prepare and give the various drinks and stimulants

From Phyllis Raybin Emert, ed., *Women in the Civil War: Warriors, Patriots, Nurses, and Spies,* Perspectives on History Series, pp. 47–49. Copyright © 1995 Discovery Enterprises, Ltd., Lowell, Massachusetts.

at such times as they were ordered by the surgeon.

I dropped into my desired sphere at once, and my whole soul was in the work. Every man wore the look of a hero in my eyes, for had they not faced the red death from thundering artillery, and braved the deadly shots of the "minnies"? Had they not stood fearlessly, when like leaves of the autumn before a howling blast, they had fallen thick and fast — bronzed and dripping with gore — faces forward in the black mud of the trenches?*

A few tents were up, for shelter, and, as fast as they were vacated by transportation to Washington, they were filled up from the numbers who were lying upon the ground, waiting to have their wounds dressed. A general and hurried care was exercised for their many and pressing wants — it was all we could under the circumstances afford them.

Death met us on every hand.... Scenes of fresh horror rose up before us each day. Tales of suffering were told, which elsewhere would have well-nigh frozen the blood with horror. We grew callous to the sight of blood....

Often they would long for a drink of clear, cold water, and lie on the hard ground, straining the filthy river water through closely set teeth.

So tortured were we all, in fact, by this thirst...that even now, when I lift to my lips a drink of pure, cold water, I cannot swallow it without thanking God for the priceless gift....

...Tents were being spread, and the ambulances came upon the field with their ghastly, bloody freight — unloading them, dying and groaning under the sun — the small number of tents being entirely insufficient to shelter the constantly arriving throngs.

...Men lay all around me, who had been left for days on the battleground, wet with the dews of night, disfigured with powder and dirt, with blood oozing from their torn flesh, and worms literally covering the festering wounds — dying with thirst, starving for food, unable to attend to nature's wants, groaning in delirious fever, praying to die, to be rid

*From *In Hospital and Camp* by Sophronia E. Bucklin. Edited by Harold Elk Straubing, Stackpole Books, PA, 1993, pp. 102–103, first published in 1869.

Mathew Brady photographed a wounded soldier receiving a drink of water in a deserted camp.

of the intense pain which wracked the poor body.

Such dreadful suffering I hope never to witness again. The field was one vast plain of intense mortal agony, tortured by the sun, and chilled by the night dews. Everywhere were groans and cries for help; everywhere were the pleading and glassy eyes of dying men who were speechless in the delirium of death. It was a scene to appall the stoutest hearts, but the excitement nerved us to shut our senses to everything but the task of relieving them as fast as possible. The dead lay by the living; the dying groaned by the dead, and still one hundred ambulances poured the awful tide in upon us....*

*Excerpts by Bucklin from *Noble Women of the North,* edited by Dannett, Thomas Yoseloff Publishers, NY, 1959, pp. 99–101, 171–173.

THE COURAGE TO SPEAK

by Joelle Runkle

Outside the meeting hall, mobs chanted, "Burn down the hall! Burn them out!" Inside, Angelina and Sarah Grimké continued speaking to their audience as the mob pelted the building with stones. Later, after the speakers and audience had left, the mob made good its threat and burned down the building.

This cartoon captures a women's rights meeting in 1857. Not all the men were jeering from the balconies. Some supported the suffragettes and sat among them.

Once, as Lucy Stone waited to speak to a church congregation, someone hurled a hymnal at her head. Another time as she spoke, a window behind her was opened, a hose was inserted, and she was drenched with icy water.

When Elizabeth Cady Stanton and Susan B. Anthony traveled the lecture circuit together, they were attacked by mobs and pelted with vegetables, rotten eggs, and clods of mud. Rowdies in their audiences hooted and jeered so loudly that the women could scarcely be heard.

What had these women done to provoke such anger and ridicule? Partly it was what they had to say — that women and men should have equal rights — and partly that they dared to speak in public at all.

In the early to mid-1800s, women who appeared on a public platform or assumed the "male" role of instructor or public speaker were considered brazen and unfeminine. Crowds gathered more to see the "crowing hens" than to hear what the women had to say.

Not only were women discouraged from speaking in public, but they also were excluded from schools and colleges. Few employers would hire them, and if they did have a paying job, they earned far less than men, and their money belonged to their fathers or husbands. Children, too, were considered the property of fathers but not mothers. Women could not inherit or own property, could not sign a contract or sue, and could not serve on juries. They could not vote or be elected to public office.

For the most part, people believed that things were as they should be. Those who called for changes in women's rights — including the Grimké sisters, Stone, Stanton, and Anthony — were considered outrageous and dangerous. They were denounced by churches, ridiculed in newspapers, and ignored or laughed at by lawmakers and politicians.

Ministers called these women "unwomanly and unchristian" and preached strong sermons against them. A council of ministers wrote a letter warning of the dangers threatening women in this new movement. God made women weak and dependent on men for their own protection, the letter said. Another religious leader said that a woman not directed or controlled by a man was unnatural, "a hideous monster." Women's rights leaders were branded infidels, and Stone was expelled from her church.

Newspapers made fun of women's rights conventions. They were called "hen conventions" and "petticoat rebellions." The women who attended were accused of being immoral and indecent and of wanting to destroy family life. They were reported to smoke black cigars, swear like men, and hang around hotel barrooms. They were called "jezebels," "vile characters," "amazons," "she-hyenas," and "mummified and fossilated females."*

Legislators, to whom feminists took their petitions and pleas for changes in the law, turned a deaf ear or turned their appeals into a joke. New York lawmakers said it was men, not women, who should be trying to get equal rights. After all, they said, "the ladies always have the best place and tidbit at table. They always have the best seat in cars, carriages, and sleighs...and their choice on which side of the bed they will lie." The lawmakers refused to change the laws, saying that husbands and wives who had signed the petitions should exchange dress, the men wearing petticoats and the women britches, so that their neighbors and the public would know who was the boss in those families.

As the fight for women's rights grew stronger, state and local societies opposed to female suffrage appeared. These merged into the National Association Opposed to Woman Suffrage (for women) and the American Constitutional League (for men). The new antisuffrage groups distributed pamphlets warning of "The Dark Side of Woman Suffrage" and called mass meetings to "Save the South" and the nation from this great evil. In their opposition literature, medical experts wrote that women's frailty and emotional nature made them unfit to bear the "burden of the ballot." Suffrage would "unsex" women, destroy marriage and the family, and "weaken the

GLOSSARY
by Elizabeth Hagner

Abolitionist	One who favored the ending of slavery (from the word "abolish," meaning to end).
Amendment	A revision of or an addition to a law or constitution.
Bloomer	A costume of baggy pants worn underneath a short skirt; named for Amelia Bloomer, one of the first women to wear the costume.
Emancipate	To free from oppression, bondage, or authority; to liberate.
Enfranchisement	Another word for the right to vote.
Feminism	A belief or movement that advocates the same rights for women as for men, as in political or economic status.
Liberal	Having social or political views that favor nonrevolutionary reform and progress.
Lobby	As a verb, to try to influence legislators to vote for or against a measure (from the noun, referring to a public room adjoining a legislative hall where interested people can talk to legislators).
Petition	A formal written document requesting a right or benefit from a person or group in authority.
Reformer	A person who seeks to make things better by correcting faults; especially involved with social, political, religious, or economic improvement.
Statute	A law enacted by a legislative body of a representative government.
Suffrage	The right to vote.
Temperance	Moderation, especially in drinking alcoholic beverages (from the word "temper," meaning to free from excess).
Women's liberation	A movement that seeks equal rights and status for women (from the word "liberate," meaning to free).

*The term "jezebel" refers to a scheming, wicked woman. It comes from the name of a Phoenician princess of the ninth century B.C. who was known for her wickedness. An amazon is a tall, vigorous, aggressive woman. In Greek mythology, the Amazons were a nation of female warriors reputed to have lived in Scythia, near the Black Sea.

WHO OPPOSED WOMAN SUFFRAGE?

by Alice P. Miller

Suffragists were opposed by strong political lobbies that had the power to defeat just about every prosuffrage candidate who ran for public office. Although suffragists eventually convinced legislators to support their cause, they did so in spite of this opposition.

Among the more powerful opponents were liquor manufacturers. They feared that women would use their votes to prevent the sale of alcoholic beverages, which they believed would hurt everyone connected with the liquor trade. These people included brewers of beer and distillers of whiskey; farmers who grew the grains used in making liquor; coopers who made barrels to hold the liquor; railroad workers who profited from the transportation of those barrels; and saloon-keepers and bartenders. Liquor manufacturers spent millions of dollars on newspaper and magazine ads, thereby gaining the power to control much of the editorial matter. Cartoons, editorials, and news stories kept hammering home antisuffrage messages.

Southerners opposed woman suffrage for a number of reasons. Many southerners resented the fact that African American men had been given the vote. If African American women also should gain the right to vote, that would double the number of eligible African American voters. Southern plantation owners also reasoned that women voters might insist on better working conditions for African Americans on plantations as well as in northern cotton mills.

It might seem odd that any woman would wish to deny herself the right to vote, yet many women prided themselves on being too "feminine" to be mixed up in politics. Suffragists often were portrayed as cigar-smoking, loudmouthed, outlandishly garbed creatures, reinforcing the notion that any woman who wanted to vote must be a freak.

Although suffragists faced many heartbreaking defeats, they finally realized their dream on August 26, 1920, when the Nineteenth Amendment gave women the vote.

moral fiber of the nation," they said.

One antisuffrage poster pictured a man coming home from work only to find the supper table bare, his children crying, and a note from his wife saying she had gone off to a suffrage meeting. "Suffrage households are suffering households," the poster read.

Cartoons, phonograph records, and silent films took up the battle against suffragists, describing them as women who wanted to be men. Cartoonists portrayed them as harsh, mannish-looking women in tailored jackets. A song titled "In the Land Where the Women Wear the Trousers" described a "funny land where woman is the boss and poor old man is second hand." Moviegoers saw women wearing "Votes for Women" banners throw men to the ground and trample them. Movies portrayed husbands of suffragists as apron-wearing men who meekly took orders from their wives.

Slowly, however, more and more people began to agree with the suffragists' ideas, and one by one they became accepted goals. Although many of these goals were eventually realized, they were accomplished only because of the courage, determination, and perseverance of many women who were willing to endure ridicule, scorn, and even physical assault to convince society of the reasonableness and justice of women's rights.

THE ROOTS OF WOMEN'S RIGHTS

by Gary K. Shepherd

The women's rights movement can trace its roots to a book titled *The Vindication of the Rights of Women* written by Mary Wollstonecraft in the late 1700s. But women's rights might never have been more than a vague idea were it not for the far more popular antislavery issue.

The year was 1840. The scene was the first World Anti-Slavery Convention in London, England. Among the American delegation were several women, including a soft-spoken Quaker named Lucretia Mott. Mott had assisted William Lloyd Garrison in founding the American Anti-Slavery Society, and for a time she and her husband kept a "station" on the Underground Railroad. Although the convention's leaders had warned that only men could attend, Mott and her group had come anyway.

Also among the delegates was Henry Stanton, who had brought along his new bride, Elizabeth. Stanton opposed women's participation in the convention, and, quite naturally, his wife went along with his ideas. But once she met and talked with Mott, Mrs. Stanton began to change her mind.

When the convention opened, Boston attorney Wendell Phillips immediately proposed that the women delegates be accepted. Henry Stanton stood to support the measure. Many more voices were raised against it, however, and the convention voted overwhelmingly to exclude the women. They were required to sit behind a curtain and were not allowed to participate in the proceedings. William Lloyd Garrison, who was to have been the keynote speaker, was so outraged that he tore up his speech and went to sit with the women. From that moment on, the women's rights and antislavery movements were almost inseparable.

Most of the early leaders of the women's movement came directly from the abolitionist cause. Not until these women had tried to become politically active did they encounter the barriers society had placed before them. "We have good cause to be grateful to the slave," said Abby Kelley, a leading abolitionist and suffragette. "In striving to strike his irons off, we found most surely that we were manacled ourselves."

Angelina and Sarah Grimké were the daughters of a wealthy southern plantation owner. Upon inheriting his estate, they freed their slaves and went north to speak against the evils of slavery. When outraged men condemned them for speaking before mixed audiences, Angelina replied, "What then, can women do for the slave when she herself is under the feet of man, and shamed to silence?"

Lucy Stone was a lecturer for the American Anti-Slavery Society and an early proponent of women's rights. The society complained about her divided loyalties, however, saying that she was paid to talk about slavery, not women's rights. Eventually, she reached a compromise with the group. She spoke against slavery on the weekends and for women's rights during the week.

Another antislavery lecturer was the escaped slave Sojourner Truth. Traveling the back roads to speak against slavery, she encountered double prejudice, since she was both an African American and a woman. She responded to her critics in her own special style:

"That man over there says women need to be helped into carriages and lifted over ditches, and to have the best place everywhere. Well, nobody ever helped

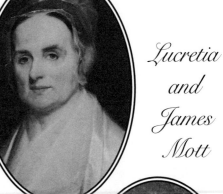

Lucretia and James Mott

Lucretia and James Mott were Quakers who supported the abolitionist cause. Lucretia also was an advocate of women's rights. Along with Elizabeth Cady Stanton, she organized the first Women's Rights Convention in 1848 in Seneca Falls, New York.

The executive board of the Pennsylvania Anti-Slavery Society, 1851. Back row, left to right: Mary Grew, E.M. Davis, Haworth Wetherald, Abby Kimber, J. Miller McKim, and Sarah Pugh. Front row, left to right: Oliver Johnson, Mrs. Margaret Jones Burleigh, Benjamin C. Bacon, Robert Purvis, Lucretia Mott, and James Mott.

me into carriages or over ditches, or gives me the best place. And ain't I a woman? I have ploughed and planted and gathered into barns and no man could head me. And ain't I a woman? I can work as much and eat as much as a man — when I could get it — and bear the lash as well. And ain't I a woman? I have borne thirteen children and seen most of 'em sold into slavery and when I cried out my mother's grief, none but Jesus heard me. And ain't I a woman?"*

Like Lucretia Mott, Susan B. Anthony was a Quaker who bitterly opposed slavery. She, like so many others, believed that the rights of women and African Americans were tied together.

For a time, the two movements acted almost as one. A special foundation called the Jackson Fund entrusted twenty-five thousand dollars to Lucy Stone, Susan B. Anthony, and Wendell Phillips to be spent equally on women's rights and abolition. During the Civil War, the women's movement was quiet, but after the war, the two movements merged briefly to form the Equal Rights Association, which advocated the right to vote for both women and African Americans.

When the Fifteenth Amendment to the Constitution was proposed in 1869, however, it referred only to African Americans. Phillips argued that if antislavery groups pushed for the inclusion of women, the amendment would never pass. Anthony and Elizabeth Cady Stanton felt betrayed by this action, and in a sense they had been. But in another sense, the women's movement might never have been born if women had not begun to fight beside men for the abolitionist cause.

*A different version of this speech appears in volume 1, page 112.

The women's rights movement owed its existence in part to the antislavery movement, just as the women's movement of today gained fresh momentum from the civil rights movement of the 1950s and 1960s.

THE GRIMKÉ SISTERS

by Carey Howes

In 1838, Sarah and Angelina Grimké stood at the center of American history, yet their names are almost unknown today. Their unusual story began on the South Carolina plantation where they were raised in luxury, surrounded by servants. As children, however, they were troubled by the system of slavery that provided their wealth. On their own, they tried to improve the lives of slaves and women in the South. When this tactic proved unsuccessful, they took the dramatic step of moving north to work with those who shared their beliefs.

Their first and most difficult task was to convince people that women had a duty to take part in government. According to tradition, they were confined to "the woman's sphere," the private world of home and family. The Grimkés argued that women had to demand the right to make speeches before mixed audiences in public, since they had no public voice in the laws that governed them.

On February 21, 1838, Angelina became the first American woman to address a legislative body. As she made her way to the podium to speak before a committee of the Massachusetts legislature in the State House in Boston, she was almost overcome by the huge responsibility facing her. She knew from experience in the antislavery movement that a crowd could suddenly turn hostile, and she was well aware that many were there only to witness the curious sight of a woman speaking in public. But after a smile and a word of encouragement from a friend, Angelina forgot her fears. Her eloquent voice, powered by deep moral convictions, filled the hall as she urged the lawmakers to end the system of slavery that kept so many children, women, and men in chains.

Newspapers nationwide reported the speech. Some nicknamed her "Devilina." One said that Angelina showed considerable talent "for a female." Another mocked her personally by saying that no man would marry such a bold woman. But as another observed, "It was a noble day when for the first time in civilized America, a Woman stood up in a Legislative Hall, vindicating [supporting] the rights of women."

Angelina took the praise and insults calmly. She knew that she was speaking

These illustrations of the Grimké sisters appeared in the book *William Lloyd Garrison*, by Wendell Phillips and Francis Jackson Garrison, published in 1885.

Sarah and Angelina Grimké

for all women, not just for herself, and she shared the victory — especially with Sarah. The two sisters worked very closely with one another and did not compete. In fact, it was Sarah who was originally scheduled to speak before the legislative committee. When she came down with a terrible head cold, Angelina took her place at the last minute.

Sarah and Angelina traveled throughout New England spreading the word that slavery was evil and that free people everywhere had a moral duty to end it. Along the way, they suffered many hardships, often going without food and sleep as they rushed from one town to another. But they got results. As southerners, they could tell many firsthand stories about the suffering of slaves, and their listeners were moved to action.

Women in every town they visited joined political groups to fight slavery. And since women at that time were not entitled to vote or run for office, they used petitions to make their opinions heard. In fact, they sent so many signed petitions to the U.S. Congress that the legislators began to pay attention to the growing movement to end slavery.

The Wesleyan Chapel (shown here under construction), where the first Women's Rights Convention took place, is part of Women's Rights National Historical Park in Seneca Falls, New York.

The Grimké sisters told American women something they had never heard before — that they were powerful. Sarah and Angelina proved that even timid, dignified women could find the courage to speak out against injustice. They showed their audiences that one voice could make a difference and that many voices raised together in protest could change society.

In addition to their pioneering work as public speakers, the Grimkés wrote a steady stream of essays and books, some of which are still in print today. Sarah's book *Letters on the Equality of the Sexes and the Condition of Woman,* published in 1838, was the first serious study of women's rights by an American woman. It appeared ten years before the Seneca Falls convention, when for the first time in history, women organized to demand their rights as citizens. The Grimkés inspired many of the early leaders in the struggle for women's rights, including Elizabeth Cady Stanton and Susan B. Anthony.

The lives of Sarah and Angelina Grimké spanned almost a century. They helped bring an end to slavery, and they advanced the rights of women to be educated and to express themselves freely. To the very end, they lived their belief that there are no men's rights and women's rights — only human rights.

SHE STOOD HER GROUND

by Karen Klos

The school bell rang. Eight-year-old Susan B. Anthony approached the schoolmaster's desk while her classmates hurriedly filed out the back door.

"Now you can teach me how to do long division, if you please, sir," she said eagerly. All afternoon, she had watched the teacher struggle as he tried to instruct the older boys.

The astonished teacher refused. "Girls don't need to know long division. Girls only need to count eggs and weigh butter. Men manage all the business of the world."

Yet Susan persisted. Instructed by her father, Daniel Anthony, she went on to master advanced arithmetic. Refusing to give in to opposition became the trademark of Susan's life.

Susan B. Anthony, born in Adams, Massachusetts, in 1820, was the child of two unusual parents. Her father, Daniel, had a courageous and broad-minded spirit. His skill in mechanics and mathematics enabled him to operate his cotton mills successfully. Daniel had been reared in a strict Quaker family, and Susan often heard him voice his opposition to slavery and alcohol. He went so far as to refuse to purchase cotton raised by slave labor.

Daniel also refused to sell alcohol in his stores after finding an old man frozen to death by the side of the road with an empty jug of rum beside him. "Men with befogged minds aren't worth their salt" was a saying Susan learned from her father.

Lucy Read Anthony, Susan's mother, had a loving and warm nature. Her upbringing was completely opposite that of her husband. She had been raised in the Baptist religion and as a young girl loved to sing and dance. Lucy gave up this lifestyle and donned the gray dress of the Quakers when she married. Susan was close to her mother and would often have long talks with her after school.

Susan had a driving ambition to learn things considered beyond a girl's capacity. The village schools in her hometown provided her with the basics in reading, spelling, and sewing, but her father recognized the need for a better education for his seven children. He organized a school in his mercantile store, employing the best teachers available. His children learned to love poetry, geography, books, and the "newfangled" calisthenics.

Along with her school tasks, Susan shared in the housework. At one point, twelve brickmakers boarded at the Anthony home. Susan's mother was responsible for the cooking and cleaning, with the help of her three older daughters, Guelma, Hannah, and Susan. Each day, the girls cooked the workers' lunch over an open fire, packed it into twelve pails, and carried it out to the men. Hiring extra help was unheard-of. The money Susan's mother received for this extra work was immediately turned over to her husband.

Susan once asked, "Why did you give the money to Father, when *you* did all the work?"

Her mother looked down at her daughter in surprise. "Why, women always do. Women can't own anything."

"Why can't they own anything?" Susan asked.

"They just can't! Not if they are married. It's the law."

"Why do they have such bad laws?" Susan wondered. "Someday I shall work to support myself — but I shall keep the money I earn."

"Liberty will not descend to a people — a people must raise themselves to liberty."

By organizing the Woman's Loyal League during the Civil War, Anthony showed her support of Lincoln and his emancipation policies.

When the Anthonys moved to New York in 1845, Susan became a member of the Society of Friends. Although parties, dancing, and singing were considered sinful, the Quakers did believe that men and women were equal in God's sight. The Quakers allowed women to speak during their meetings, while other churches did not, and Susan's grandmother was an important elder in her local church. Growing up in this atmosphere of healthy self-expression and respect for all people inspired Susan in her later struggles for equality.

Armed with her natural persistence, Susan B. Anthony emerged in the 1850s as a leading figure in the fight for women's right to vote. A quick intelligence, loving spirit, respect for *all* persons, and hard-working drive were her weapons. "Liberty will not descend to a people — a people must raise themselves to liberty" became her motto and the goal to which she devoted her life.

Susan B. Anthony

THE PARTNERSHIP

by Jean McLeod

It is difficult to speak of Susan B. Anthony without mentioning Elizabeth Cady Stanton. For more than fifty years, the two were the best of friends and close partners in the women's rights movement.

Anthony and Stanton first met in the spring of 1851 in Seneca Falls, New York, where Stanton was living with her abolitionist husband and young children. Anthony had come to the city to attend some antislavery meetings, and the women met after one of those meetings.

"There [Anthony] stood," wrote Stanton years later, "with her good earnest face and genial smile.... I liked her immediately."

The feeling was mutual. Anthony later called at the Stanton home, where the two women spent the next several hours sharing thoughts on abolition, temperance, and women's rights. Anthony was particularly interested in hearing Stanton talk of the Women's Rights Convention that she and four other women had organized in 1848 (see page 72). The visit passed quickly, each woman finding in the other a friend with whom she could share her ideas. Leaving Seneca Falls, Anthony promised that she would keep in touch and visit the Stanton home again.

In the next few years, as Anthony became more interested in women's rights, she visited Stanton frequently. During those visits, she grew to share Stanton's conviction that the right to vote was the most important step in gaining equal rights for women. Together, they committed themselves to that goal.

Not being married, Anthony was freer to travel, attend conventions, and organize groups of people to work for suffrage. She also was skilled in raising money for expenses such as hiring halls and printing posters and pamphlets. Stanton was tied to her home by a family of small children, but she had a way with her pen. She could write speeches, resolutions, and newspaper articles in a crisp style that caught people's attention.

Elizabeth Cady Stanton

They made a good team, having more impact together than they could have had separately. Stanton helped Anthony with the speeches she gave. Anthony produced the facts; Stanton prepared the text. Sometimes Anthony would stay at the Stanton home to "hold the baby and make the puddings" while Stanton shut herself away to work on a speech or resolution.

At first, Anthony felt uncomfortable speaking in front of groups, but Stanton encouraged her. "In reference to 'thinking on one's feet,' I have no doubt that a little practice will render you an admirable lecturer.... If you are attacked in your meetings, be good-natured and keep cool."

Likewise, Anthony encouraged Stanton, who later confessed that at times she was tired and thought of retiring from public view. But Anthony would then show up with a bag "stuffed with facts...the statistics of women robbed of their property, shut out of some college, half paid for their work, the reports of some disgraceful trial; injustice enough to turn any woman's thoughts from stockings and puddings."

When Stanton's children were older, she and Anthony campaigned for suffrage together. As soon as they reached a town, Anthony would begin organizing — hiring a hall, putting up posters, handing out leaflets. When meeting time arrived, she would step back and let Stanton do what she did best — give a fine, humorous, well-planned address. Together they founded equal rights and suffrage associations, organized annual conventions, campaigned in several states, and coedited the first three volumes of *The History of Woman Suffrage*.

With the passage of years, Stanton grew impatient with the slow progress toward woman suffrage and

The Revolution's purpose was "principle, not policy: justice, not favors. — men, their rights and nothing more: women, their rights and nothing less."

THE REVOLUTION
by Paula Mitchell Marks

For most of her life, Susan B. Anthony had longed to publish a women's rights journal. In January 1868, with the help of entrepreneur George Francis Train, her dream came true when the first edition of *The Revolution* appeared.

The newspaper included information about woman suffrage, working women's problems, and women's rights. But *The Revolution* had problems from the beginning, the most serious of which was money. Although Train had been generous in establishing the paper, he soon departed for England, and the small fund he left behind quickly disappeared. Anthony struggled to meet rent payments and the cost of paper and printing. But without the necessary advertising and subscription support, *The Revolution* began to slip into debt.

One reason the paper was having trouble attracting subscribers was Train. To Anthony and Elizabeth Cady Stanton, one of the paper's editors, Train was the man who had helped them in their Kansas campaign for woman suffrage. But to their eastern friends, Train was a crackpot.

Even without Train, many people felt that the newspaper was too radical. Harriet Beecher Stowe agreed to write for it if they would change the name. Many suffragists even avoided the paper.

As *The Revolution* went more deeply into debt, Stanton advised Anthony to sell out. She did, assuming a ten-thousand-dollar debt. "I feel a great, calm sadness," she wrote, "like that of a mother binding out a dear child that she could not support."

MARGARET FULLER

by Beth Turin Weston

Margaret Fuller, born on March 23, 1810, began her education in the classics and the three Rs at the age of three. When her formal education ended at age sixteen, her goal was to support herself by writing. She was told, however, that she had three choices: She could marry, be a governess, or teach young children. Because she thought it unlikely that she would marry, she stayed at home, assuming more and more of the responsibilities of rearing her eight siblings. When her father died in 1835, she began to teach the younger children at home. She also gradually became acquainted with a group later known as the transcendentalists.

In 1837, Fuller taught briefly at Bronson Alcott's Temple School in Boston and then in Providence, Rhode Island. When she returned to Boston, she joined an informal discussion group, from which grew her "conversations for women," a series of discussions on education, fine arts, and Greek mythology. In 1839, Fuller was asked to edit *The Dial*, a journal that grew out of the transcendental movement (see volume 1, page 157). In 1843, she traveled to the Great Lakes, keeping a detailed journal that became her first book, *Summer on the Lakes*.

After her book was published, Horace Greeley, editor of the *New York Tribune*, asked her to move to New York, write for his paper, and expand her essay on the role of women into a book. She accepted, and this second book was called *Woman in the Nineteenth Century*. After contributing numerous articles to the *Tribune*, Fuller became this country's first female foreign correspondent, writing for the *Tribune* from England, Scotland, France, and Italy. While in Italy, she met Giovanni Angelo Ossoli, a nobleman whom some sources say she secretly married. In 1850, on a voyage to the United States, Ossoli, Fuller, and their young son were killed in a shipwreck.

began to expound on other concerns of women. "The fact is," she wrote Anthony, "that I am tired of bubbling on one issue." Anthony remained convinced that working for suffrage should come before other matters and stayed committed to that goal. Despite their different attitudes, the two continued to help each other and remained close friends.

Two weeks before Stanton's eighty-seventh birthday, Anthony received word of her friend's death. She retired to her room for several hours to grieve in private. Later when a reporter called, she felt unable to express herself adequately. "For fifty years, there has been an unbroken friendship between us.... If I had died first, she would have found beautiful phrases to describe our friendship, but I cannot put it into words."

THE WOMAN CALLED MOSES

by Peg Mims and Walter Oleksy

In the year 1835, on a large plantation located in Bucktown, Maryland, a fifteen-year-old African American girl lay awake on the dirt floor of the windowless one-room cabin she shared with her parents in the slave quarters. The room was hot — almost too hot to bear. Softly, so as not to waken her sleeping parents, Harriet Tubman got up and walked to the open doorway of the chinked-log cabin and listened to the sounds of music and laughter that floated down through the heavy night air from the mansion where her owners were celebrating the harvest of a bumper cotton crop.

It was a beautiful clear night, with millions of twinkling stars and a silver moon. Many years later, Tubman would recall that night and describe it as the turning point in her life — the night the wind quieted and some unseen force reached down from the star-studded heavens and stripped away the terror that kept her mind and body in servitude. That night, Tubman's fear was replaced with a single focus: to escape from slavery and live free.

From the spoken and written words of Harriet Tubman, we can learn much about who she was and how she felt about being a slave.

"I grew up like a neglected weed — ignorant of liberty, having no experience of it. I was not happy or contented: every time I saw a white man I was afraid of being carried away. I had two sisters carried away in a chain gang — one of them left two children.

"We were always uneasy. Now I've been free, I know what slavery is. I have seen hundreds of escaped slaves but I never saw one who was willing to go back and be a slave. I have no opportunity to see my friends in my native land. We would rather stay in our native land if we could be as free there as we are here (in the North). I think slavery is the next thing to hell. If a person would send another into bondage he would, it appears to me, be bad enough to send him to hell if he could."

Fourteen years of backbreaking, dawn-to-dusk labor in the cotton fields would pass before Tubman would make her escape from the bonds that held her and almost four million other African American slaves as the "nonhuman" property of their white owners.

She told how much freedom meant to her: "There's two things I've got a right to, and these are Death or Liberty. One or the other I mean to have. No one will take me back alive; I shall fight for my liberty, and when the time has come for me to go, the Lord will let them kill me."

In 1849, Tubman escaped. She made her way to the North and freedom aided by the Underground Railroad. This was a system invented by a loosely organized group of white people who hated the practice of slavery and actively fought against it by aiding and protecting runaway slaves. Tubman remembered the moment when she finally reached the free soil of Pennsylvania: "When I found I had crossed that line, I looked at my hands to see if I was the same person. There was such a glory over everything; the sun came like gold through the trees, and over the fields, and I felt like I was in Heaven."

Many people risked their lives by providing aid and shelter to runaways at farms and houses located a night's travel apart. Runaways risked flogging and sometimes death at the hands of professionals who made a living hunting them down. Those who were captured alive and uninjured were returned to their owners. Slaves represented a substantial investment. A prime male field hand could bring up to eighteen hundred dollars on the auction block.

Tubman soon realized that she could not be free until all her people were free. She wrote later, "I had crossed the line. I was *free;* but there was no one to welcome me to the land of freedom. I was a stranger in a strange land; and my home, after all, was down in Maryland, because my father, my mother, my brothers, my sisters, and friends were there. But I was free and *they should be free!* I would make a home in the North and bring them there!"

A year after her escape, Tubman sneaked back onto the same Maryland plantation and assisted in rounding up members of her family, including her aging parents. She conducted them through the Underground Railroad to the comparative safety of the northern states.

Once Tubman's relatives were safe, she embarked upon a series of daring and courageous forays into other southern states, becoming one of the Underground Railroad's most famous "conductors." Huge rewards were offered for her capture, and she became the object of an intense hunt. Tubman and the three thousand or so sympathizers who provided aid and shelter led some seventy-five thousand slaves to freedom. Tubman personally brought two hundred of those to safety.

Harriet Tubman

"There's two things I've got a right to, and these are Death or Liberty. One or the other I mean to have."

Tubman defiantly led the frightened, weary slaves northward, maintaining order with a rigid military discipline to protect their lives and her own. Often she would keep them moving by threatening them with a loaded revolver. She did not want to be cruel, but she knew that if she relaxed for a second, her mission would be over and her freedom and the freedom of her followers would be lost. "As a conductor of the Underground Railroad for eight years, I can say what most conductors can't say — I never ran my train off the track and I never lost a passenger," Tubman said.

With the outbreak of the Civil War in 1861, Tubman ceased her activities with the Underground Railroad and became a spy for the Union army. Posing as a laundress, she managed to cross back and forth between the lines of the Confederate and Union forces stationed along the coast of North Carolina, carrying information that greatly aided Union troops. In one raid, Tubman actively participated in the fighting against the Confederate troops, and the story of her exploits was carried on the front pages of northern newspapers.

After the Civil War, Tubman made her home in Auburn, New York. On March 10, 1913, at the age of ninety-three, this remarkable woman died. A year later, the city of Auburn placed a bronze tablet in her memory at the entrance to the courthouse, where it remains today.

Harriet Tubman had the courage to make a decision and to set her life's course against the forces and beliefs of her day. By her devotion to her cause, she helped make available the full benefits of our democracy to all Americans.

MOSES

*P*erhaps the most famous "conductor" on the Underground Railroad was Harriet Tubman. After escaping from slavery herself in 1849, she returned to the South again and again, at great risk, to lead others to freedom. Thus, she earned the title *Moses*. The following article about Harriet Tubman was published by the New-England Freedmen's Aid Society in their monthly publication *The Freedmen's Record.**

One of the teachers lately commissioned by the New-England Freedmen's Aid Society is probably the most remarkable woman of this age. That is to say, she has performed more wonderful deeds by the native power of her own spirit against adverse circumstances than any other. She is well known to many by the various names which her eventful life has given her; Harriet Garrison, Gen. Tubman, &c.; but among the slaves she is universally known by her well-earned title of *Moses*, — Moses the deliv-erer. She is a rare instance, in the midst of high civilization and intellectual culture, of a being of great native powers, working powerfully, and to beneficient ends, entirely unaided by schools or books.

Her maiden name was Araminta Ross. She is the granddaughter of a native African, and has not a drop of white blood in her veins. She was born in 1820 or 1821, on the Eastern Shore of Maryland. Her parents were slaves, but married and faithful to each other, and the family affection is very strong.

From Ellen Hansen, ed., *The Underground Railroad: Life on the Road to Freedom,* Perspectives on History Series, pp. 37–43. Copyright © 1993 Discovery Enterprises, Ltd., Lowell, Massachusetts.

*From *The Freedmen's Record,* Vol. 1, No. 3 (Boston, March, 1865): 34–38.

Harriet Tubman (1823—1913)
nurse, spy and scout

She claims that she was legally freed by a will of her first master, but his wishes were not carried into effect.

She seldom lived with her owner, but was usually "hired out" to different persons. She once "hired her time," and employed it in rudest farming labors, ploughing, carting, driving the oxen, &c., to so good advantage that she was able in one year to buy a pair of steers worth forty dollars.

When quite young she lived with a very pious mistress; but the slaveholder's religion did not prevent her from whipping the young girl for every slight or fancied fault. Araminta found that this was usually a morning exercise; so she prepared for it by putting on all the thick clothes she could procure to protect her skin. She made sufficient outcry, however, to convince her mistress that her blows had full effect; and in the afternoon she would take off her wrappings, and dress as well as she could....

In her youth she received a severe blow on her head from a heavy weight thrown by her master at another slave, but which accidentally hit her. The blow produced a disease of the brain which was severe for a long time, and still makes her very lethargic. She cannot remain quiet fifteen minutes without appearing to fall asleep. It is not refreshing slumber; but a heavy, weary condition which exhausts her. She therefore loves great physical activity, and direct heat of the sun, which keeps her blood actively circulating. She was married about 1844 to a free colored man named John Tubman, but never had any children. Owing to changes in her owner's family, it was determined to sell her and some other slaves; but her health was so much injured, that a purchaser was not easily found. At length she became convinced that she would soon be carried away, and she decided to escape. Her brothers did not agree with her plans; and she walked off alone, following the guidance of the brooks, which she had observed to run North. The evening before she left, she wished very much to bid her companions farewell, but was afraid of being betrayed, if any one knew of her intentions; so she passed through the street singing, —

"Good bye, I'm going to leave you,

Good bye, I'll meet you in the kingdom," —

and similar snatches of Methodist songs....

[After escaping across the Mason-Dixon Line into a free state,] she remained two years in Philadelphia working hard and carefully hoarding her money. Then she hired a room, furnished it as well as she could, bought a nice suit of men's clothes, and went back to Maryland for her husband. But the faithless man had taken to himself another wife. Harriet did not dare venture into her presence, but sent word to her husband where she was. He declined joining her. At first her grief and anger were excessive.... [B]ut finally she thought..."if he could do without her, she could without him," and so "he dropped out of her heart," and she determined to give her life to brave deeds. Thus all personal aims died out of her heart; and with her simple brave motto, "I can't die but once," she began the work which has made her Moses, — the deliverer of her people. Seven or eight times she has returned to the neighborhood of her former home, always at the risk of death in the most terrible forms, and each time has brought away a company of fugitive slaves, and led them safely to the free States, or to Canada. Every time she went, the dangers increased. In 1857 she brought away her old parents, and, as they were too feeble to walk, she was obliged to hire a wagon, which added greatly to the perils of the journey. In 1860 she went for the last time, and among her troop was an infant whom they were obliged to keep stupefied with laudanum to prevent its outcries. This was at the period of great excitement, and Moses was not safe even in New-York State;

but her anxious friends insisted upon her taking refuge in Canada. So various and interesting are the incidents of the journey, that we know not how to select from them. She has shown in them all the characteristics of a great leader: courage, foresight, prudence, self-control, ingenuity, subtle perception, command over others' minds....

A clergyman once said, that her stories convinced you of their truth by their simplicity as do the gospel narratives. She never went to the South to bring away fugitives without being provided with money; money for the most part earned by drudgery in the kitchen, until within the last few years, when friends have aided her. She had to leave her sister's two orphan children in slavery the last time, for the want of thirty dollars. Thirty pieces of silver; an embroidered handkerchief or a silk dress to one, or the price of freedom to two orphan children to another! She would never allow more to join her than she could properly care for, though she often gave others directions by which they succeeded in escaping. She always came in the winter when the nights are long and dark, and people who have homes stay in them. She was never seen on the plantation herself; but appointed a rendezvous for her company eight or ten miles distant, so that if they were discovered at the first start she was not compromised. She started on Saturday night; the slaves at that time being allowed to go away from home to visit their friends, — so that they would not be missed until Monday morning. Even then they were supposed to have loitered on the way, and it would often be late on Monday afternoon before the flight would be certainly known. If by any further delay the advertisement was not sent out before Tuesday morning, she felt secure of keeping ahead of it; but if it were, it required all her ingenuity to escape. She resorted to various devices, she had confidential friends all along the road. She would hire a man to follow the one who put up the notices, and take them down as soon as his back was turned. She crossed creeks on railroad bridges by night, she hid her company in the woods while she herself not being advertised went into the towns in search of information. If met

The U.S. government often employed slaves who escaped to Union lines as drivers of horse teams or as laborers. This group posed for the photographer in front of their roughly built shanty.

on the road, her face was always to the south, and she was always a very respectable looking darkey, not at all a poor fugitive. She would get into the cars near her pursuers and manage to hear their plans....

The expedition was governed by the strictest rules. If any man gave out, he must be shot. "Would you really do that?" she was asked. "Yes," she replied, "if he was weak enough to give out, he'd be weak enough to betray us all, and all who had helped us; and do you think I'd let so many die just for one coward man." "Did you ever have to shoot any one?" she was asked. "One time," she said, "a man gave out the second night; his feet were sore and swollen, he couldn't go any further; he'd rather go back and die, if he must." They tried all arguments in vain, bathed his feet, tried to strengthen him, but it was of no use, he would go back. Then she said, "I told the boys to get their guns ready, and shoot him. They'd have done it in a minute; but when he heard that, he jumped right up and went on as well as any body." She can tell the time by the stars, and find her way by natural signs as well as any hunter; and yet she scarcely knows of the existence of England or any other foreign country.

When going on these journeys she often lay alone in the forests all night. Her whole soul was filled with awe of the mysterious Unseen Presence, which thrilled her with such depths of emotion, that all other care and fear vanished. Then she seemed to speak with her Maker "as a man talketh with his friend"; her child-like petitions had direct answers, and beautiful visions lifted her up above all doubt and anxiety into serene trust and faith. No man can be a hero without this faith in some form; the sense that he walks not in his own strength, but leaning on an almighty arm. Call it fate, destiny, what you will, Moses of old, Moses of to-day, believed it to be Almighty God....

Her efforts were not confined to the escape of slaves. She conducted them to Canada, watched over their welfare, collected clothing, organized them into societies, and was always occupied with plans for their benefit....

She has a very affectionate nature, and forms the strongest personal attachments. She has great simplicity of character; she states her wants very freely, and believes you are ready to help her; but if you have nothing to give, or have given to another, she is content. She is not sensitive to indignities to her color in her own person; but knows and claims her rights. She will eat at your table if she sees you really desire it; but she goes as willingly to the kitchen. She is very abstemious in her diet, fruit being the only luxury she cares for. Her personal appearance is very peculiar. She is thoroughly negro, and very plain. She has needed disguise so often, that she seems to have command over her face, and can banish all expression from her features, and look so stupid that nobody would suspect her of knowing enough to be dangerous; but her eye flashes with intelligence and power when she is roused....

A Nineteenth-Century Childhood: Harriet Beecher Stowe

by Kathleen Burke

In 1852, the year *Uncle Tom's Cabin* was published, the name Harriet Beecher Stowe became well-known throughout the United States. Stowe was the author of this controversial novel, which stirred strong reactions in readers from both North and South with its startling portrayal of the cruelties of slavery. Stowe's fame would remain with her throughout the rest of her life.

But fame probably never occurred to Stowe during her girlhood in Connecticut. She grew up in a large, rambling house overlooking Prospect Hill in the small town of Litchfield. Small and blue-eyed, Harriet was the sixth of eight children born to Roxana Beecher and her husband, Lyman, the pastor of the Litchfield Congregational Church. She was a quick-witted and observant girl, and later in life she would write vividly of her early days in New England.

Eight children must have made the Beecher household a lively place. But in 1816, when Harriet was five years old, her mother died, and a deep sorrow settled over the Beecher clan. Many children of Harriet's generation knew this tragedy, for women often died young because of disease or difficulty with childbirth.

After her mother's death, Harriet was taken to her grandmother's near Guilford, Connecticut. There was no shortage of rules in her grandmother's household. Harriet wrote later that she was expected to behave as a well-brought-up New England girl, to "move very gently, speak softly and prettily, say 'yes ma'am' and 'no ma'am,' never tear clothes, to sew, to knit at regular hours, to go to church on Sundays."

Nevertheless, good times and gaiety were plentiful. Harriet's grandmother told eloquent, compelling tales from the Bible. And when Harriet's Uncle Sam, a sea captain, came home from voyaging, Harriet was spellbound by the blustering old salt. She listened for hours on end to his tales of pirates and thundering storms, marauding Turks and exotic ports.

After a year, Harriet returned to the parsonage in Litchfield. Her father remarried, and a warm-hearted stepmother took charge of the household. The familiar commotion of children and visitors resumed.

Stowe's memories of that parsonage were so sharp that in her imagination, the house nearly took on a life of its own. Her favorite hideaways were the three attics where she and her brothers explored on winter afternoons.

In the attic over the kitchen, heaps of pumpkins covered the wide-plank floor. Great bins held the stores of shelled corn and oats. But most exciting of all for Harriet was her discovery of barrels of old sermons and pamphlets stored in a corner. From these

Harriet Beecher Stowe

After *Uncle Tom's Cabin*, Stowe wrote a second book on slavery titled *Dred: A Tale of the Great Dismal Swamp*, published in 1856. In addition to her work for the abolitionist movement, she was involved in the temperance and women's rights movements.

Henry Ward Beecher with his sister Harriet Beecher Stowe in New York City, 1868. Their father, Lyman Beecher, held many church positions. He was pastor of the Congregational Church in Litchfield, Connecticut, helped found the American Bible Society, and was president of Cincinnati's Lane Theological Seminary.

She remembered sitting in the Meeting House and hearing about man's "inalienable rights…life, liberty, and the pursuit of happiness."

musty barrels, she retrieved a treasure: a copy of *The Arabian Nights.* Very few books for children were to be had in those days, and she cherished the collection of tales. Whenever her brothers set out on an adventure in the countryside and left her behind, she had only to open the book and journey to an enchanted world.

The second attic, she remembered, was equally wonderful for rummaging. It held a hodgepodge of "bed-quilts and old bonnets, spinning wheels and old pictures," and "dried herbs hanging from their different nails." Here her brothers whittled away the hours, carving toy windmills, boats, and rabbit traps.

Reverend Beecher converted the third attic into his library, to which Harriet loved to retreat. This room gave her "a kind of sheltered feeling as I sat and watched my father writing." In her father's library, "high above all the noise of the house," where there were "books of all sorts, sizes, and bindings," Harriet discovered exciting tales of an earlier New England — of Indians, witches, and her Puritan forefathers. As she went to sleep each night, she dreamed of the fantasy world she had found in her books and of someday writing exciting stories herself.

The village of Litchfield also held its share of happy memories for Harriet. She remembered setting out with her family for church at the Meeting House on the village green, observing the seasonal changes in the hills surrounding the town, and tramping into the woods on fishing expeditions with her brothers. Lively debates on all kinds of theological and political issues resounded at the family's table. Harriet listened to the grownups with keen curiosity.

But nothing captured Harriet's imagination as surely as a village holiday. The Fourth of July especially was a day of pageantry not to be forgotten. All the local boys reenacted a Revolutionary War battle. The town cannon boomed, and the entire village set out tables on the green for a magnificent picnic. In the Meeting House, Colonel Benjamin Tallmadge, who had fought under George Washington, read the Declaration of Independence. Harriet was thrilled at the sight of the old soldier, resplendent in his blue-and-buff uniform. She remembered the "resounding majesty" of his voice. "I was ready to pledge my life, fortune, and sacred honor for such a cause."

When Harriet was eight years old, she entered Miss Pierce's Academy in Litchfield. Her father held the view that girls should receive an education and should be encouraged to use their talents. Most men at that time believed that girls should be prepared only for lives as homemakers. At Miss Pierce's, Harriet absorbed all her lessons, especially those taught by her favorite instructor, Mr. Bunce. "Much of the inspiration of my early days," she wrote, "consisted not in things I was supposed to be studying, but in hearing Mr. Bunce with the older classes."

Mr. Bunce also taught composition. Harriet began writing essays for him and realized how much she loved putting her thoughts and ideas on paper. When she was twelve, teachers were reading her compositions aloud at the annual school exhibitions. Her dream for the future was formed in that New England classroom: She wanted to be a writer.

In the years that followed, Harriet wrote essays, stories, poems — whatever she had time for between her other studies. As she grew to young womanhood, she began to address the great issue of the day, slavery, in her work. Her writing later helped spread her reputation across the country.

But in all her years as a writer, as she labored over twenty-three books and countless articles, Harriet Beecher Stowe never forgot Litchfield, for there she had learned to trust her imagination and to enjoy the rhythm of a well-turned sentence. She remembered sitting in the Meeting House and hearing about man's "inalienable rights...life, liberty, and the pursuit of happiness." In word and in deed, she crusaded for those freedoms throughout her life.

DOROTHEA DIX: QUIET CRUSADER

by Lucie Germer

Dorothea Dix was so shy and quiet that it is hard to believe she had such a tremendous impact on nineteenth-century America. Yet almost single-handedly, she transformed the way people with mental illness were treated.

Dix was born in Maine in 1802 to a neglectful father and a mother who had trouble coping with daily activities. She ran away at the age of twelve to live with her grandmother, a cold, inflexible woman who nevertheless taught her the importance of doing her duty, as well as the organizational skills to help her do it.

Dix grew into an attractive woman, with blue-gray eyes, wavy brown hair, and a rich, low speaking voice. As a young adult, she spent her time teaching, writing books for children, and fighting the effects of tuberculosis. Despite her poor health, by age thirty-nine she had saved enough money that she had no financial worries. Afraid that her health was too poor for her to continue teaching, she looked forward to a lonely, unfulfilling life.

Then a friend suggested that she teach a Sunday school class for women in a Massachusetts jail. It would be useful without overtaxing her. On her first day, she discovered that among the inmates were several mentally ill women. They were anxious to hear what she had to say, but she found it impossible to teach them because the room was unheated. Dix, angry at this neglect on the part of the authorities, asked noted humanitarian Samuel Howe for his help in taking the case to court. The court ordered the authorities to install a wood stove.

Almost single-handedly, she transformed the way people with mental illness were treated.

Dorothea Dix

This sparked Dix's interest in the way mentally ill people were treated. Encouraged by Howe and education reformer Horace Mann, she spent two years visiting every asylum, almshouse, and jail in Massachusetts, quietly taking notes on the conditions. Her grandmother had trained her to be thorough, and the training paid off.

Dix put her findings into a memorial (a report) that Howe presented to the Massachusetts legislature: "I tell what I have seen.... [I]nsane persons confined...in cages, closets, cellars, stalls, pens; chained, naked, beaten with rods and lashed into obedience."

The memorial caused an uproar: What kind of woman would be interested in such a subject and insist on discussing it in public? Gradually, the personal attacks abated, primarily because Dix's research had been so thorough and her results were so complete that no one could argue with them. Howe was able to push a bill through the Massachusetts legislature to enlarge the state insane asylum.

Dix spent the next few years systematically studying conditions and getting legislation passed in other states. Her health did not keep her from putting in long hours of hard work and travel. First, she studied the psychological and legal views of mental illness and its treatment. Before she went into a state, she examined local laws and previous proposals for change. Then she visited every institution, small or large, and met with administrators, politicians, and private citizens. She put all this information together in a memorial that was presented to the legislature.

She also wrote newspaper articles to inform the public of her findings. By this time, she knew what kind of opposition to expect, and she could help deflect it by appealing to the citizens' sense of pride or desire for economy. She met privately with small groups of politicians to answer their questions and try to persuade them to come around to her point of view. She was usually successful, and public institutions to house and treat people with mental illness were established.

Unfortunately, that success did not carry over to her next goal: national legislation to improve living conditions for people with mental illness. In the 1850s, Congress passed a bill setting aside land for the establishment of national hospitals for those with mental illness, but President Franklin Pierce vetoed the bill on constitutional grounds.

Dix was shattered. Her health, which had been surprisingly good during her struggles, took a turn for the worse, and doctors recommended she take a long voyage. Dix was unable to relax, however, and her vacation turned into a marathon journey through Europe, as she examined the living conditions of mentally ill people in each place she visited. She spoke with doctors, government officials, and even the pope, pleading for humanitarian treatment for those who were mentally ill. She went as far east as Constantinople (now Istanbul) in Turkey and as far north as St. Petersburg in Russia. She was greeted respectfully everywhere she went, and many of her recommendations were followed.

She returned to the United States in 1857 and was appointed superintendent of women nurses during the Civil War. Dix was the only woman to hold an official position in the U.S. government during the war.

During the Civil War, Dorothea Dix served as superintendent of Union nurses. She is shown here helping a soldier.

After the war, Dix continued her work on behalf of mentally ill people both in the United States and abroad. She died in 1887 at the age of eighty-five. Between 1841, when she began her crusade, and the year she died, thirty-two new hospitals for those who were mentally ill were built, most of them directly because she had brought the problem to the attention of people in power. Several other institutions in Canada and Europe, and even two in Japan, were established because of her influence. She also left a legacy of concern: No longer was mental illness treated as a crime, and her enlightened and tireless work led to more humane living conditions for people with mental illness.

FEDERAL SPY, PAULINE CUSHMAN

by Phyllis Raybin Emert

Born in New Orleans, Louisiana, Pauline Cushman was the dark-haired attractive daughter of a French mother and Spanish father. She left home at age 18 for a life in the theatre and by the time she was 20, was appearing on stages in cities throughout the country.

When the Civil War broke out in 1861, Pauline was a 28-year-old actress married to a fellow actor named Charles Dickinson. He enlisted in the Union Army as a musician but died after a short illness. Although a Southerner by birth, Pauline's sympathies were with the North.

In March of 1863, she was appearing in a production of *The Seven Sisters* at Wood's Theatre in Louisville, Kentucky. Although Kentucky was a Union state, the city of Louisville was filled with Southern supporters. Pauline was approached by two men who assumed the popular actress also supported the Confederate cause. They dared her to drink a toast to the South during her performance in one of the show's skits that night, and even offered her money.

Pauline loved being the center of attention but her loyalties were with the Union. She visited Colonel Moore, the Federal Provost marshall in Louisville, for his opinion. Moore urged her to make the toast. Publicly, everyone would think Pauline was a Confederate but privately she could help identify spies and Southern sympathizers for the North.

That night's performance was standing room only. Pauline, dressed as a man in this particular skit, lifted a champagne glass in her hand and walked away from the other performers to the edge of the stage. Everyone was silent as she raised her glass to the audience and said loudly, "Here's to Jeff

Cushman was a widely known New York City actress before helping the Union army as a spy. Although she was discovered, she escaped punishment. After the war, dressed in uniform, she shared her wartime experiences with the public.

Pauline Cushman

Braxton Bragg

....

Bragg (1817–1876), the general who brought down Pauline Cushman, was one of the most unpopular and controversial Confederate generals. After he lost at Missionary Ridge in 1863, he resigned his command.

From Phyllis Raybin Emert, ed., *Women in the Civil War: Warriors, Patriots, Nurses, and Spies,* Perspectives on History Series, pp. 31–32. Copyright © 1995 Discovery Enterprises, Ltd., Lowell, Massachusetts.

Davis and the Southern Confederacy. May the South always maintain her honor and her rights."

Shouts and cheers mingled with boos and hisses rang out in the theatre. Fights started in the audience and women screamed. In one night, Pauline had become a Southern heroine. No one suspected she was really a Federal spy and in the months that followed, her fame spread. People flocked to theatres in Louisville and Nashville to see her perform. Southerners rushed to her side, confiding Confederate secrets and important information, never doubting her loyalty to the Southern cause. For months, she passed on this valuable material to Union officials.

One day, Colonel William Truesdail, head of intelligence for the Union's Army of the Cumberland, gave Pauline her most dangerous assignment. She was to visit the camps of Confederate General Bragg and the Army of Tennessee and get all the information she could about troop numbers, movements, and fortifications. Her excuse in visiting was that she was searching for her long lost brother (who really was a member of the rebel army). Truesdail's order to Pauline was to remember everything and put nothing down on paper.

It was May of 1863 when the young actress was escorted out of the city of Nashville with other women who were suspected of aiding the Confederate cause. Her fame and beauty gave Pauline immediate access behind Confederate lines. She befriended Rebel officers, who gave in to her charms and talked to her openly about military strategy, troop movements, and regiment strength.

Living a spy's life finally caught up with Pauline. Disobeying orders, she made notes and drawings and stole enemy blueprints which she hid in the lining of her shoes. Pauline was caught once and escaped, then caught again. The papers were found and used as evidence against her.

Pauline was tried before General Bragg and a military court. She was found guilty and sentenced to death by hanging! A few days later, Union forces attacked Bragg and the Rebels pulled out quickly, retreating south to Chattanooga. In the confusion, Pauline, who by now was very ill from her ordeal, was left behind. Union soldiers who learned quickly that she was a Northern spy, were thrilled to liberate her from her Southern jailers. Pauline gave the Union officers much valuable information about what she had seen and heard before her capture.

REBEL ROSE

by Phyllis Raybin Emert

A native of Maryland who grew up in Washington, Rose O'Neal Greenhow was a strong secessionist and devoted to the Southern cause. When her husband, Dr. Robert Greenhow, died in 1854, Rose used her political friendships and influence to support herself and her four daughters. She knew senators, generals, congressmen, and statesmen from both the North and the South. Even President James Buchanan (1857–1861) was a frequent visitor to Rose's home.

The dark-haired and beautiful widow was always surrounded by male admirers, and when the Civil War broke out, Rose used her power as a famous Washington hostess to obtain important information for the South. Within weeks, she was the head of a secret spy ring and was directly responsible for General Beauregard's

Confederate victory at the battle of Bull Run (First Manassas) in July 1861. The "Rebel Rose," as she was called, supplied important dates and information to Beauregard in several messages.

Shortly after the Confederate victory, Rose was placed under house arrest by the Federal government for five months. In January, 1862, she was transferred to Old Capitol Prison where she remained until her release on June 2nd. At that time, Rose signed a document promising "not to return north of the Potomac River during the present hostilities without the permission of the Secretary of War of the United States."

When Rose arrived in the Confederate capital of Richmond, Virginia on June 4, Rebel President Jefferson Davis declared, "But for you there would have been no battle of Bull Run." The successful spy was next sent as an ambassador to England and France in order to gather support for the Confederate cause. While returning from that mission to Europe in 1864, Rose drowned when the boat which was rowing her ashore overturned.

ROSE O'NEAL GREENHOW AND DAUGHTER

MY IMPRISONMENT AND THE FIRST YEAR OF ABOLITION RULE AT WASHINGTON*

by Rose O'Neal Greenhow

On the morning of the 16th of July, 1861, the Government papers at Washington announced that the [Union] "grand army" was in motion and I learned from a reliable source (having received a copy of the order to McDowell) that the order for a forward movement had gone forth....

At twelve o'clock on the morning of the 16th of July, I dispatched a messenger to Manassas, who arrived there at eight o'clock that night. The answer received by me at midday on the 17th will tell the purport of my communication —

"Yours was received at eight o'clock at night. Let them come: we are ready for them. We rely upon you for precise information. Be particular as to description and destination of forces, quantity of artillery etc."

Signed, "Thomas Jordan, Adjt Gen."

On the 17th of July, I dispatched another message to Manassas, for I had learned of the intention of the enemy to cut the Winchester railroad, so as to intercept Johnston and prevent his reinforcing Beau-

From Phyllis Raybin Emert, ed., *Women in the Civil War: Warriors, Patriots, Nurses, and Spies,* Perspectives on History Series, pp. 32–35. Copyright © 1995 Discovery Enterprises, Ltd., Lowell, Massachusetts.

*From *Heroines of Dixie*, by Jones, Bobbs-Merrill Company, NY, 1955, pp. 62–66, originally published in 1864.

The great Battle of Bull Run (Manassas), July 21, 1861.

regard who had comparatively but a small force under his command at Manassas....

On Sunday (21st) the great battle of Manassas was fought — which ended in the total defeat of the entire "Grand Army." In the world's history such a sight was never witnessed: statesmen, Senators, Congressmen, generals and officers of every grade, soldiers, teamsters — all rushing in frantic fright, as if pursued by countless demons.... The news of the disastrous rout of the Yankee Army was cried through the streets of New York on the 22nd. The whole city seemed paralyzed by fear....

On Friday, Aug. 23, 1861, as I was entering my own door in returning from a promenade, I was arrested by two men, one in citizens clothes and the other in dress of an officer of the United States Army. This latter was called Major

Allan, and was the chief of the detective police of the city. They followed close upon my footsteps. As I ascended my steps the two men ascended also before I could open the door and asked, "Is this Mrs. Greenhow?" I answered "Yes. Who are you and what do you want?" "I come to arrest you" — "By what authority?" The man Allan, or Pinkerton (for he had several aliases) said: "By sufficient authority." I said: "Let me see your warrant." He mumbled something about verbal authority from the War and State Department and then they followed me into the house. By this time the house had become filled with men, and men also surrounded it outside like bees from a hive. Men rushed with frantic haste into my chamber. My beds, my wardrobes were all upturned. My library was taken possession of and every scrap of paper was seized....

The work of examining my papers had commenced. I had no reason to fear of the consequences from the papers which had as yet fallen into their hands. I had a right to my own political opinions. I am a Southern woman, born with Revolutionary blood in my veins, Freedom of speech and of thought were my birthright, guaranteed, signed and sealed by the blood of our fathers.

...I was allowed to go to my chamber and I then resolved to destroy some important papers which I had in my pocket, even at the expense of my life. (The papers were my cipher, with which I corresponded with my friends at Manassas.) Happily I succeeded without such a painful sacrifice....

A very large sum had been offered for my cipher. This stimulated the zeal of the employees of the Government to a very remarkable degree. The tables were filled with fragments of old letters and scraps in cipher, in several languages, from early morning till late at night. For seven days they puzzled over them. I had no fear. — One by one they allowed the clue to escape them. Only once was I frightened. Miss Mackall [McCall], who like myself was always on the alert, abstracted from a heap of papers a sheet of blotting paper upon which was the whole of my dispatch to Manassas on July 16.

On Friday the 30th of August I was informed that my house was to be converted into a prison....

Farming families in Virginia head to the Federal commissary for provisions.

A Virginia Girl in the Civil War*

by Myrta L. Avary (also known as Nellie Grey)

I joined mother at the Arlington.... Mrs. Fry before our arrival had informed her boarders that they could continue to rent their rooms from her, but that they must provide their own meals. We paid her $25 a month for our room — the price of a house in good times and in good money. During my absence...mother, to reduce expenses, had rented half of her room and bed to Delia McArthur, of Petersburg. I now rented a little bed from Mrs. Fry for myself, and set it up in the same room.

We had become so poor and had so little to cook that we did most of our cooking ourselves over the grate, each woman often cooking her own rations.... Sometimes we all put what we had together and ate in company.... Sometimes we would all get so hungry that we would put together all the money we could rake and scrape and buy a bit of roast or something else substantial and have a feast....

...Bags of peas, rice, and potatoes were disposed around the room, and around the hearth were arranged our pots, pans, kettles, and cooking utensils generally. When we bought wood, that was put under the beds....

Sometimes our guests were boys from camp who dropped in and took stewed apples or boiled peas, as the case might be. If we were particularly fortunate we offered a cup of tea sweetened with sugar.

The soldier who dropped in always got a part — and the best part — of what we had. If things were scant we had smiles to make up for the lack of our larder, and to hide its bareness.

How we were pinched that winter! How often we were hungry! and how anxious and miserable we were! And yet what fun we had! The boys laughed at our crowded room and we laughed with them....

...Hungry and shabby as we were, crowded into our one room with bags of rice and peas, firkins of butter, a ton of coal, a small wood-pile, cooking utensils, and all of our personal property, we were not in despair. Our faith in Lee and his ragged, freezing, starving army amounted to a superstition. We cooked our rice and peas and dried apples, and hoped and prayed. By this time our bags took up little room. We had had a bag of potatoes, but it was nearly empty. There were only a few handfuls of dried apples left — and I must say that even in the face of starvation I was glad of that! — and there was a very small quantity of rice in our larder. We had more peas than anything else....

There were hunger and nakedness and death and pestilence and fire and sword everywhere, and we, fugitives from shot and shell, knew it well, but, somehow, we laughed and sang and played on the piano — and never believed in actual defeat and subjugation....

From Phyllis Raybin Emert, ed., *Women in the Civil War: Warriors, Patriots, Nurses, and Spies,* Perspectives on History Series, pp. 58–59. Copyright © 1995 Discovery Enterprises, Ltd., Lowell, Massachusetts.

*From *Ladies of Richmond,* by Jones, Bobbs-Merrill Company, NY, 1962, pp. 258–262, originally published in 1903.

Testing the Fourteenth Amendment

by Linda S. Berg

No American woman had voted in a national election before, but Susan B. Anthony was determined to do so. On November 1, 1872, Anthony and fifteen other women arrived at the voter registration office in Rochester, New York, to register for the upcoming presidential election.

By this time, Anthony was a leader in the women's rights struggle and had campaigned nationwide for women's voting rights. During the previous few years, women had won the right to sue in court, inherit money and property, and keep their wages for themselves. Still, many did not receive even a high school education, and it was illegal for women to vote.

In 1868, the states had ratified the Fourteenth Amendment to the U.S. Constitution. Anthony believed that women were included in the amendment. By actually voting and risking fines or imprisonment, she could test her belief in court instead of waiting years for Congress to approve woman suffrage.

In the Rochester registration office, Anthony read the Fourteenth Amendment aloud: "All persons born or naturalized in the United States...are citizens of the United States.... No State shall make or enforce any law which shall abridge the privileges or immunities of citizens of the United States."

"I think, sirs, that no one would say that women are neither persons nor citizens," she concluded. The registrars, aware of her influence, allowed the women to register.

On November 5, Anthony returned with her fifteen followers and voted. It was a giant step for women, and Anthony wrote gleefully in a letter, "Well, I have been and gone and done it!"

As she expected, however, trouble soon followed. On November 28, Thanksgiving Day, the U.S. chief marshal came to her home to arrest her for voting illegally. He hoped to convince Anthony to go quietly to the courthouse by herself, but she refused. She insisted that her group be taken to court like any other criminals, and the

The trial of Susan B. Anthony took place in this courthouse in Canandaigua, New York, in 1873.

marshal was forced to parade them publicly through the streets.

Once at the courthouse, the women were ignored. They later complained that they had been kept in a cramped, grimy room all day for no reason. The next morning, all the women except Anthony pleaded not guilty and were released on bail.

Anthony refused to leave and was sent to jail to await trial. She wanted to remain in prison to make a political statement, but to her dismay, her lawyer paid her one-thousand-dollar bail. Anthony lectured all over New York during the six months between her arrest and trial, always insisting that women could vote according to the Fourteenth Amendment.

The trial location was changed because of protests that Anthony's speeches were influencing possible jury members. In June 1873, the trial finally took place in Canandaigua, New York. The judge was J. Ward Hunt, a man chosen by politicians who regarded Anthony as a nuisance and wanted to get rid of her case quickly.

The district attorney first moved that women were incompetent to testify in court. Justice Hunt agreed, so Anthony could not speak in her own defense. Her lawyer was furious but could do nothing. On the second day of the trial, the judge came to court with his verdict already prepared. He stated that the Fourteenth Amendment did not protect Anthony's right to vote.

"I have also decided that her belief and the advice she took do not protect her in the act which she committed. The result must be a verdict of guilty," he added.

Susan B. Anthony is buried in Rochester, New York's Mount Hope Cemetery. Fellow reformer Frederick Douglass also is buried there (see page 225).

He fined Anthony one hundred dollars and dismissed the jury before they had heard the case. Anthony was outraged by the unfair trial and cried that she would never pay the fine. Her furious outburst to the courtroom audience appeared in newspapers nationwide.

Anthony could have been arrested for not paying the fine, but she was not. Public opinion was in her favor, and the government did not want to arouse further anger. Anthony lost her case, but her cause and trial attracted public sympathy. Letters and money poured in to support her, and the national attention gave the suffrage movement a needed boost.

Progress in woman suffrage occurred gradually after Anthony's attempt to vote. Beginning in the late 1860s and 1870s, some western territories allowed women to vote in territorial elections.

The movement spread to eastern states, but it was not until 1920 that the Nineteenth Amendment to the U.S. Constitution gave women the right to vote in all elections. The amendment was known as the "Susan B. Anthony Amendment" out of respect for the determined woman who had brought it to life with one daring vote.

WYOMING: THE LAND OF THE FREE

by Sandra E. Guzzo

In the mid-1800s, the rest of the United States knew little about Wyoming Territory. But in December 1869, the territory's first legislature became the first government in the world to give women the right to vote and hold public office.

How did such a controversial measure pass in this "Wild West" territory? Although some legislators believed that giving women the vote was the right thing to do, many others were interested only in attracting more people — especially women — to the territory. Whatever the motives, Wyoming set America on a course that eventually led to the passage of the Nineteenth Amendment to the U.S. Constitution.

William H. Bright, a forty-five-year-old saloonkeeper from South Pass City, Wyoming, introduced the suffrage bill. Many credit his wife, Julia, with persuading him to present the bill. Esther Morris, another woman who lived in the same gold-mining town, also might have influenced "Colonel" Bright. Legend has it that she invited Bright to a tea party and made him promise to introduce the bill. Although historians have disputed Morris's role in this matter, she did play a part in Wyoming history when she later became the nation's first female justice of the peace.

A true friend of woman suffrage in Wyoming was Edward M. Lee, a thirty-two-year-old lawyer from Connecticut who was appointed secretary of Wyoming Territory by President Ulysses S. Grant. He, too, believed that woman suffrage was just, but he used another argument to win the legislature's support. He told them that it would attract settlers. Wyoming Territory had only eight thousand residents at this time, and men outnumbered women six to one. What better way, he argued, to increase the population and encourage more women to settle in Wyoming?

Lee also knew that it was easier to pass such a bill in a territory than it would be in a state. In a territory, simple majority vote by the legislature with the approval of the governor would do. In a state, however, the citizens voted on new laws. Lee became the spokesman for prosuffrage views at a time when Wyoming women did not even have a suffrage organization and were not accustomed to speaking in public.

Nationally known suffragist speakers also played an important role in the bill's passage. Anna Dickinson was considered to be a "celebrated lady" by the *Cheyenne Leader,* one of the territory's better-known newspapers, and her visit was hailed as "quite an event in our city." Redlia Bates, another suffragist leader, spoke in Cheyenne in November 1869, just before the legislators met. Audiences found Dickinson and Bates to be attractive and charming, two qualities that appealed to the predominantly male population.

The suffrage bill was not without its opponents, however. Representative Ben Sheeks led the attack against

William H. Bright

Above: Bright was president of the first Wyoming Council in 1869. Below: As the first woman voter in Wyoming, Swain became the first woman in the world to vote in a general election.

Eliza Swain

woman suffrage, expressing some of the popular notions of the time. He believed that a woman's place was in the home; only bad and ignorant women would vote; politics was dirty business; and suffrage would result in conflict in the home. Despite this opposition, the bill passed the house of representatives and the territorial council. All that remained was the governor's approval.

Most of the legislators knew that Governor John A. Campbell was not a women's rights sympathizer. Many thought that he would use his power to veto the bill, but they were wrong. Governor Campbell took the issue seriously. Deciding that "an experiment" was justified, he signed the bill in December 1869.

On September 6, 1870, Mrs. Eliza Swain, a woman of "high social standing" in Laramie, became the first of the one thousand eligible female voters to cast her ballot. Many believed that the women's presence "reduced drunkenness and fighting" at the polls. Pronouncing the experiment a success, Governor Campbell said that the women had conducted themselves with "as much tact, sound judgment, and good sense as men." Susan B. Anthony would later praise Wyoming as "the first place on God's green earth which could...claim to be the land of the Free!"

VICTORIA C. WOODHULL: FIRST WOMAN PRESIDENTIAL CANDIDATE

by Carole Joyce Davis

Our Constitution says that anyone who is born in this country and who is at least thirty-five years old can run for president. Anyone. When Ohio-born Victoria Woodhull ran for the nation's highest office more than one hundred years ago, women were not even allowed to vote. Nevertheless, the name of this outspoken and remarkable woman appeared on the November ballot in 1872: Victoria C. Woodhull — The Equal Rights Candidate.

In the summer of 1850, The Claflin Traveling Medicine Show rolled into a small Ohio town. The tired horse hung its head. Pulling the heavy wagon over the bumpy dirt roads all day was hard work. Maybe the Claflin family (all ten of them) would take in enough money this time for an extra ration of feed. If they did, they could thank Victoria, twelve, and Tennessee, only five.

A crowd started to form as soon as the wagon came to a halt in the town square.

"Be sure and have young Victoria tell your fortune," one man said.

"I hear she's got the gift," added another.

"Yes, and so does little Tennessee, who goes into trances just like her ma and Victoria."

"That Buck Claflin is one lucky man. Imagine havin' two daughters with the psychic powers."

Talk like this buzzed around the hot, dusty square. Most of the townspeople already knew about Victoria's and Tennessee's amazing abilities. Now they could hardly wait to see whether what they had heard was true.

Roxanna Claflin, the girls' mother, was fascinated with spiritualism, as it was called. Young Victoria had the same "gift," and from early childhood she, like her mother, had "visions" — an ability to predict future events. Victoria was the

Victoria C. Woodhull

Woodhull (1838–1927) was an editor, a presidential candidate, and an unconventional reformer.

103

seventh child in the Claflin family, and some think that is a lucky number.

When the Claflins found that daughter Tennessee possessed the same ability, they decided to use their talents to help the family earn money. The scene with The Claflin Traveling Medicine Show was repeated many times. The "medicine" part of their show was a one-dollar bottle of vegetable juice, Elixir of Life, which, they assured everyone, would cure anything from a toothache to cancer.

Victoria was fifteen when she married Dr. Canning Woodhull. She divorced him twelve years later. This was in 1865, the year the Civil War ended and President Abraham Lincoln was shot.

The next year, Woodhull met and married Colonel James Blood, a handsome Civil War veteran. Freedom, of course, was a much-talked-about subject, and Woodhull liked what Blood had to say on this subject, especially his ideas about freedom and equal rights for women. Woodhull's decision not to take her husband's name must have shocked most people of the day, but she reasoned that people recognized her more easily as Victoria Woodhull.

Woodhull shocked many people with her liberal ideas and behavior. In 1868 she, Blood, and the whole Claflin family heeded her vision, which, she said, told her to go to New York City. Almost at once, she and Tennessee met the great railroad king Cornelius Vanderbilt, who was deeply interested in mystic wisdom. "The Commodore," as he was known, also had the sense to see that Woodhull and Tennessee would be smart businesswomen.

In January 1870, he helped the sisters start their own business. Their firm, Woodhull, Claflin and Company, sold stocks and bonds. They were the first women ever to own and run such a company, and business boomed. Men called them "the bewitching brokers."

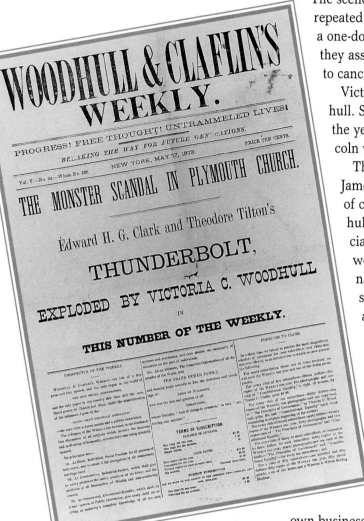

Woodhull & Claflin's Weekly promised "progress, free thought, untrammeled lives, and to break the way for future generations."

Three months later, on April 2, Woodhull put this amazing announcement in the *New York Herald:* "While others argue the equality of women with men, I proved it by successfully engaging in business. I therefore speak for the (unliberated) women in the country. I now announce myself as candidate for the U.S. presidency."

Woodhull had thought for some time how unfairly existing laws treated women. She decided to try and change these injustices.

The next thing she did was begin to publish her own newspaper, *Woodhull & Claflin's Weekly,* so that she could tell people how she would work for equal rights for women. In January 1871, she was invited to give a speech before the House Judiciary Committee, the first woman ever to do so. In a loud, clear voice, she asked that women be given full rights of citizenship and that these rights be made legal.

Susan B. Anthony heard of Woodhull's speech. At first, Anthony thought that Woodhull would be good for the cause. She thought that people would listen to this woman who not only spoke of equal rights but also urged that women be allowed to wear shorter, more comfortable skirts. Later, however, Anthony expelled Woodhull from her national woman suffrage organization on the grounds that her views were too radical.

In 1872, Woodhull formed her own political party and held her own convention in May. She was the official nominee for the Equal Rights party.*

Woodhull, of course, was way ahead of her time. Women had to wait almost fifty years before they could vote. As for rights, Woodhull found out the hard way what a battle lay ahead.

She had a violent argument with well-known preacher Henry Ward Beecher about whether her divorce from Dr. Woodhull was legal. Reverend Beecher was very popular, as was his sister, Harriet Beecher Stowe, who had written *Uncle Tom's Cabin,* a book that greatly influenced the antislavery cause. Woodhull dared to voice her arguments against Reverend Beecher just three days before the national election. She printed all her objections in her newspaper, hoping that people would side with her. Instead, she and her sister, Tennessee, were thrown into jail.

On Election Day, November 5, 1872, America reelected the country's great Civil War hero Ulysses S. Grant. Woodhull actually received a few thousand votes — cast, of course, by men.

Frederick Douglass and Women's Rights

by Karen E. Hong

Two hundred people filled Wesleyan Chapel in Seneca Falls, New York, on July 19, 1848. It was the Women's Rights Convention, the first such gathering in the world, and Frederick Douglass was prominent among the thirty-two men present.

Elizabeth Cady Stanton called for an end to women's social inferiority, changes in laws oppressing women, educational opportunities for women, the end of a double standard for men and women, and the right of women to vote. The call for female suffrage was radical, but Douglass supported Stanton and her demands.

Douglass realized that the situations of African Americans and women were similar. Arguments used to justify slavery also supported male supremacy. Many people felt that women were naturally inferior to men, just as they believed that African Americans were inferior to whites. In some places, women could not own property. Their wages, like those of hired-out slaves, legally belonged to the man responsible for them, usually their husband or father. Higher education and certain occupations were denied them. And women, like African Americans, were subject to laws they were powerless to change.

Just as Douglass recognized the importance of the demands for women's rights, many women were working to end slavery. Both Stanton and Susan B.

*Woodhull knew that the minimum age for a U.S. president is thirty-five, and she would not be thirty-five until September 1873, almost a year after the election. Even if she had been elected, she would not have been able to serve.

Frederick Douglass

Douglass realized that the situations of African Americans and women were similar.

helped found in 1870), Douglass promoted the women's cause. He praised Victoria Claflin Woodhull for arguing that women were guaranteed the vote by the Fourteenth and Fifteenth amendments.

When the Equal Rights party nominated Woodhull for president of the United States in May 1872, Douglass was named her vice-presidential running mate. Although Woodhull accepted the nomination in early June, Douglass's attention was so consumed by a fire that had burned his home to the ground that he was unable to notify the party that he could not accept the nomination.

As Woodhull's influence diminished, Douglass, Stanton, and Anthony reconciled their differences. Douglass was a frequent speaker at women's rights conventions, and in 1885 he listed woman suffrage second only to full freedom for African Americans as a cause to which he intended to devote the rest of his life.

Douglass spent his last day, February 20, 1895, at a meeting of the National Council of Women in Washington. Although many newspapers marked his passing with headlines such as "Great Negro Leader Dies," some papers carried the headline "Friend and Champion of Women Dies." Indeed, Frederick Douglass was a humanist. He was intensely involved in securing freedom and equality for all.

In 1889, Jane Addams and Ellen Gates Starr established Hull House, shown here in the 1890s, in the slums of Chicago to serve as a neighborhood center for the poor.

JANE ADDAMS AND CHICAGO'S HULL HOUSE

by Caryl Simon-Katler

Jane Addams, founder of Chicago's Hull House, was born only months before the Civil War began. Raised in the small town of Cedarville, Illinois, more than one hundred miles from Chicago, she was two when her mother died. Jane idolized her father, John Addams, a prosperous miller who was active in community affairs, organizing the construction of a local railroad and serving as a state senator.

After a village school education, Jane hoped to attend Smith College in Massachusetts. Instead, her father insisted that she study at Rockford Seminary in Illinois. Enrolling in 1877, Jane studied Greek, Latin, French, history, and literature. She was elected class president and named editor of the school magazine, and she developed a close friendship with Ellen Gates Starr.

When John Addams died in 1882, Jane, longing for a change of scenery, decided to study medicine in Philadelphia. Severe back pain forced her to discontinue her training, however. Following an operation, she was bedridden for six months and wore a steel and whalebone back support for another year.

On doctor's orders, Addams traveled to Europe with family and friends in 1883. In her journal, she recorded despair at seeing the "masses of ill-clad people." Again in 1887, she traveled abroad with her college friend, Ellen Gates Starr. They visited Toynbee Hall and the People's Palace in England, their first encounter with community education and recreation centers, or settlement houses.

On their return to Chicago, Addams and Starr discussed what they had seen. Seeing herself as a "missionary," Addams determined to rent a house in a poor neighborhood. Money was no problem, as she had inherited an income from her father. She spoke with clergymen and officials from local charities to gain support. Addams's ambition created conflicts with her family, however, who did not believe in careers for women. "It has always been difficult for the family to regard the daughter, otherwise than as a family possession," she noted.

Addams and Starr toured the city for days, looking for a suitable place. Finally, they located an old house at 800 South Halsted Street. Constructed by Charles Hull in 1856, the house had served as a factory, furniture warehouse, and home for the aged. Addams and Starr rented the second floor, moving to Hull House in September 1889.

Jane Addams

Hull House was located amid tenements and small wooden houses originally intended for one or two families. During the late 1800s, six to twelve families occupied one house. People often slept in windowless rooms, without fire escapes or indoor plumbing. "One is overpowered by the misery and narrow lives of so large a number of city people," Addams wrote. In sweatshops, tailors worked twelve to fourteen hours a day, earning only five to ten dollars a week. Four-year-old children often worked with their mothers, removing threads from garments.

Ellen Gates Starr

Addams's new neighbors were immigrants — Italians, Germans, French Canadians, Irish, Bohemians, and Russian and Polish Jews. Addams wanted Hull House to meet the needs of the immigrants while they adjusted to city life. Nevertheless, the first Hull House event was a reading from a literary novel, followed by slides of Italian art. The visitors were baffled but returned anyway in the coming weeks.

Over the years, Hull House responded more directly to the community's needs, eventually expanding into a complex comprising a dozen buildings. The neighborhood urgently needed a kindergarten, as young children were forced to stay alone in tenement apartments while their mothers worked. Within three

weeks of its opening, the Hull House kindergarten had twenty-four children enrolled, with seventy more on a waiting list. Hull House also offered ethnic evenings, sewing courses, art classes, and debating and social clubs. There was a music school and theater, a gymnasium, and a reading room. A public kitchen provided food for women workers who had no time to cook for their families. Activities for every age and interest were provided.

Hull House also opened a labor museum. Crafts such as spinning, weaving, embroidery, basketry, pottery, and woodworking were demonstrated. The labor museum restored the immigrants' pride in their workmanship, and Addams also believed that it was important for the immigrants' children to learn about their cultural traditions.

Addams promoted Hull House in local newspapers and spoke at nearby colleges. Young, educated men and women volunteered at the settlement house, and many famous individuals also assisted, including ministers, professors, and the widely known educator John Dewey. Addams was convinced that helpers often benefited more than those they helped. In fact, her own health improved through vigorous work at Hull House.

Addams and Hull House were leaders in the settlement house movement. In the first year, fifty thousand people came to Hull House. By 1890, that number had doubled. Two years after Hull House opened, there were six settlements in the United States; by 1900, there were more than a hundred. The University of Chicago, founded in 1892, worked closely with Hull House. Together they studied disease, juvenile delinquency, and the local immigrant populations.

Addams became increasingly involved in Chicago politics. She served on the local school board, advocated a juvenile court, helped advance the cause of labor unions, initiated construction of a playground, and worked for child labor laws. Realizing that garbage piled outside tenements promoted disease, she even became the local garbage inspector.

Her popularity diminished somewhat during the First World War, however. As an advocate of peace, Addams was labeled the "most dangerous woman in America." Continuing to raise funds for Hull House in the 1920s, she traveled throughout the world, later regaining her popularity. In 1931, she received the Nobel Peace Prize for her work among the poor.

Although Jane Addams died in 1935 at the age of seventy-four, Hull House continued. The myth of Addams continued, too. In her autobiography, *Twenty Years at Hull House,* Addams called herself an "ugly duckling" and described her concern for the poor. As a result, the public came to view her as a self-sacrificing saint. Although it is true that Addams alleviated much suffering, she derived tremendous personal satisfaction from her work.

As she freely admitted, in helping Chicago's poor,
she and those who worked with her
also helped themselves.

A NEW KIND OF SOLDIER

The Civil War was *not fought* by professional armies.

Children, inventors, scientists, immigrants, and even Native Americans all took part in the conflict.

The most remarkable development of all, however, was the rise of the African American soldier after the Emancipation Proclamation took effect on January 1, 1863. Until then, the only African Americans helping the Union cause were laborers working at menial tasks in army camps. Beginning in 1863, African Americans were actively recruited. They went on to fight bravely in segregated units led by white officers.

By the end of the war, the U.S. Colored Troops, as they were officially known, numbered two hundred thousand soldiers. They fought in some four hundred fifty battles.

Lincoln called these troops the Union's "sable arm." He gave them much credit for helping to win the war. Their value to the entire North became clear in an angry message the president sent to his hometown of Springfield, Illinois, to be read aloud at a public meeting in support of the war.

Many residents had objected strongly when Lincoln had transformed the war from a fight to save the Union into a fight to end slavery. Lincoln told them sharply, "You say you will not fight to free negroes. Some of them seem willing to fight for you."

TWO FIGHTERS FOR FREEDOM

by Virginia Calkins

Frederick Douglass was pleased when Abraham Lincoln was elected president in 1860. Of the three main candidates — John Breckinridge, Stephen Douglas, and Lincoln — Lincoln was the only one who had spoken out against slavery. But Douglass was disappointed by Lincoln's inaugural address. Lincoln said that he

The Army Post Office of the chief ambulance officer, Petersburg, Virginia, August 1864.

would abide by the Republican platform and not interfere with slavery in the South. Although he was personally opposed to slavery, he wanted above all to preserve the Union.

On April 12, 1861, the Confederates fired on Fort Sumter, and the South was in open rebellion against the Union. Lincoln called for seventy-five thousand troops to suppress the rebellion, but African American men were not allowed in the army. This upset Douglass, who believed that the real issue in the war was slavery and that African Americans should be able to fight for their freedom.

Douglass wanted Lincoln to move against slavery. The president had plans for freeing the slaves, but since the Union did badly in the early days of the war, Lincoln felt that he should move slowly. Furthermore, he did not want the border states to leave the Union.

On April 16, 1862, Lincoln signed a bill that outlawed slavery in the District of Columbia. The bill also set aside funds for the voluntary colonization of freed African Americans in Haiti and Liberia. Lincoln felt that colonization was a solution to the problem of slavery, but Douglass was outraged by the idea. Douglass believed that African Americans had helped build the United States and were entitled to live in it.

When Confederate forces suffered a defeat at Antietam on September 17, 1862, Lincoln decided that the time had come to move toward emancipation of the slaves. On September 22, he issued a proclamation stating that if the Confederates did not stop fighting by January 1, 1863, he would free all the slaves in the

Confederate states. Douglass was overjoyed, but he worried that Lincoln would not keep his promise.

African Americans planned gala celebrations for the signing of the Emancipation Proclamation on January 1. Douglass was asked to speak that day at the Tremont Temple in Boston, taking part in a program arranged by the Union Progressive Association. A crowd of three thousand people gathered to await the news of the signing of the proclamation. The hours dragged on, and people became restless and worried that Lincoln would not keep his promise. Shortly after ten o'clock that night, a messenger burst into the Tremont Temple. Word from Washington had come over the telegraph wires. Late that afternoon, Lincoln had signed the Emancipation Proclamation.

There were tears and shouts of joy as the proclamation was read. Voices were raised in songs of rejoicing. The celebration continued for two hours, then the crowd moved to the Twelfth Baptist Church on Phillips Street, where the singing and celebrating went on until dawn.

The wording of the proclamation satisfied Douglass. Colonization of African Americans was not mentioned, and African American men would be welcomed into the Union army. Douglass regarded the proclamation as an important symbol that the rights of African Americans were finally being recognized.

Soon Douglass was involved in recruiting African Americans for the army. John A. Andrew, the governor of Massachusetts, had been authorized by Secretary of War Edwin Stanton to raise two African American regiments. Douglass was enrolled as an agent. His first recruit was his own son Charles. Another son, Lewis, joined the army shortly after.

Recruiting became difficult. African American soldiers resented the fact that they were paid less than white soldiers and that they could not become commissioned officers. Potential recruits were frightened because the South refused to exchange African American soldiers as prisoners of war and African American prisoners were usually executed.

There were tears and shouts of joy as the proclamation was read.

Above: American artist A.A. Lamb's *The Emancipation Proclamation,* painted around 1863, attempts to make the proclamation ceremony more dramatic by moving it outdoors and picturing Lincoln on horseback. Left: The far more realistic engraving *The First Reading of the Emancipation Proclamation Before the Cabinet* was taken from the original picture painted by Francis Bicknell Carpenter at the White House in 1864. From left to right are Edwin Stanton, secretary of war; Salmon Chase, secretary of the Treasury; Abraham Lincoln; Gideon Welles, secretary of the Navy; Caleb Smith, secretary of the interior; William Seward, secretary of state; Montgomery Blair, postmaster general; and Edward Bates, attorney general.

Douglass decided to take his problems to the president. Late in July 1863, he had an interview with Lincoln, the first meeting of the two leaders. Lincoln listened carefully to Douglass's complaints. Then he explained that many people objected to African American men in uniform and that the lower pay was in response to "popular prejudice." Because Douglass believed that it was important for African American men to fight for their freedom, he was willing to accept this injustice. Lincoln promised that African American and white soldiers would eventually receive equal pay.

Douglass suggested that when the Confederates shot or hanged African American prisoners of war, the Union army should execute an equal number of Confederate prisoners. Lincoln would not agree to punishing innocent men for the deeds of others.

Finally, the president promised to sign any commission for an African American soldier recommended by the secretary of war. Douglass left the White House impressed with Lincoln's sincerity and hopeful that conditions would improve for African American soldiers.

On August 25, 1864, Douglass was summoned to the White House. The war was not going well, and Lincoln was afraid that he would have to sign a peace treaty without a provision for freeing the slaves. The president wanted Douglass to organize a band of African American men to go into the Confederate states and help slaves cross into free territory. Douglass reluctantly agreed to the dangerous plan, but fortunately the tides of war turned in favor of the Union, and the plan was dropped.

When Lincoln was inaugurated for his second term, Douglass decided to attend the reception and congratulate the president. African Americans were not expected to attend such an event, and two policemen at the door of the White House tried to keep Douglass from entering. Douglass insisted that Lincoln would want to see him. To prevent a scene, the officers let him in but tried to trick him into leaving by another door. Lincoln saw Douglass in the crowd and exclaimed, "Here comes my friend Douglass!" The two chatted for a short time, and Douglass told Lincoln how moved he was by the president's inaugural address.

The assassination of Lincoln was a terrible blow to Douglass, as the two men had developed a special bond. Lincoln's widow sent her husband's walking stick to Douglass, saying that Lincoln had wanted Douglass to have a token of his regard. The cane became Douglass's most prized possession.

FIGHTING FOR 'GLORY': AFRICAN AMERICAN TROOPS AT FORT WAGNER

by Harold Holzer

Abraham Lincoln's Emancipation Proclamation, issued in its final form on January 1, 1863, did more than grant freedom to slaves in the rebellious states. It also declared that for the first time, African Americans would be "received into the armed service of the United States."

MEMBERS OF THE 107TH U.S. COLORED TROOPS

Ever since the beginning of the Civil War, free northern African Americans had been trying to enlist in the Union army and navy. They had always been rejected. Now things would change dramatically.

African American recruits poured into the armed services. By war's end, some two hundred thousand African American men bore arms for the Union. But at the outset, they were treated unfairly. Until 1865, for example, African American soldiers were paid less than white soldiers. African Americans also could not rise in the ranks. They were always commanded by white officers. Worst of all, for a time African Americans were assigned to do manual labor instead of fighting. Many northerners seemed convinced that African Americans could not be trusted to carry weapons into battle or fight and die as bravely as whites.

All this changed in the summer of 1863 on a sandy beach near Charleston, South Carolina. The Union was determined to capture the city where the war had begun two years earlier. But first Union troops had to reach a nearby patch of land called Morris Island, located only a mile or so below the famous Fort Sumter.

The northern tip of Morris Island was protected by an unusual obstacle known as "Battery Wagner." Officially, Battery Wagner was a "redoubt" — the military term for a small extension of a nearby fort, built to protect a more important position. Redoubts were usually made of earth and logs, not stone walls, and they were often well armed with heavy cannon. Battery Wagner was such a redoubt. It boasted several deadly guns and some twelve hundred Confederate troops to defend it against attack.

Members of the 107th U.S. Colored Troops stand outside their guardhouse.

After hearing about the Emancipation Proclamation, freed slaves cross Union lines at Newbern, North Carolina.

Augustus Saint-Gaudens's *Shaw Memorial*, located in the Boston Common, celebrates the bravery of Colonel Robert Gould Shaw and the Fifty-fourth Massachusetts Colored Infantry. Shaw is on horseback in the foreground. The cast of the memorial (shown here) is located at Saint-Gaudens National Historic Site in Cornish, New Hampshire.

Union forces first tried to attack Battery Wagner on the morning of July 11, 1863. After a brave charge, 108 of the 196 men were killed or wounded. The Union retreated.

Refusing to give up, the North planned a second assault. This time, a huge force of six thousand men would be sent against Battery Wagner. It was almost certain that the first wave of troops would suffer the worst casualties. Union commanders offered the risky honor of leading the charge to a young officer named Robert Gould Shaw.

Colonel Shaw, just twenty-five years old, commanded the Fifty-fourth Massachusetts Colored Infantry. The son of Boston abolitionists, Shaw had been handpicked by the governor of his state to lead the unit. Its roster of volunteers became the first all–African American regiment from the North. Its men included the son of the great African American leader Frederick Douglass. Reluctant at first, Shaw ultimately accepted the offer to lead them. He referred to himself unhappily as a "nigger colonel," but he quickly gained respect for both his assignment and his men.

The Fifty-fourth headed for South Carolina. On July 16, 1863, the unit lost forty-six men in action around Morris Island. Two days later, Shaw accepted the challenge of sending his troops against Battery Wagner. If they succeeded, Shaw knew that African American soldiers might never again be treated as second-class citizens in the military. This challenge presented a grave danger but also a great opportunity. Shaw told his troops that it was their chance to "prove yourselves men." He also believed that "God isn't very far off."

At 7:45 on the morning of July 18, 1863, Shaw marched his men along the beach and directly into the flaming guns of Battery Wagner. As the Confederates

inside the redoubt opened fire, Shaw and the Fifty-fourth began running at full speed toward the fortress. Bullets filled the air, smoke covered the hot beach, and men fell dead all around. Still, the determined soldiers raced on.

Somehow, most of them managed to reach the top of the fortress. Boldly, Colonel Shaw shouted, "Onward, Fifty-fourth!" But just then, an enemy bullet hit him squarely in the chest, and he fell dead. Confederate bullets filled the air, killing dozens more. When the fighting was over, the Fifty-fourth had lost 272 of its 650 men. One officer on the scene reported, "The men were slaughtered, but fought like demons." Within minutes, more than 1,100 Union troops lay dead and wounded, and once again the assault on Battery Wagner was abandoned.

The victorious defenders of Battery Wagner were angry and embarrassed when they discovered that African Americans had been part of the unsuccessful charge against them. They disrespectfully dumped all the African Americans' bodies into a common grave and threw in the corpse of Robert Gould Shaw as well. Although the Confederates intended this as an insult, Shaw's parents later said that he would have been most proud to be buried with his men.

For seven weeks thereafter, Union troops bombarded Battery Wagner with heavy guns. Only hours before they were ready to charge its walls once more, Confederate troops abandoned the battery and escaped into the harbor in boats. Battery Wagner was finally captured, but at an enormous cost in human life.

PETER D. THOMAS

Thomas was an escaped slave who was picked up by the Fifteenth Wisconsin Volunteer Infantry during the war. He later joined the Eighteenth U.S. Colored Infantry. After the war, Thomas moved to Wisconsin, where he eventually became the Racine County coroner.

The bravery of the Fifty-fourth Massachusetts proved a victory in itself. Never again did Americans doubt the ability of African American troops to fight side by side with white troops.

Over the next two years, African American soldiers would serve in more than four hundred battles. Studies show that they were killed and wounded at a far greater rate than white troops, probably because Confederates made them their special targets whenever they could. At the Battle of Fort Pillow, Tennessee, in 1864, unarmed African American troops who had surrendered were massacred by Confederates, outraging the North. And many captured African American soldiers were illegally shipped into slavery in the South. Yet they fought on.

Eventually, African American troops were granted equal pay with whites. They also deserve equal credit for the Union victory. African American soldiers fought for their own freedom and helped win it.

No one should underestimate the importance of African American soldiers to the war effort — or the importance of Battery Wagner in proving how well African American troops could fight. "We hear nothing but praise of the Fifty-fourth," Colonel Shaw wrote home to his father only a few hours before he was killed. There has been nothing but praise ever since. More than 125 years later, the heroism of the Fifty-fourth Massachusetts became the subject of the popular film *Glory*.

canoe, and paddled swiftly up the Chippewa River.

Two days later, Chief Sky came to a farm owned by Daniel McCann, hoping to sell him the eaglet. The farmer was out working in his fields, but his wife thought that she would like to keep the bird as a pet. She traded the chief a bag of corn and took the eaglet.

When McCann came home and saw the eaglet, he said the bird would have to go. He would be too much trouble to keep. The next day, McCann took the bird to the town of Eau Claire and showed him to some young Wisconsin recruits on their way to Camp Randall at Madison. One of them, a young man named Johnny Hill, took a special liking to the bird.

"We need a mascot in this war we're going to," Hill told his comrades. "Let's buy him and take him along with us."

"How much?" the other recruits asked.

McCann decided that he wanted to be rid of the eaglet more than he wanted to make a lot of money, especially off recruits going to war. "Two dollars and a half?" he asked.

Hill and his companions dug into their pockets and came up with the money. The sale was made, and the eaglet now found himself going off to war. Hill christened him Old Abe, after President Abraham Lincoln, and they took the eaglet in as a full-fledged recruit in the Union army.

A few days later, they marched into Camp Randall with Old Abe. They were a little afraid that they might get their mascot killed and themselves court-martialed for bringing a wild eagle into the army. But the commander, knowing the importance of morale, thought that an eagle for a mascot was a fine idea. A perch was made for Old Abe in the form of a shield on which the stars and stripes were painted along with the inscription "Eighth Regiment, Wisconsin Volunteers."

The metal perch was mounted on a five-foot pole. A bearer, by setting the staff in a belt socket, held up Old Abe at a station assigned him at the center of the line of march, behind the Union flag. A short time later, the commander nicknamed the regiment "The Eagles," and Old Abe was formally sworn into the army and bedecked in red, white, and blue ribbons. His fame had already begun to spread, and a businessman in St. Louis offered to buy Old Abe for five hundred dollars, but he was not for sale.

Old Abe went with the Wisconsin Eagles to war. After he overcame his initial surprise at the sound of enemy gunfire, he would scream fiercely, especially when the company advanced. He would jabber raucously and often soar overhead as if scouting, then return to his perch and call noisily, as if urging the men to action.

Everywhere the regiment marched, it became famous — not only because of its mascot but also because of its bravery. Old Abe was always there, in the thick of thirty-six battles and skirmishes, a symbol of courage to Johnny Hill and every other soldier. One Confederate general remarked that he would rather capture "that sky buzzard" than a whole brigade of soldiers.

Old Abe suffered two minor battle wounds, at Corinth and Vicksburg, Mississippi, before the war ended. When the Wisconsin Eagles returned to Madison, the soldiers marched through the streets carrying Old Abe bobbing on his perch, hale and hearty as ever. Crowds cheered him as a hero, and he flapped his wings as a sign of recognition.

With the war over, Old Abe was presented to the State of Wisconsin and given a room in the basement of the capitol, where a soldier comrade became his private caretaker. Johnny Hill, who also survived the war, visited him often.

The next time you see a little brass eagle mounted atop a flagpole in a parade, remember Old Abe, the eagle who went to war.

Thousands of people from all over the country came to see the famous war eagle who had survived so many battles and spurred so many soldiers on to victory. His molted feathers sold for five dollars apiece, and the famous circus owner P.T. Barnum offered twenty thousand dollars to feature him as a circus performer. But other work was in store for Old Abe.

By special act of the Wisconsin legislature in 1876 and with the governor's approval, Old Abe was exhibited at the United States Centennial Exposition in Philadelphia. His chaperon was none other than his old army buddy, Johnny Hill.

After returning from Philadelphia, Old Abe went on tours of the country. He helped raise thousands of dollars for war relief charity and became a national hero all over again.

Old Abe was almost twenty years old when he died. A granite statue of the valiant eagle stands over the arched entrance to Old Camp Randall in Madison. If you are ever in the Midwest, you can stop in and pay your respects to Old Abe. And the next time you see a little brass eagle mounted atop a flagpole in a parade, remember Old Abe, the eagle who went to war.

ELY S. PARKER: GRANT'S MILITARY SECRETARY

by Bonnie Geisert

Ely S. Parker

In General Ulysses S. Grant's recommendation to extend a commission to Seneca chief Ely* S. Parker, he praised Parker as a highly educated "full blooded Indian" and an engineer of "considerable eminence."

Parker received notice of his appointment as assistant adjutant general with the rank of captain at Tonawanda Indian Reservation, New York. With the Senecas' blessing, Parker accepted the commission.

He joined General John E. Smith's division at Vicksburg, Mississippi, in 1863 and renewed his friendship with General Grant, whose army had just captured Vicksburg. Parker had met Grant in 1860 in Galena, Illinois, while working as an engineer there.

Parker's duties as adjutant general included handling correspondence and keeping records. His mastery of the English language served him well in this capacity. His legal and engineering training also benefited the army. In September 1863, he was assigned to Grant's personal military staff. Parker's glowing account of Grant's bravery, stamina, and military economy during the Battle of Chattanooga, Tennessee, was published in several northern newspapers.

In August 1864, Parker was appointed Grant's military secretary with the rank of lieutenant colonel. Until the end of the war, Parker wrote Grant's orders and maintained his papers. Perhaps the most important paper he copied for Grant was the terms of surrender presented to General Robert E. Lee at Appomattox Court House, Virginia, on April 9, 1865. After Grant and Lee agreed to the terms of surrender, Parker wrote the official copy of Grant's letter in ink in his fine handwriting. Grant and Lee then signed the document.

Two accounts of the surrender at Appomattox note that when Grant introduced Parker, Lee hesitated before shaking his hand. When Lee realized that Parker was an American Indian, he extended his hand and, according to Parker, said, "I am glad to see one real American here." Parker then shook Lee's hand and replied, "We are all Americans."

A PROUD TRADITION

by John P. Langellier

A letter dated June 1872 said, "The Indians called the African American troops [they encountered in the West] 'buffalo soldiers,' because their woolly heads are so much like the matted cushion that is between the horns of the buffalo." It is believed that the

Right: Parker was commissioner of Indian affairs from 1869 to 1872 under President Ulysses S. Grant. He worked to improve conditions for the Plains Indians, who were being displaced.

Below: On June 15, 1877, Henry Flipper became the first African American to graduate from West Point. After graduation, he joined the Tenth Cavalry as a second lieutenant on the western frontier. Unfortunately, he was dishonorably discharged on June 30, 1882, for conduct unbecoming an officer. Flipper went on to become a surveyor, mining consultant, land claims investigator, and assistant to the secretary of the interior. In 1976, through the efforts of Flipper's niece, he was granted an honorable discharge.

The buffalo soldiers were often given poor equipment and difficult assignments, and they regularly encountered prejudice. Yet despite the hardships they faced, their record of service is impressive.

Indians used the nickname out of respect for the fighting spirit of the soldiers, which reminded the Indians of the courage of the buffalo. The buffalo, a source of food, shelter, and clothing, was sacred to the Plains Indians.

African Americans had proven their patriotism and ability as soldiers since the Revolutionary War, but they had been unable to join the U.S. Army. This policy began to change during the Civil War. By the end of the war in 1865, more than 180,000 African Americans had served in the Union army as members of "colored volunteer" regiments.

In 1866, the U.S. Congress passed a law allowing African Americans to join the peacetime Army in special units: the Ninth and Tenth Cavalry regiments and the Thirty-eighth, Thirty-ninth, Fortieth, and Forty-first Infantry regiments. Three years later, the four infantry regiments were merged into the Twenty-fourth and Twenty-fifth Infantry regiments.

What made African American men want to join the military after the Civil War? Some of them, like Jacob Wilks, had served in the Union army and found that they liked being soldiers. Others, such as Horace Wayman Bevins, had never been in the Army. After Bevins finished school, he decided to become a soldier, "having a great desire for adventure and to see the wild West." Charles Creek

Frederic Remington's *Captain Dodge's Black Cavalrymen.*

PEACHES AND RATTLESNAKE
by Mary Kay Morel

Even a skilled cook could not solve the problem of terrible Army food. Limited supplies delivered to Army posts made any cooking difficult. Eggs, milk, cream, and butter were uncommon luxuries. Instead, Army cooks worked with staples such as beans, hard crackers, flour, coffee, bacon, coarse bread, salt, vinegar, brown sugar, and occasionally low-grade beef or game.

Because soldiers ate the same food over and over again, meals could be boring. Breakfast often consisted of beef hash, dry bread with no butter, and coffee with no milk. Dinner, served at midday, might be sliced beef, dry bread, and coffee. Supper usually consisted of more bread and coffee.

Often supplies arrived at Army posts in poor condition. Yellow or green bacon was common. Mice frequently lived in the flour supply. At Fort Concho, Texas, soldiers were given canned peas that were not fit to eat. Their bread was sour, the flour made of suet (fatty tissue from the kidneys of cattle and sheep).

One remedy for the food problem was gardening. Where a water supply and decent soil existed, homegrown vegetables provided nutritious feasts at Army posts. Enlisted men planted, weeded, cultivated, and harvested crops of spinach, cabbage, peas, onions, lettuce, okra, celery, pumpkins, turnips, beets, carrots, potatoes, tomatoes, peppers, and corn. These fresh foods kept the men from getting diseases caused by malnutrition.

Sometimes officers ate better than enlisted men. At one officers' luncheon during the 1870s, the menu included treats such as buffalo berry jelly, chokecherry (a bitter fruit) pie, and lemonade made with citric acid crystals.

The campaign trail offered the true test of a soldier's taste buds. When troopers traveled, they were accompanied by wagons full of greasy salt pork, dried beans, coffee, and sugar. The soldiers carried knapsacks full of hard crackers. One soldier described these crackers as a cross between a soda cracker and a firebrick.

The Seminole Negro Indian Scouts, under the command of John Bullis, added variety to their diet from the landscape around them. They lived on canned peaches and rattlesnake meat.

turned to the Army as a chance to escape farming. "I got tired of looking at mules in the face from sunrise to sunset," he said. At twenty-six, George Bentley stated that he "joined the army simply to get away from his mother and a brother, neither of whom he liked."

Some African Americans thought that serving in the Army would be a good way for them to earn money (they were paid thirteen dollars a month). The desire to receive an education (the Army provided an opportunity for soldiers to learn how to read and write) was another reason they enlisted. Other African Americans looked to the West for a better life, hoping to leave behind their past and the places where they had been forced to work against their will.

After a period of training at midwestern forts such as Fort Leavenworth, Kansas, African American soldiers were sent to the Great Plains, the western mountains, and the southwestern deserts. They were expected to maintain order between the Indians and the settlers, help build forts and roads, patrol borders, and protect mail coaches and railroad construction crews.

The buffalo soldiers were often given poor equipment and difficult assignments, and they regularly encountered prejudice. Yet despite the hardships they faced, their record of service is impressive. The cavalry boasted the lowest desertion rate in the entire Army. As Rayford Logan, a famous African American professor, wrote, "Negroes had little at the turn of the century to help sustain faith in ourselves except the pride that we took in the Ninth and Tenth Cavalry, the Twenty-fourth and Twenty-fifth Infantry."

Above: The emblem of the Tenth Cavalry.
Below: A dismounted buffalo soldier from the Tenth Cavalry.

COURAGE IN ACTION

by Janet Fick

As settlers moved west following the Civil War, they were in constant conflict with American Indians, who were determined to fight to protect and maintain their rights to live on the land as their ancestors had. With orders to keep the peace in these unsettled areas, African American soldiers proved their ability as fighting men and leaders. During the Indian wars, eighteen men of the Ninth and Tenth Cavalry units won our country's highest military award for bravery, the Medal of Honor.

Sergeant Emanuel Stance of the Ninth Cavalry, a young man barely five feet tall, was an excellent scout and one of the first buffalo soldiers to win the Medal of Honor. In May 1870, near Kickapoo Springs, Texas, Stance bravely led his men in several charges against Indians and recovered a number of stolen horses.

One of the fiercest foes the buffalo soldiers faced was the Apache chief Victorio. The Ninth Cavalry and some of the Tenth Cavalry in Texas, as well as white infantry and cavalry, pursued the Apaches. On September 18, 1879, they thought they had the Apaches trapped in the canyons at Las Animas Creek, New Mexico, but could not drive them out from the bushes and rocks. From their hiding places, the Apaches shot at the soldiers, killing eight men. The officer

VICTORIO

The Apache chief Victorio was one of the buffalo soldiers' fiercest foes.

in charge ordered a retreat. Sergeant John Denny of the Ninth Cavalry noticed that Private Freeland had been shot in the leg and was dragging himself toward his comrades. Under heavy fire, Denny dashed to Freeland and carried him to safety. For his bravery, Denny received the Medal of Honor.

Later that month, there was trouble with another American Indian tribe, the Utes, on the White River Reservation in Colorado. Captain Francis S. Dodge and forty buffalo soldiers of the Ninth Cavalry rode to the aid of four hundred fifty white infantrymen and cavalrymen. The buffalo soldiers arrived at daybreak on October 2, to the cheers of their fellow soldiers. As the fight continued, nearly all of their horses were killed, and the soldiers used them and the wagons as a barricade. With bullets whistling past him, Sergeant Henry Johnson went to each sentry post, making sure all was well. When water began to run low, Sergeant Johnson once more left the safety of his rifle pit and shot his way to the river. He brought back water to his companions, both African American and white.

When Colonel Wesley Merritt and his force of about three hundred fifty soldiers arrived on the morning of October 5, the Utes withdrew. This was one of the last battles the Army had with the Utes, as they soon moved to reservations. For his acts of bravery, Sergeant Johnson won the Medal of Honor, as did Captain Dodge for his role in the fight.

Dodge and his soldiers were soon on their way southwest, where Sergeant George Jordan of the Ninth Cavalry received the Medal of Honor for driving back an attack by Victorio against a small settlement near Fort Tularosa, New Mexico, on May 14, 1880. Victorio retreated to Mexico and was killed by Mexican soldiers on October 15, but the Apache wars were not over. Chief Nana, over seventy years old, took Victorio's place in July 1881. Several buffalo soldiers of the Ninth Cavalry won the Medal of Honor in battles against Nana, who eventually surrendered in March 1886.

A couple of months later, Lieutenant Powhatan H. Clarke, a white officer with the Tenth Cavalry, won the Medal of Honor for rescuing Corporal Scott, who had been wounded by the Apache leader Geronimo's forces. Sergeant William McBryar, also of the Tenth, won the medal in a skirmish with Apaches on March 7, 1890. Ten days later, the Apache campaign came to a close.

While the Tenth Cavalry was fighting Apaches in the Southwest, the Ninth was on the northern plains battling the Lakota Sioux. Corporal William O. Wilson received the Medal of Honor for a battle against Chief Big Foot in 1890. Wilson was the last buffalo soldier to win the medal during the conflict between the U.S. government and American Indians.

NINTH CAVALRY BALLAD

by Michael Nethercott

I think I could travel forever,
on these waves of wild grass,
which tremble a good hundred
    miles
if the slightest breeze should
    pass.

As a boy born into slavery,
I only had journeyed such
as an hour's walk would take
    me,
which doesn't add up to much.

But see how this prairie
    awaits me,
stretching so far and so wide;
they call me a buffalo soldier,
and with Colonel Hatch I
    ride.

Years back, some among us
    saw battle
in the war that broke our chains.
Our motto is "We Can; We Will!"
here now upon these Great Plains.

Sometimes on patrol I get thinking,
as winds are stirring the morn,
how sunrise might look in Africa,
where Ma's and Pa's folks were born.

And at times standing guard in the darkness,
I feel like the King of Night,
alone on a prairie of moon fire,
keeping a world safe and right.

5

· · · · · · · · · · · · · · · · · · ·

THE WAR AND THE ARTS

"During the war," a writer noted in 1866, *"the Fine Arts witnessed a very considerable development."*

Indeed, writers and artists alike reported on every aspect of the Civil War: its battles, its leaders, and its enormous social changes. The relatively new art of photography flourished as well. When Mathew Brady and his cameramen took the first pictures of dead soldiers littering a battlefield, the horrors of war were brought home with disturbing power.

Many Civil War artists and writers participated in the war directly. Poet Walt Whitman nursed wounded soldiers. Author Louisa May Alcott also volunteered for hospital duty. Painters like the Union's Julian Scott and the Con-

federacy's Conrad Wise Chapman served in the army.

Even those who did not serve, such as the great artist Winslow Homer, got close enough to the action to create pictures of it. Homer was sent to the front to record the war for the pictorial newspapers.

The Civil War produced a record in art and literature almost as important as the record of the fighting itself. With works ranging from Alcott's still-popular *Little Women* to the Gettysburg Cyclorama that remains on view at the battlefield park today, writers and artists preserved both the gore and the glory of war for future generations.

This chapter traces the development of American art and literature, beginning long before the war and continuing on through the new century.

PRINTING PAST AND PRESENT

by Karen Zeinert

America's first printing presses were made from wood and operated by hand. Colonial printers handpicked type (the letters and numbers) and arranged it into words and sentences on a rulerlike tool called a composing stick. The type was slipped from the stick into a wooden frame that, when full, was locked and

JOIN or DIE

Benjamin Franklin designed this woodcut, which appeared in *The Pennsylvania Gazette* on May 9, 1754.

New Hampshire's *Peterboro' Transcript* of January 13, 1876, advertised cheap dry goods, clean beds, money loans, and investments in Kansas and Nebraska.

placed on the press.

If printers wanted to include an illustration in their newspapers, they had to make a woodcut. A woodcut was made by drawing a picture on a block of wood. The wood was then carved until only the picture remained on top.

Printing a paper on early presses was not easy. To make one copy, a printer blackened the type and woodcut surfaces with a large leather ink ball and pinned a sheet of paper over the frame. Then he pressed the frame and paper together by lowering the platen, a heavy, flat form on the press. When the platen was raised, one copy was removed.

The process obviously was slow. Even the best Colonial printers had to work very hard to produce enough copies for the public.

At first, all printing supplies, even printing styles, were imported from England. In 1773, however, Christopher Sower II brought type-making machinery from Germany to Pennsylvania. His apprentice, Jacob Bay, was the first to make and sell type to American printers. By the early 1800s, almost all paper and presses, including iron presses, were made in the United States. It was not until the mid-1800s that major changes began to take place in printing. While some printers experimented with horsepower to operate their presses, it was machine power that changed the industry.

Robert Hoe developed a rotary press that used type set on a large cylinder rather than in a flat frame. The cylinder and type turned so fast that it was possible to make eight thousand copies per hour. Because of this speed, rotary presses rapidly replaced flat presses.

In the late 1800s, halftones (pictures composed of shaded dots) replaced woodcuts. Instead of carving wood, photographers used chemicals and negatives from specially equipped cameras to etch the halftones in metal plates for printing.

In 1886, setting type by hand was no longer necessary thanks to Ottmar Mergenthaler's invention, the linotype. His machine had a keyboard similar to a typewriter's. When the keyboard operator typed, letters and numbers automatically fell into line. Molten lead was poured around the line, which could be used for printing or making printing plates.

Because the linotype could set type quickly, duplicates could be made easily, allowing several presses to run the same page at the same time. This greatly increased the number of copies printed per hour. By the mid-1900s, printers who used linotypes, several rotary presses, automatic paper feeders, and ink pumps could produce more than seventy thousand copies per hour.

Today computers have replaced linotypes. Headlines and stories are written on computers and sent to special printing equipment. From the days of hand-set type, printing has developed into a modern technology.

PAPERS FOR A PENNY

by *Beth Turin Weston*

On September 3, 1833, the modern newspaper was born. The first issue of the *New York Sun* was published that day, and it was different from any American newspaper before. Also, the people who paid a penny to read it were, for the most part, a new class of newspaper readers.

These new readers included the increasingly literate working class and European immigrants who filled the cities in the early 1800s. They were hungry for news about their neighborhoods and cities as well as the political news of the country. They also were eager to read entertaining stories, especially human-interest stories and police and court reports.

Before the 1830s, American newspapers were of the "commercial press" or the "party press." These newspapers were printed for special groups, especially politicians and merchants interested in business news. They consisted of shipping lists and long political editorials. They also sold at a price the common person could not afford — six cents per issue or eight to ten dollars per year. This was more than a week's wages for a working person. The *Sun,* however, appealed to everyone, and it cost only one cent.

The Sun also was sold in a new way. Newsboys hawked in the streets selling the latest news.

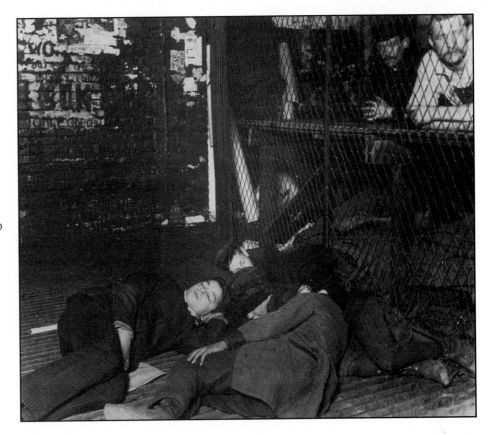

At the *Sun*'s office, newsboys catch some sleep at 3 A.M. The men in the background are not so lucky.

Within a few months, the *Sun* had a larger circulation than any paper before it. The price and the corner newsboy changed American journalism. Following the *Sun*'s example, "penny papers" began appearing in cities throughout the country.

As these new papers competed with each other to provide the most interesting and up-to-date news, they hired reporters to seek out stories. This idea, although fundamental to newspapers today, was shocking to editors of that period.

Advertising also promoted the growth of the penny press. For the first time, merchants had a way to reach widespread buyers. Therefore, the penny press is indirectly responsible for starting the new era of advertising.

In its early days, the penny press often sensationalized the news to sell more papers. The papers played up human-interest stories, murders, and local gossip to shock and thrill their readers and convince them to come back for more the next day. But as the penny press became more established, both the press and the readers began to take news more seriously.

The independent press grew out of the penny press. Newspapers such as the *New York Herald* and *New York Tribune* broke their ties to political interests and began improving their reporting. These newspapers increased their value as a news source and also increased their price. Throughout these transitions, the modern newspaper developed.

THE LIKENESS MEN
by Debbie Felton

When photographers first traveled to the rural areas of America, they packed more than their cameras and processing chemicals. They also took a talent for storytelling and an appetite for adventure.

Along the way, these photographers captured thousands of daguerreotype portraits of American pioneers. Those likenesses of the living and the dead earned these early photographers the title "likeness men."

Traveling photographers took to America's roads and rivers beginning in 1840, as soon as they could buy the daguerreotype equipment introduced by French artist Louis Daguerre. But they soon found that traveling to these barely settled areas took some ingenuity.

The main ingredient for a successful daguerreotype, besides a camera and some luck, was plenty of natural light. Some photographers rented the best-lighted room they could find in a local boarding house or hotel. There they set up a temporary gallery and advertised that customers were welcome only when the sky was clear.

Other photographers solved the problem of light by creating their own galleries. They started with a wagon or flatboat, then built in a skylight, plus a reception area and a "chemical room" if there was enough space. Some wagon studios, called daguerreotype saloons, were designed so that the wagon could be lifted off its wheels and placed on a vacant lot. Handbills and samples of the likeness man's work usually were hung on nearby fences.

The likeness men who traveled on rivers were ready for business as soon as they docked. And if business or cash was hard to come by, the photographers

Louis Daguerre

....

Daguerre's invention, the daguerreotype, was introduced in the United States by J.W. Draper and Samuel Morse. Draper's 1840 photograph of his sister is said to be one of the earliest daguerreotypes produced in the United States. His photograph of the moon is said to be the first one ever taken.

THE DAGUERREOTYPE IN AMERICA

by June L. Sargent

Joseph Nicéphore Niépce took the earliest existing photograph in 1826 in France. Other experimenters, like Thomas Wedgewood, had produced images, but Niépce was the first to make them permanent.

Louis Jacques Mandé Daguerre was a stage designer in Paris who coproduced the diorama, a highly successful picture show that used special lighting effects. In an effort to find a mechanical method of producing pictures, Daguerre became Niépce's partner in 1829. But before Niépce's heliographic (etched by sunlight) process could be perfected, he died.

By 1837, Daguerre produced a permanent photographic image. The daguerreotype, a silver-coated copper plate (sensitized by fuming with vapors of iodine), recorded a sharp image within a half hour when exposed to sunlight. Although the daguerreotype was expensive and laborious to prepare, it produced amazingly fine detail and became extremely popular, especially in America.

Making a daguerreotype took a long time. A person could be required to sit still for approximately three minutes (some sittings could be longer). Any slight movement could distort the daguerreotype's image. To ensure that a subject did not move, a chair was developed that held the neck securely with a vise (a clamping device). Sometimes wrists and ankles also were strapped to the chair. In full-length daguerreotypes, a metal base can be seen behind the subject's feet.

The daguerreotype was important in the cultural development of America. It also helped the country make the transition from an agricultural to a technological society. Families afraid of separation by death could now obtain permanent images of themselves together. Portraits of such famous personalities as Andrew Jackson, Edgar Allan Poe, Jenny Lind, and Tom Thumb made them more real to the public. (The spread of images of celebrities, however, is more closely related to paper photographs than to the daguerreotype.) With the aid of the camera, the average American family could view such exotic and faraway places as Africa, China, and Japan for the first time. The daguerreotype also became the eye of history, recording many important events.

Frontier photographers like Robert H. Vance were pioneers in a double sense. They explored a wild and unsettled country and practiced a new science. Their daguerreotypes (prints made from negatives on glass also were used) of frontier towns, riverboats, miners, and Indians captured and preserved the adventurous flavor of life in the American West. As a result, hundreds of thousands of people migrated westward in search of golden opportunities.

The work of daguerreotypists helped educate the American people about themselves, their society, and the world. These early photographers can be considered artists, scientists, and historians all at the same time.

could always catch their supper without even going ashore.

In the late 1840s, many itinerant photographers began promoting themselves as professors and masters of a scientific craft. Some of the likeness men were masters. Many of them had kept up with advances in daguerreotypy and were experimenting with dramatic poses and highlights to enhance their portraits. But many of the likeness men were as baffled by photography as their customers.

They could not understand how an image suddenly appeared on the metal plate.

If a daguerreotype failed, these likeness men often blamed the subject for moving too much or breathing too hard. Then they would retreat to the chemical room and try to figure out the real reason, usually without much success.

Many things could go wrong with a daguerreotype. The plate could be dirty, one of the chemicals could be spoiled, the plate could have been exposed to one of the chemicals for too long or too short a time, or the sun could have ducked under a cloud at the wrong moment. Often a likeness man relied on trial and error to figure out which factor was responsible for a failed photograph.

The likeness men photographed all kinds of subjects — from little girls with their pets to parents in their frontier finery. Each subject had to sit perfectly still for the exposure, which took anywhere from twenty seconds to three minutes, depending on the process and available light. The lengthy exposure shows in the solemn, serious looks typical of daguerreotype portraits.

If likeness men were not masters of their craft, some of them did master the art of advertising. Many attracted subjects with ads that played on sentiment. "How

many have lost a father, a mother, a sister, a brother, or an innocent little prattling child," asked one ad, "and have not even a shadow to look upon after the separation?" The perfect remembrance, of course, was a portrait.

If loved ones were not photographed while they were alive, death did not stand in the way. Photographing the dead became a lucrative sideline for the likeness men, who could order special black mast and gaudy cases to set off the portraits. This somewhat morbid trend in photography was short-lived.

The careers of the likeness men continued into the 1850s, when advances in photography put an end to their colorful lifestyle. But they left behind a valuable collection of portraits that provide a true look at America's pioneers.

NEWSPAPER ILLUSTRATION

by Julia F. Lieser

Newspaper illustrations were rare in Colonial times, although each paper had its own pictorial touches. Colophons, or printers' trademarks, usually appeared at both ends of a newspaper's title and sometimes in the middle of it. These emblems ranged from crude to artistic. Some colophons included royal or provincial arms, a ship in full sail, or a mail carrier galloping on his horse.

Factotums also were commonly used as front-page decorations. Factotums are large, artistically designed first letters of the first word of a story. Along with an occasional line drawing of an item being advertised, factotums and colophons were the only illustrations used in early American newspapers. Woodcuts were used to reproduce these illustrations, although frequently used emblems and letters were made of metal.

During the time before the American Revolution, newspaper editors discovered that pictures could be more effective than the printed word. It was during this period that a cartoon of a sectioned snake (representing the Colonies) facing a dragon (representing Great Britain) came into common use. The cartoon's caption read "Join, or Die." It was the forerunner of the political cartoon. It was designed by Benjamin Franklin, who was the first to print it in 1754.

Another early political cartoon, used in the *Boston Gazette*, illustrated a story on the Boston Massacre. The cartoon showed four coffins, each scratched with a death marking and the initial of the victim.

Wood engraving was expensive, and the process was much too slow for timely news illustration. Carving the picture into a block of wood often took a week or more after the artist finished his sketches. Newspapers, however, began using more illustrations due to popular demand.

Special events were often illustrated extensively. For example, the Whig victories in 1838 and 1840 were celebrated by an Albany, New York, newspaper with a woodcut of a large eagle covering nearly a page. Also, in 1845 the *New York Herald* created a sensation by publishing a full page of engravings on Andrew Jackson's funeral. Since woodcuts still took time to prepare, the illustrations appeared two weeks after Jackson's death.

In spite of the time element and expense, woodcuts were used extensively throughout the Civil War to report to a news-hungry nation. A small army of artists worked on the battlefields drawing pictures, sometimes under fire, for publication in the nation's newspapers. Frequently, large war maps illustrated news of the latest battles, and pictures of generals and forts were often included.

It was during the Civil War that plates and zincographs (a picture obtained from prepared

REPORTING FROM THE FRONT

At Boonesboro, Maryland, a great stone arch honors 147 reporters who covered the Civil War. That number is only a small fraction of the army of newsmen who accompanied the soldiers into battle. Every newspaper that could afford the expense sent a correspondent to cover the war. To separate the professionals from the pests, commanders insisted that correspondents be approved and accredited to travel with the troops. The flood of stories they sent to editors in both the North and South turned a generation of Americans into avid newspaper readers.

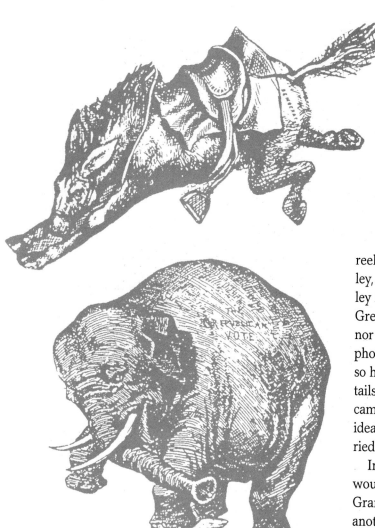

Nast was responsible for creating the symbols of the Republican (the elephant) and Democratic (the donkey) parties.

he is helpless. Even the donkey feels safe, so he kicks the lion.

The donkey first appeared in a cartoon in January 1870, after the death of Republican Edwin Stanton, who had been secretary of war under Lincoln and Andrew Johnson. Democratic newspapers began attacking Stanton's reputation. Nast came to the rescue with his cartoon showing the newspapers (donkey) kicking the dead Stanton (lion).

Nast supported Grant when he ran for reelection in 1872. Opposing Grant was Horace Greeley, editor of the *New York Tribune.* Cartoons of Greeley showed that he would do anything to beat Grant. Greeley's vice-presidential running mate was Governor Gratz Brown of Missouri. Nast did not have a photograph of Brown to use for drawing his cartoons, so he drew Brown as a tag attached to Greeley's coattails. Just before the election, Greeley said that his campaign was "on the home stretch." Nast used this idea to create a cartoon showing Greeley being carried off on a stretcher. Grant won reelection.

In 1874, the *New York Herald* thought that Grant would be running for a third term. The *Herald* called Grant a dictator. To defend Grant, Nast borrowed another of Aesop's fables, "The Donkey in the Lion's Skin." In that fable, a donkey finds a lion's skin, puts it on, and frightens animals on his way to the village. Nast's cartoon, "The Third Term Panic," was printed in November 1874. The *New York Herald* is the donkey frightening the other New York papers. The Republican party is the elephant about to fall into a pit. This was the first time the elephant appeared as the symbol of the party. The Republicans eventually adopted the elephant symbol. They said it showed their size and strength.

In the 1876 election, Republican Rutherford B. Hayes ran against Samuel Tilden in what was one of the most hotly contested elections in our history. Nast's cartoons backed Hayes, and he won by one electoral vote. Nast's cartoon of a wounded elephant shows the Republican party's close victory.

In that cartoon, the Democratic party is represented by a dead tiger. Nast used other animals, such as a fox and a wolf, to represent the party, but the Democrats liked the image of the donkey best and accepted the animal as their symbol. The donkey and the elephant first appeared together in the 1879 cartoon "Stranger Things Have Happened."

Nast faced an unpleasant choice in the 1880 election. The Republican candidate, James A. Garfield, had been involved earlier in a railroad scandal. Nast disliked him. The Democratic candidate, Winfield Scott Hancock, was a friend Nast admired and respected. The editors at *Harper's* tried to convince Nast to support Garfield. Nast finally agreed to support the Republican party but not the candidate. In his cartoons, he attacked the Democratic party but was gentle with candidate Hancock.

The 1884 election was a turning point for Nast. The Republicans had nominated James G. Blaine, former Speaker of the House of Representatives. Blaine was accused of having used his office for personal gain. "Speaking for myself," Nast said, "I positively decline to support Blain, either directly or indirectly even if the Democrats should nominate the Devil himself."

The Democrats nominated Grover Cleveland, and Nast supported him. *Harper's* went along with his choice. This was the first time in twenty-five years that the magazine had backed a Democrat.

Nast and *Harper's* came under fire for their choice, but Nast would not change his mind. One of his cartoons shows Blaine as a "magnetic candidate" with his head resting on a barrel of campaign money. This election was very close, but Cleveland won. And Thomas Nast had become known as a maker of presidents.

BRADY OF BROADWAY

by Jean-Rae Turner

Mathew B. Brady, a native of Warren County, New Jersey, was born in 1823. When he was only sixteen, he moved to New York City with a friend, William Page, who was an artist. Brady worked as a jeweler's helper during the day and studied the new art of daguerreotype photography at night with another artist, Samuel F.B. Morse (who would later become famous as the inventor of the telegraph).

In 1844, Brady believed that he knew enough to establish his own studio, and he soon became known as "Brady of Broadway." Many rich and famous people — John Quincy Adams, Edgar Allan Poe, singer Jenny Lind — came to his studio to have their portraits made. They had to sit very still for long periods of time because the cameras Brady used needed a long exposure.

Just before the start of the Civil War, Brady opened a second studio in Washington, D.C. Even though he was busy photographing princes, presidents, and poets, he wanted to go to war when the Civil War began.

"I felt I had to go," he told a friend later, "to preserve the moment of experience for the future." Brady began to dog the steps of General Winfield Scott, head of the Army of the Potomac, to get permission to accompany him to face the Confederate army. When Brady learned that Scott was going to be replaced, he went to President Abraham Lincoln and Allan Pinkerton, the famous detective, for the desired permission. President

This photo was taken on July 22, 1861, as Brady returned from Bull Run.

Mathew B. Brady

Brady's photographic outfit near Petersburg, Virginia, 1864.

Lincoln scrawled "Pass Brady" on a piece of paper for him, but he told Brady that he must stay out of the troops' way and pay for his own equipment.

Brady did. Before the war's end, Brady had twenty-two of his odd-looking, hearselike "What-is-it?" wagons assigned to many of the battlefields, including First Bull Run, Antietam, Fredericksburg, Gettysburg, and Second Bull Run. One of his photographers, J.F. Coonley, even photographed the last days of the Confederacy from a specially equipped train. He accompanied General William T. Sherman.

Each of Brady's photographic teams included a driver, the "What-is-it?" wagon pulled by two horses, the photographer, the photographer's assistant, and the printer to make the photographs from the glass plates.

The cameras were huge and heavy by today's standards. Instead of film, glass plates were used. Since no enlarging to speak of was done at the time, the camera's plates were the same size as the photographs. Most of these plates were eight by ten inches in size, but some were as big as twelve by sixteen inches. Because an exposure took about thirty seconds, there were no action photographs, and photographers had to use heavy tripods to hold their cameras still during the exposure.

Each team's equipment was extensive. There were glass plates, bottles containing the various chemical solutions, dishes in which to mix the solutions and develop the plates and photographs, measuring cups for the solutions, funnels, and a pail for rinse water. Some of the teams even carried barrels with their own water supply.

Brady and his men faced danger daily in their marches, and more than once a "What-is-it?" wagon team found itself caught between the two armies. Brady told his photo teams, "The camera is the eye of history...you must never make bad pictures."

Brady wore a white linen duster (long coat), an artist's straw hat, and sturdy military boots, called jackboots, that reached above his knees. Because the name "Brady" was stamped on most of the photographs, it is difficult to determine which ones he took and which ones E.L. Handy, his nephew-in-law, and other assistants took.

Brady's health and eyesight, which had always been poor, became worse after the Civil War. In addition, he was faced with many debts from outfitting the photography wagons. Although he had published two earlier photo books, he was unable to find a backer to publish his Civil War photographs during his lifetime. In 1871, he went bankrupt. He died in 1896 and was buried in Arlington National Cemetery.

After his death, many of his famous "wet plates" were seized by people in lieu of debts. Some of them were broken and chipped when improperly stored in various government warehouses. Others were found in a barn in upstate New York. Still others were lost forever.

In 1954, Brady's heirs sold a large collection to the Library of Congress for five thousand dollars. The library also has acquired all the other known plates. They have been cataloged and in 1964 were finally made available to the public as Brady had wished.

Mathew Brady was not the first war photographer, but he was the first to put teams of photographers into the field to photograph all aspects of the battle. His teams were the forerunners of today's press photographers. Brady's photographs captured the utter desolation and cruelty of war for the first time. They show the grotesquely sprawled bodies of men, horses, and dogs in death; roofless, crumbled houses, barns, and fences; the wounded; wrecked wagons and unmanned cannon. They preserve the facts of war for historians and have carved a permanent niche for Brady in American history.

On April 17, 1953, Brady was remembered when the U.S. government named the *RB 36*, the largest photo reconnaissance plane in the world at the time, for him. The five-dollar bill is another testament to Brady. He took the portrait of Abraham Lincoln that appears on the bill.

Mathew Brady in old age. His lecture book (below left) includes mention of a ceremony that took place at Fort Sumter on April 14, 1865, after Major General Robert Anderson's victory there. The ceremony featured a speech by Harriet Beecher Stowe's brother Henry Ward Beecher.

SEEING THE GLORY: ART AND ARTISTS OF THE CIVIL WAR

by Harold Holzer

While the Civil War raged, and long after the last guns were fired, Americans at home wanted to see what its battles and leaders looked like.

Photographs could show battlefields only *after* the armies had left. They portrayed casualties and survivors, but not the action itself. No photographer could safely set up his camera while bullets and artillery shells exploded around him.

Engravings and lithographs were able to picture the great battles, but the scenes were more often than not invented by artists working in studios located in large cities far from the action. Few engravers or lithographers ever saw a Civil War battle.

Winslow Homer's great 1865 painting *Prisoners From the Front* shows three war-weary Confederate captives meeting their young Union captor.

The one form of art that could truly portray battles and heroes alike was paintings. The Civil War artists of the North and South marched, camped, and fought alongside the soldiers of the Union and the Confederacy. Some actually served in the ranks, carrying rifles when they were not carrying sketchbooks and pencils; drawing when they were not marching. Those who followed the armies just to paint them were called "combat artists."

When these on-the-spot artists took their sketches home and produced the very first paintings of the Civil War, they found few customers for their works. Americans seemed uninterested in celebrating the bloodshed and the sacrifice with paintings. Besides, America had few museums at the time of the Civil War. The art of painting was still restricted to those very rich patrons who could afford to commission works of art for display in their private homes.

All that soon changed. Once the war ended, Americans decided that they must have paintings of its battles and heroes for their public buildings. Veterans hospitals and lodges were decorated with such pictures. In 1870, the American art museum was born with the establishment of two great institutions: the Metropolitan Museum of Art in New York and the Museum of Fine Arts in Boston. Soon America's walls were covered with paintings that portrayed not only the famous battles but also the everyday life of soldiers in camp and the great heroes of the Union and the Confederacy.

Finally, the country came to appreciate the work of its Civil War artists. As one editor wrote of them, "A noble army of artists [were] part of it all, and their faithful fingers...made us a part also."

Many of these paintings can still be found in American museums. Two of the most famous Civil War battle paintings are located exactly where the action they show first took place. They are the cycloramas of Gettysburg and Atlanta.

Cycloramas are huge, circular paintings displayed inside cylinder-shaped buildings. The buildings are dark except for the light that shines directly on the pictures. In the days before movies and television, these gigantic, dramatic paintings thrilled viewers. They made people feel as if they were standing in the middle of the action, with the battle raging all around them.

The Atlanta Cyclorama is located in a special National Park Service building not far from where the fighting took place in 1864. The Gettysburg Cyclorama, which opened in late 1884 in Boston, is in the cyclorama center of Gettysburg National Military Park, just a few feet from where the third day of fighting reached its climax. The painting, created by Paul Philippoteaux (1846–1913), is 26 feet high and 356 feet around. It contains 400 gallons of paint and weighs 2 to 9 tons.

Following are brief biographies of the greatest artists of the Civil War and their fondly remembered works.

Winslow Homer (1836–1910) went to war as a "special artist" for the illustrated New York newspaper *Harper's Weekly*. He covered several campaigns of the Union army in Virginia. Homer did not portray battles. He preferred to picture soldiers in camp — playing horseshoes, whittling homemade pipes, or huddling around campfires. His most famous wartime painting, *Prisoners From the Front,* shows a young Union officer capturing three war-weary Confederates. Homer had such trouble selling his early Civil War canvases that his brother occasionally purchased them secretly to encourage him. In later years, Homer painted famous seascapes.

Conrad Wise Chapman (1842–1910), son of a famous painter, grew up in Rome but returned to the South when war broke out. He fought for the Confederacy in Kentucky, but after suffering a head wound at Shiloh, he was assigned to make an artistic record of the Confederate defenses in Charleston, South Carolina. He produced beautiful oil paintings of ironclad ships, soldiers on guard duty, and battered forts. The works are now on display at the Museum of the Confederacy in Richmond, Virginia.

Paul Philippoteaux's Gettysburg Cyclorama is 26 feet high and 356 feet around and contains 400 gallons of paint. In the days before movies, thousands of viewers paid fifty cents each to see this huge circular picture.

The Boston Museum of Fine Arts opened its doors to the public on July 4, 1876.

Thomas Nast (1840–1902) had been an illustrator for six years when the war broke out. He continued to sketch for *Harper's Weekly* and other papers and produced several important paintings as well, including his large canvas of New York's Seventh Regiment marching down Broadway on their way to war. In later years, Nast became a political cartoonist. He is most famous for inventing the symbols of the nation's political parties — the Republican elephant and the Democratic donkey. (See page 144.)

William D. Washington (1834–1870) was a successful landscape and portrait painter in the nation's capital when the war broke out. The Virginia-born artist resettled in Richmond and attempted to paint pictures celebrating the Confederacy. His landscape paintings of soldiers fighting in the Shenandoah Valley are unrealistic, but he achieved fame with *The Burial of Latane,* which shows a hastily arranged funeral service for a Confederate hero killed in action in 1862. After the war, the picture was displayed in Richmond to raise money for wounded veterans.

Julian Scott (1846–1901) not only served in the Union army during the war but also won the Medal of Honor — the only Civil War artist to do so. He was a camp musician for a Vermont regiment when he rushed into enemy fire to save his wounded comrades. Scott made many sketches while serving and later painted dramatic battle scenes.

Adalbert Johann Volck (1828–1912) might have become the most famous of all Confederate artists had he lived in the Confederacy. But he resided in Union Baltimore and was forced to publish etchings of his pictures in secret, for fear of arrest for treason. His *Cave Life in Vicksburg,* which became famous after the war, shows a heroic southern lady praying inside a cave during the Union bombardment of the Mississippi city. Volck also produced a series of vicious pictures attacking Lincoln.

THE CONFEDERATE IMAGE: ART OF THE CIVIL WAR SOUTH

by Mark E. Neely, Jr., Harold Holzer, and Gabor S. Boritt

The Civil War was a grueling experience for most southerners — not only for the tens of thousands of soldiers who were wounded or killed in battle, but also for the women, children, elderly, and infirm left behind to care for their homes and families. As the war dragged on, they suffered widespread shortages in food and other vital supplies. Even paper supplies dwindled, forcing several newspa-

pers to print the news on wallpaper.

It is difficult to imagine that in this atmosphere of desperation, southerners could maintain their love for art, but they did. Unfortunately, however, supplies of art and the materials needed to produce it, like supplies of bread and sugar, grew increasingly scarce.

Such shortages were not evident at the start of the conflict. In early 1861, the Confederacy won the first battle of the war at Bull Run in northern Virginia. During the battle, Confederate president Jefferson Davis rode out from the capital of Richmond to observe his troops in action. In the flush of victory, reports reached home that Davis had taken to the field in uniform and had actually led the army. The story was untrue, but within weeks artists had produced pictures showing Davis as a general on horseback at "Bull's Run."

In the era before newspapers could print photographs, and long before the invention of movies, television, and slick magazines, "prints" were cherished display pieces for family parlors. Pictures were drawn with a special crayon on a slab of stone (lithographs) or carved with a sharp tool onto a steel plate (engravings), then printed by the hundreds on durable, heavy paper. The relatively inexpensive prints decorated homes the way movie star posters would in generations to come.

For a variety of reasons, southern printmakers virtually ceased issuing pic-

An early Confederate lithograph of Jefferson Davis at the Battle of Bull Run is inaccurate. Davis was at Bull Run, but after the fighting ended and not in uniform.

tures for the home within a year after Bull Run. In fact, not until the war was over did southerners finally get to see and own pictures of their most beloved hero, General Robert E. Lee. Incredibly, not one print of Lee was published while the Confederacy was still alive.

Why did Confederate printmaking decline so swiftly? Chronic shortages of ink and paper were part of the reason, but the shortage of manpower was the main cause of the decline. Many artists were drafted into the army, and those who were spared were ordered to focus on a different kind of printmaking. The new government needed postage stamps and money, and artists who had created large portraits to hang above family fireplaces now created tiny ones to grace dollar bills and penny stamps.

Baltimore and New Orleans, two southern cities where art flourished, were soon deprived of their artistic influence. Baltimore was cut off from the Confederacy when Maryland chose to remain in the Union, and local artists with southern sympathies were forced to abandon Confederate printmaking or work in secret. One who chose secrecy was a dentist named Adalbert J. Volck. His prints — such as a scene showing Vicksburg's women living in caves during the Union siege — were masterful examples of political art that was strictly censored. In New Orleans, opportunities were no greater. The city was captured by the Union army early in the war, and from that point on, artistic "disloyalty" was not tolerated. When one local painter was caught working on a portrait of Confederate general "Stonewall" Jackson, he was arrested.

One notable exception to the shortage of art was a painting titled *The Burial of Latane.* When a Richmond artist named William D. Washington heard the story of a Confederate cavalry officer killed in a skirmish outside the city in 1862, he could not help but capitalize on the situation. The victim had been denied a formal funeral when Union troops surrounding the plantation to which the body had been carted refused to allow a minister to pass through the lines. Undaunted, the women and African American slaves on the plantation buried the officer. Washington painted a sentimental scene of full-skirted women in prayer, suggesting the courage and sacrifice of southern women and perpetuating the myth of the steadfast loyalty of the slaves.

The painting was a sensation in Richmond. Wherever it was displayed, an empty pail was set beneath it so that southerners could donate money to care for the war wounded. Because southern printmakers were no longer able to copy paintings for mass distribution, however, the work remained virtually unknown throughout the South until after the war.

Following the war, northern engravers and lithographers entered the southern market, taking up where the ravaged southern picture industry had left off. By 1868, a New York publisher was selling engravings of *The Burial of Latane* for the then-hefty sum of twenty dollars apiece. Not long afterward, when Virginians organized an effort to build a statue of Lee in Richmond, they too hired a New Yorker to engrave a print that could be sold to raise funds for the project. And the fierce "Stonewall" Jackson, seen in wartime only in British-made prints showing him without his famous beard, became immortalized in prints made in New York, Philadelphia, and Boston. Even Jefferson Davis, whom many southerners blamed for the defeat of the Confederacy, enjoyed a comeback in the 1870s and 1880s, thanks in part to a series of prints that portrayed him as a hero.

Thus, much of what we identify as the Confederate image was a product not of the South, but of its bitter enemy, the North. The Confederate "cause" had been ill served by its artists, through no fault of their own, but the "lost cause" would be romanticized in dozens of prints made, ironically, in the North.

A TASTE FOR ART

by Harold Holzer

Frederick Douglass had an enormous influence on the American people, even concerning the unlikely subject of art. Although slavery was dead after the Civil War, Douglass still worried that the chance for African Americans to be accepted as equals was being hurt by certain works of art portraying them as grotesque jokes. Douglass believed that the image of his people could be dramatically improved through more realistic art. He also believed that now that African Americans were setting up their own homes as free men and women, they needed inspiring art to decorate them.

One such picture was finally offered in 1870, when a Boston company issued thousands of copies of a handsome portrait of a new leader named Hiram Revels. Revels had recently been elected as a U.S. senator from Mississippi. Not only was he the first African American senator from that southern state, but he also was elected to the Senate seat previously occupied by Jefferson Davis, the former Confederate president who had led the unsuccessful fight to save slavery during the Civil War. The irony was not lost on many Americans, and Revels became the object of curiosity among whites and admiration among African Americans.

To Douglass's delight, the publishers of the Revels picture sent him an advance copy and asked for his opinion. They hoped he would have something flattering to say so that they could print his comments in advertisements for the picture. Douglass probably realized that he was being used to help profit the publishers, but he seized the opportunity anyway. As he explained bluntly, "We colored men so often see ourselves described and painted as monkeys, that we think it a great piece of good fortune to find an exception to the general rule."

Hiram R. Revels

Not only was he the first African American senator from Mississippi, but he also was elected to the Senate seat previously occupied by Jefferson Davis.

Here at last, Douglass said enthusiastically, was "a faithful presentation" not of a monkey but of a man.

"Every colored householder in the land should have one of these portraits in his parlor," Douglass went on. "He should explain it to his children, as the dividing line between the darkness and despair that overhung our past, and the light and hope that now beams upon our future as a people."

Before emancipation, Douglass admitted, African Americans had seldom enjoyed the luxury of thinking of "adorning their parlors with pictures." He observed, "Pictures come not with slavery and oppression and destitution, but with liberty, fair play, leisure, and refinement. These conditions are now possible to colored American citizens." Douglass predicted, "I think the walls of their homes will soon begin to bear evidence" of their new equality.

The great African American leader was right. Not only did ex-slaves purchase and display the Revels portrait by the thousands, but its success inspired publishers to issue pictures of other African American heroes as well. Before long, pictures of Douglass also adorned the parlors of many people. There they came to symbolize "liberty, fair play, leisure, and refinement," just as Douglass had hoped.

EMILY DICKINSON'S CORRESPONDENCE
by Toni A. Watson

Writing letters was one of American poet Emily Dickinson's greatest passions. She wrote letters not only to keep in touch with people who lived far away but also to communicate with those close by, enabling her to remain emotionally connected but physically distanced.

One of her first pen pals was Abiah Root, an Amherst Academy school chum. Events in Dickinson's early life are revealed in her long letters to Abiah.

Her brother, Austin, received a letter once a week while he was attending Harvard Law School and teaching in Boston. She kept him informed about life in Amherst, Massachusetts, where she lived. Austin said her letters were "the next best thing to talking to her."

Susan Gilbert, a friend who later married Austin and became her "sister Sue," was another early pen pal. Dickinson continued to write to her sister-in-law even after she moved into the house next door. She often included poems in her letters, and Sue was one of the few people close to Dickinson who recognized her talent.

In several cases, Dickinson's correspondence developed into good friendships, even though she rarely met or visited with these friends. Both Sam Bowles, editor of the *Springfield Republican,* and Dr. Josiah Holland, literary editor of the *Republican,* were charmed by Dickinson and her poetry. Bowles printed one of her poems in the May 1861 issue of the newspaper. The poem was heavily edited, and Dickinson regretted allowing it to be published, but she continued a friendly correspondence with Bowles until his death in January 1878. Her correspondence with Holland and his wife, Elizabeth, also continued for years.

In April 1862, Dickinson responded to an article by literary critic Thomas

O.A. Bullard's 1840 portrait of Emily Dickinson as a young girl.

Wentworth Higginson in *The Atlantic Monthly.* The article gave advice to would-be writers. Dickinson sent him four of her favorite poems. A kind, thoughtful man, Higginson called Dickinson's thoughts and words "beautiful," but he did not recognize the originality and genius of her work and tried to get her to fit her poems into the perfectly rhymed and metered modes of the time. Fearing that the public and critics would reject her work, he discouraged her from trying to get it published.

For more than twenty years, Dickinson continued to write to Higginson because he showed genuine interest in her work. She asked for his advice, but she never made the slightest change to please him. She once wrote him, "You were not aware that you saved my Life."

Dickinson and Helen Hunt Jackson (a childhood friend) corresponded on and off over the years. By the 1870s, Jackson had become one of the most popular writers of the day with the publication of *Ramona.* She saw that Dickinson was a talented poet and pleaded with her to submit some of her work to an anthology of poems. Dickinson did, and again her work was changed. The editors made five changes in a twelve-line poem. It was her last poem to be published while she was alive.

In 1876, Jackson wrote to Dickinson, "You are a great poet — and it is a wrong to the day you live in, that you will not sing aloud." It was perhaps the most encouraging assessment of her verse that Dickinson ever received.

In 1886, bedridden and dying, Dickinson wrote her last note to her young cousins Louise and Frances Norcross: "Little Cousins, Called back. Emily." She was buried on May 19 of that year. Her words and thoughts, however, are still heard in the more than one thousand letters she left behind.

'KINSMEN OF THE SHELF'

by Meg Greene

"There is no Frigate like a Book / To take us Lands away / Nor any Coursers like a Page / Of prancing Poetry —."

So wrote Emily Dickinson. Reading books and magazines gave her a strong connection to the world, since she lived most of her adult life avoiding people and rarely leaving her parents' house. She called books her "Kinsmen of the Shelf." In them, she could visit foreign lands, travel in time, and read about current events.

Encouraged by her father, Dickinson began to read at an early age. Her schooling at Amherst Academy and later Mount Holyoke Female Seminary fed her appetite for books. As she grew older, her reading material included the Bible, classical and popular literature, and newspapers and magazines.

Critics have long debated the inspiration for many of Dickinson's poems. Some believed that her physical isolation deprived her of ideas and that her poems were simply the products of an agile but undisciplined mind. They could not have been more wrong. Dickinson marked many of the books she read, indicating passages that held a special meaning for her. These books sharpened her mind and tell us a lot about the poems she wrote.

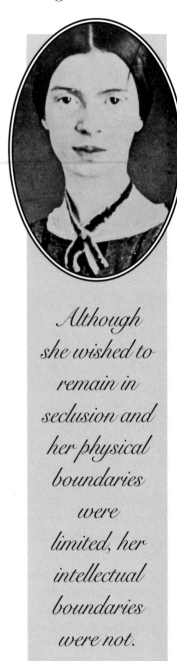

Emily Dickinson

Although she wished to remain in seclusion and her physical boundaries were limited, her intellectual boundaries were not.

Massachusetts. The patients and the hospital staff were sad to see her go, but she was so ill that she hardly knew what was happening.

Alcott's parents and sister May took care of her during her slow recovery. Her hair had fallen out and had to be cut off, so she wore a wig or cap until it grew back. She had to learn to walk again.

Some of Alcott's letters to her family from the hospital had been sent to the magazine *Commonwealth.* The editors wanted to publish them and urged Alcott to get them into shape for publication. By late spring, she was well enough to work on the letters. She disguised the names of the patients and hospital staff, and she called herself Nurse Tribulation Periwinkle. The hospital was called Hurly-burly House.

Commonwealth began to publish the letters in late May. They were called "Hospital Sketches" and were very well received. (See page 67 for an excerpt from these sketches.) Alcott cared deeply about the patients she tended at the hospital, and she made her readers care about them, too. The sketches also contain bits of humor, which people enjoyed.

The Alcott home, Orchard House (above), is now a museum located on the site of Bronson Alcott's School of Philosophy in Concord, Massachusetts. This is where Louisa May Alcott (opposite) wrote *Little Women.* Among its collections are manuscripts and publications by Louisa and Bronson Alcott and paintings by Louisa's sister May.

Other magazines and newspapers reprinted "Hospital Sketches," and a couple of publishers wanted to put them into book form. Alcott chose James Redpath to publish the book. It was a big success, and her work became known all over the country. She received many letters praising the book. What pleased her most, though, was the approval of her former comrades, the people who had been her patients and coworkers when she was an army nurse.

ONE OF THE 'LITTLE WOMEN'

by Gloria T. Delamar

When a publisher first asked Louisa May Alcott to write a book for girls, she did not like the idea. When he asked again, she said, "I'll try."

In May 1868, she settled down at the small half-moon desk her father had built between the two front windows of her bedroom in Orchard House, their home in Concord, Massachusetts. On the window frames above the desk were colorful flowers hand-painted by her sister May. The thirty-five-year-old writer got her paper and pencil and began to write. In four sentences, she introduced four girls and showed something about their lives and their personalities:

" 'CHRISTMAS won't be Christmas without any presents,' grumbled Jo, lying on the rug.

spear, after messes of eels. We would cut holes in the ice, sometimes striking quite an eel bonanza, and filling our baskets with great, fat, sweet, white-meated fellows."

He remembered the beaches, where he had some of his "happiest hours": "I went regularly every week in the mild seasons down to Coney island, at that time a long, bare unfrequented shore, which I had all to myself, and where I loved, after bathing, to race up and down the hard sand, and declaim Homer or Shakespe[a]re to the surf and seagulls by the hour."

WALT WHITMAN, JOURNALIST

by Barbara Hall

It is the summer of 1839, and for two hours a tall young man has been stretched out under an apple tree, dozing as if the world is his apple and clocks do not exist. A "printer's devil" — a messenger sent by newspaper publisher James J. Brenton — approaches the sleeping man and jostles him awake. The young man, dressed simply in black, slowly trails the messenger back to the *Long Island Democrat* press. The man is Walt Whitman, who in his own good time will become one of the great journalists of his day.

Dozens of newspapers were published in and around New York City during the mid-1800s. For about thirty years beginning when he was twelve years old, Whitman wrote for many of them, including *The Brooklyn Daily Eagle, Brooklyn Times, Brooklyn Standard, Brooklyn Advertizer, Brooklyn Evening Post, The New York Times, New York Post, Long Island Democrat, Long Island Patriot, Long Island Farmer, Evening Signal, Evening Tattler, Aurora, The Sun, Long Island Star, New Mirror, Statesman, The Weekly Freeman*, and *New World*. He also wrote briefly for the New Orleans *Crescent* in Louisiana.

One of his biographers, Henry Seidel Canby, says Whitman was "a roving reporter such as seldom comes out of a newspaper office." He was a free spirit, and he was full of curiosity, an important journalistic trait. He hated what he saw as injustice and championed the common people. He used language as if it flowed like music, and he loved life.

What makes a journalist? For Whitman, it might have been an incident he saw at age ten — the explosion of the steam frigate *Fulton*, which killed forty to fifty people and which he later described in exact detail. Or maybe it was the influence of William Hartshorne, the quiet, kindly *Long Island Patriot* newsman who taught a twelve-year-old boy to set type and told wonderful stories about George Washington and Thomas Jefferson, whom he had known. Whatever it was, Whitman was a journalist long before he became a celebrated poet.

For Whitman, journalism was education and more. Schools in Long Island and Brooklyn did not teach him what newspapers would. He learned to spell and punctuate sentences by setting type, in effect feeling the words with his hands. Once on the *Patriot* staff, he began traveling to New York City, where the world of books, theater, art, politics, and people opened before him.

The *Patriot's* motto was "The right of the people to rule in every case." Like most newspapers in the region, it was a political paper, a mouthpiece for Tam-

Walt Whitman

The earliest portrait of Whitman, taken in 1854 when he was in his thirties (above), looks a great deal like a later one taken when he was much older (opposite).

many Hall, which at that time was a powerful local branch of the Democratic party. Whitman's support of the Democrats (but not always of Tammany) and his faith in the masses may have been born at the *Patriot.*

While his journalism career began with the *Patriot,* Whitman soon developed a habit of newspaper hopping. For a short time between papers, he taught school in a series of one-room schoolhouses on Long Island. While teaching there, he wrote a series of articles called "Sun-Down Papers From the Desk of a School-Master," which was published by the *Long Island Democrat.* This teaching experience would resurface later as he neared the peak of his journalism career.

Whitman might have ventured into the Jefferson Country Market on Sixth Avenue and West Tenth Street, shown here about 1830, for inspiration for his stories about New York City's butchers, horse-car drivers, firemen, and others.

At age twenty-six, he became a special correspondent for the *Long Island Star.* By then he knew the territory and the trade. Before joining the *Star,* he had written page one stories about New York City's cast of characters — butchers, firemen, horse-car drivers, and others. As an editor at one paper, he had quoted Homer and Shakespeare in his pleas for better treatment of the poor and the helpless, and he had crossed swords with the city's leading politicians and publishers. "Editing a daily paper, to be sure, is arduous employment," he wrote during those years, "...but it is a delight."

While working on the *Star,* he remembered his year of teaching and decided to "clean up" Brooklyn's schools. He criticized the "miserable slovenliness in the plan of appointing [Brooklyn] teachers." He declared that "the instructor who uses the lash in his school at all, is unworthy to hold the power he does." (Lashing often was used to enforce classroom discipline.) He also wrote on other subjects, and one story unexpectedly brought him notoriety as a journalist.

Brooklynite William B. Marsh died on February 26, 1846, leaving his widow and children poverty-stricken. Characteristically openhearted, Whitman came to their rescue. His call for financial help was printed in the *Star,* and readers responded with generosity.

William Marsh had been editor of *The Brooklyn Daily Eagle,* a young but respected daily. The *Daily Eagle's* owner heard about Whitman's deed, and within a week the paper had a new editor: Walt Whitman.

At the *Daily Eagle,* Whitman opposed capital punishment and expressed shock at poor working conditions for the city's "sewing-women." He led a successful crusade for more churches in Brooklyn and warned that bitter division between North and South on the slavery issue could destroy the nation. As his thoughtfulness grew at the *Daily Eagle,* so did his talent for communicating his thoughts. While he still chased fires and hobnobbed with city politicians, it became more and more evident that here was a writer to be reckoned with. He led the *Daily Eagle* for two years but was fired for his belief that slavery should be kept out of Kansas, a stand that went against that of his boss.

While he was out of work, Whitman met J.E. McClure, who, with a partner, happened to be starting a journal in New Orleans. Would Whitman be interested in joining the enterprise? Within two weeks, Whitman and his brother Jeff were in Louisiana. Whitman worked for the New Orleans *Crescent* for only three months and was soon back in New York, hopping newspapers but also seriously writing poetry.

Whitman made one more important stop on his journey from journalist to poet. The Civil War he had feared finally came. In 1862, Whitman left New York to view the southern battlefields. He went directly to Fredericksburg, Virginia, then stopped in Washington, D.C., on his return. Deeply moved by the thousands of dying and wounded soldiers, he stayed in Washington, working at the Bureau of Indian Affairs and caring for the sick and wounded in his free time. While in Washington, he described the horrors of war in reports that were published in *The New York Times* and other city papers.

As a journalist, Whitman is best remembered for matching strong words with strong feelings, always showing character and courage in his work. As a poet, he would express the same attitude toward people, freedom, and democracy.

A Poem of the People

by Louise Classon and Camille Floyd

Walt Whitman has been called a genius and is recognized as one of America's greatest poets. Yet for thirty or more years, he labored over only one book, *Leaves of Grass.* In that book, however, he not only broke all the rules of traditional verse, but he also wrote of everyday subjects in a scientific, realistic way, which was a definite departure from the more romantic poetry popular at the time.

The subject of his poetry was America itself. Whitman wanted to capture the country's democratic spirit. He strove to write an epic that embraced the whole of life and death, focusing on the common people. He wanted *Leaves of Grass* to reflect the growth of both the individual and America, so he included his personal experiences in the book. He revised and rearranged the book through six editions, signing an update of the last edition on his deathbed.

The first edition of *Leaves of Grass,* published in 1855, was a departure from the typical form of that time. Whitman believed that "words are alive and sinewy — they walk, look, step with an air of command." He used words from diverse sources such as foreign languages, street language, science, the Bible, carpentry, and opera. He even made up his own words when he could not find ones that suited him. Examples of this language can be found in lines such as the following:

Allons! the road is before us!

My foothold is tenon'd and mortis'd in granite.

The blab of the pave, tires of carts, sluff of boot-soles, talk of the promenaders....

This photo of Whitman dressed as a carpenter was used in the first edition of *Leaves of Grass.*

His originality of language is one reason that *Leaves of Grass* is such a great collection of poems.

Whitman abandoned more conventional meters and wrote in a free-verse style that had no regular meter or rhyme. His poetry was written to be spoken aloud or sung, and it stands today as one of the better examples of free verse, a style that emphasizes the democratic ideals of his poetry.

Whitman wrote about the values of the common people and their everyday experiences. He wrote about the butcher boy, the blacksmith, the lunatic, the machinist, the policeman, the deck hand, and the president in a new, more realistic way. This was so revolutionary that his poetry was criticized by many people at the time and was not appreciated until much later. Whitman recognized this and wrote the following lines:

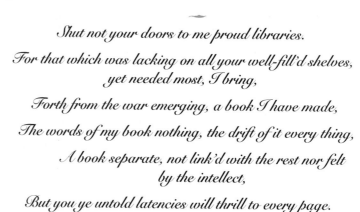

> *Shut not your doors to me proud libraries.*
>
> *For that which was lacking on all your well-fill'd shelves,*
> *yet needed most, I bring,*
>
> *Forth from the war emerging, a book I have made,*
>
> *The words of my book nothing, the drift of it every thing,*
>
> *A book separate, not link'd with the rest nor felt*
> *by the intellect,*
>
> *But you ye untold latencies will thrill to every page.*

Despite criticism, Whitman continued to expand and revise *Leaves of Grass*. The Civil War erupted in the United States in 1861 and proved to be very influential in Whitman's poetry. He spent part of the war years in Washington, D.C., nursing and comforting wounded soldiers. The emotions expressed in his war poetry range from the first excitement and glory of war to the awareness of its terrible waste. This war poetry was originally published separately under the title *Drum Taps*.

President Abraham Lincoln's assassination immediately following the war greatly affected Whitman. He felt that Lincoln was a hero and personified democracy. After Lincoln's assassination, Whitman wrote four elegies (poems expressing sadness or grief), later collectively called *Memories of President Lincoln*. His poem "O Captain! My Captain!" is probably the most famous of these, but "When Lilacs Last in the Dooryard Bloom'd" is considered by many to be Whitman's best poem. *Drum Taps* and *Memories of President Lincoln* were included in revised editions of *Leaves of Grass*. In fact, many consider them to be the cornerstones of the book.

Whitman's obsession with *Leaves of Grass* continued for the remainder of his life. He revised and rearranged his poems, adding some and dropping others, always striving toward a more perfect order. When he signed the final edition on his deathbed in 1892, he was satisfied and pleased with his lifelong work. He had reached his goal, stated in the preface of the first edition: "...the genius of the

United States is not best or most in its executives or legislatures, nor in its ambassadors or authors or colleges or churches or parlors, nor even in its newspapers or inventors...but always most in the common people."

CIVIL WAR SERVICE

by Karan Davis Cutler

By 1862, the second year of the Civil War, Washington, D.C., was dotted with hospitals. Despite the number of hospitals, however, the wounded and sick overflowed into private homes, churches, hotels, barracks, lodges, schools, warehouses, and even the Patent Office and the Capitol Building. Hundreds of civilians also poured into the city to help care for the casualties. Among those volunteers was Walt Whitman.

The U.S. Capitol around 1848. The Capitol was used to house wounded soldiers during the Civil War.

Whitman had already visited the battlefront when he arrived in the capital in December 1862. He had seen the wounded, "all mutilated, sickening, torn, gouged out." Friends helped him find a secretarial job at the Bureau of Indian Affairs, a job that left him time for another task: visiting the "vast army of the wounded and sick." He was, he wrote, "a regular self-appointed missionary.... My poor, poor boys occupy my time very much." It was a job, Whitman insisted, "which deeply holds me."

The hospitals were crowded, constantly receiving new "loads and trains and boatloads of poor, bloody, and pale and wounded men." The hospitals were disorganized, and there were too few doctors and nurses. The truth was, Whitman wrote his mother, that "the largest proportion of worst cases get little or no attention. We receive them here with their wounds full of worms — some all swelled and inflamed. Many of the amputations have to be done over again." The sights were so terrible, he declared, that "you must be on your guard where you look. I saw...a visitor...look at an awful wound.... He turned pale and in a moment more he had fainted away and fallen on the floor."

He asked friends for money to buy small gifts such as fruit, candy, tobacco, newspapers, stationery, and stamps for the patients. Even more, Whitman explained, the soldiers "hunger and thirst for attention; this is sometimes the only thing that will reach their condition." Armed with "as cheerful an appearance as possible," he visited the hospital wards nearly every day. "I adapt myself to each case...some need to be humored, some are rather out of their head — some merely want me to sit down near them & hold them by the hand — one will want a letter written...some like to have me feed them...some want a cooling drink...others want writing paper."

Edwin Forbes's sketch of bringing in the wounded after a battle.

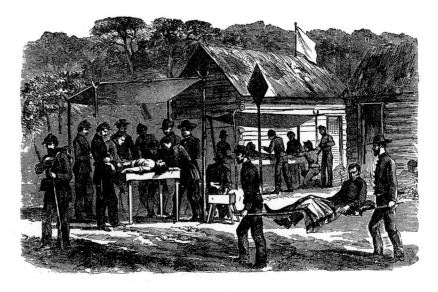

Washington, D.C., as seen from the portico of the Capitol in the 1850s, about ten years before Whitman came to the city. The Washington Monument is in the mid-distance.

Whitman's hospital visits gave him a view of war that was sharply different from the call of drum and bugle that had stirred him the year before. Now he saw the "butcher sights": "Surgeons operating, attendants holding lights, the smell of ether, the odor of blood, / The crowd, O the crowd of the bloody forms." The horrible suffering of the "million unwrit names" was the important fact of war, not the names of generals or battles. It was the simple, quiet bravery of unknown Americans that deserved attention, but that "real war," Whitman feared, "will never get in the books."

The real war has gotten in the books; moreover, Whitman put it in his books — his journals, letters, essays, and poems. *Specimen Days,* for example, includes his eyewitness accounts of battlefield and hospital life. On June 18, 1863, he noted, "Thomas Lindly, 1st Pennsylvania Cavalry, shot very badly through the foot — poor young man, he suffers horribly, has to be constantly dosed with morphine...I give him a large handsome apple...I write two letters for him."

Whitman became friends with many of the soldiers he nursed: "I have formed attachments here in hospital, that I shall keep to my dying day." His collected letters include dozens written to soldiers' families. "Dear Friends," he wrote a New York family, "I thought it would be soothing to you to have a few lines about the last days of your son Erastus...he was a noble boy.... I think you have reason to be proud." Whitman wrote these letters because he wanted to honor the "thousands...about whom there is no record or fame, no fuss made about their dying so unknown." These soldiers, he insisted, were "the real precious & royal ones of this land."

In his poetry, too, Whitman told of the "real war" and its "unwrit heroes": "A special verse for you... / Each name recall'd by me.... / Henceforth to be, deep, deep within my heart recording, for many a future year, / ...Embalm'd with love in this twilight song." In the poem "The Wound-Dresser," Whitman describes the work of an old man much like himself:

Bearing the bandages, water and sponge,

Straight and swift to my wounded I go,

Where they lie on the ground after battle brought in,...

I dress the perforated shoulder, the foot with the bullet-wound,

Cleanse the one with a gnawing and putrid gangrene, so sickening, so offensive,...

The hurt and wounded I pacify with soothing hand,

I sit by the restless all the dark night.

He wrote more than fifty poems relating to the war, never forgetting the pain and suffering, always celebrating the quiet bravery of the "divine average," the ordinary, unselfish soldiers who represented the best of America.

Whitman stayed in Washington after the war and continued to work as a clerk in the attorney general's office. He oversaw the publication of new editions of *Leaves of Grass* and wrote several new poems. In 1873, he had a serious stroke, and the next year he moved to New Jersey to live with his brother. Despite bad health, Whitman continued to write and to lecture until he died in 1892.

Whitman estimated that he made six hundred hospital visits and saw between eighty thousand and one hundred thousand soldiers. His numbers may have been exaggerated, but there is no way to exaggerate the importance to him of his wartime service. "Those three years," he later wrote, "I consider the greatest privilege and satisfaction...and the most profound lesson of my life." His hospital work gave him a vivid and lasting picture of the strength and goodness of the average American citizen. It renewed his faith in the United States and allowed him to serve his country. Most of all, it provided new experiences about which he could write. And because Whitman put those experiences in books, we, too, can know the "real war."

Whitman's brother George fought in the Union army. Walt moved to Camden, New Jersey, in 1874 after suffering a stroke and lived there for the next eleven years with George.

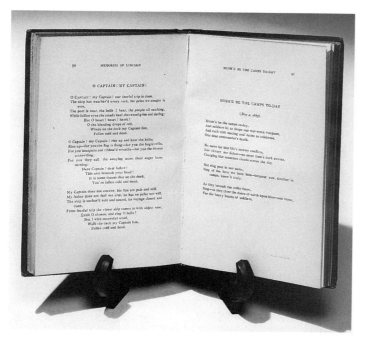

A POET AND A PRESIDENT

by Karan Davis Cutler

They began on different sides, Abraham Lincoln and Walt Whitman. The westerner, Lincoln, was a Whig congressman, his party descended from George Washington and John Adams. Whitman, an easterner, edited a Democratic party newspaper and admired the ideas of Thomas Jefferson and Andrew Jackson. "Free soil" (the question of allowing slavery into new territories) split their parties and joined them for the first time.

Both men were champions of liberty, democratic government, and the average citizen. Both hated tyranny and injustice. They devoutly hoped to avoid civil war, believing that keeping the nation together was paramount. He would "accept war," Lincoln said, "rather than let it [the Union] perish." Whitman echoed his view: "The chief thing was to stick together." The most lasting connection between the two men, however, was not political.

For nearly three years, they lived near each other, yet they never met. There are stories that Lincoln read and liked *Leaves of Grass,* but they cannot be verified. Whitman read Lincoln's speeches and saw him on the streets of Washington. In 1863, he wrote his mother, "I had a good view of the President...he looks more careworn even than usual — his face with deep cut lines...his complexion gray...a curious looking man, very sad." He attended the 1865 inaugural reception at the White House, where the president was "drest all in black, with white kid gloves...shaking hands, looking...as if he would give anything to be somewhere else." Lincoln faced harsh criticism, even the threat of impeachment, but Whitman "believed fully" in him and thought "better of him than many do."

Whitman felt Lincoln "particularly belonged" to him, that they were "afloat on the same stream...rooted in the same ground." It was this invisible bond that led Whitman to write about Lincoln after the president had been killed. He prepared an article for a popular magazine and lectured on "The Death of Abraham Lincoln." The Boston *Transcript* reported that at his last lecture, in 1890, the old poet had "crawled out of his sickbed...hoarse and half blind, to deliver his memorable essay."

Those articles and speeches are now forgotten. It is Whitman's poems about Lincoln that endure and that forever join these two nineteenth-century men. "O Captain! My Captain!" is probably Whitman's most famous poem about Lincoln. In it, Lincoln, the captain of a ship, has brought his vessel safely home (just as President Lincoln brought his nation through the war): "For you the bugle trills, / For you bouquets and ribbon'd wreaths." But Lincoln, the captain, cannot "rise up and hear the bells"; he has "fallen cold and dead."

Whitman's masterpiece and his greatest tribute to Lincoln is the long, complicated elegy "When Lilacs Last in the Dooryard Bloom'd." Lilacs were blooming when Lincoln was shot, and the flower always reminded Whitman of that terrible event. The poem pictures a funeral train moving through the United States, very much as Lincoln's did: "Coffin that passes through lanes and streets / Through day and night, / ...With countless torches lit, with the silent sea of faces and unbared heads." The train moves west to Illinois, "Carrying a corpse to where it shall rest in the grave," carrying the man Whitman called "the sweetest, wisest soul of all my days and lands."

Until he died, Whitman "annually gather[ed] a few friends to hold a tragic reminiscence" of Lincoln's assassination and to recall the president's great service to his country. Today Whitman's verse continues "to hold a tragic reminiscence" of Abraham Lincoln, and it reminds us again and again of the enduring connection between a poet and a president, two representatives of the American spirit who never met.

BORN ON THE TAIL OF A COMET

by Mary Lou Burket

On November 30, 1835, while Halley's comet streaked across the starry sky, Samuel Clemens was, as he later recalled, "born excited." His birthplace was the "almost invisible village" of Florida, Missouri, a settlement of only twenty houses. A few years after his birth, the family moved to growing Hannibal, Missouri, a place Clemens would remember again and again in his famous books.

Hannibal was paradise for Clemens. From Holliday's Hill, he could look down on the Mississippi River to Jackson's Island, where he liked to take a raft and hide away. He also liked to swim and fish in Bear Creek and explore McDowell's Cave, which was filled with bats, passages, and mysteries. One day he would write about these scenes in *The Adventures of Tom Sawyer*. In that story, the hero, Tom,

Samuel Clemens

Notice what fifteen-year-old Samuel Clemens is holding in his hand. This photograph was clearly taken before he started using the pen name "Mark Twain," which refers to the cry given as the depth of water is measured from the bow of a ship. During this time, Clemens was an apprentice printer.

attends a school much like the one where Clemens was a "fitful" student, and the frightening character Injun Joe is a man Clemens knew and feared as a boy in Hannibal.

Hannibal was a town where "everybody was poor but didn't know it; and everybody was comfortable and did know it," according to Clemens. Some people were comfortable with slavery. His own father had owned slaves before he was born, and, as Clemens said, "I was not aware that there was anything wrong about it." He spent long and happy summers on his uncle's farm, where fifteen to twenty slaves were kept. One of them possibly was the model for Jim in *Adventures of Huckleberry Finn*.

Among the delights of this farm was a lightning rod attached to the roof of the room where Clemens slept. It was "an adorable and skittish thing to climb up and down, summer nights," Clemens thought, "when there were duties on hand of a sort to make privacy desirable."

He loved a prank and often tried to do the wrong thing. "My mother," he said, "had a good deal of trouble with me, but I think she enjoyed it." (She emerges in his writing as Aunt Polly.) During a cholera epidemic in 1849, she made him take medicine every day to prevent him from catching the disease. Fortunately for Clemens, the floor "had cracks in it, and I fed the Pain-Killer to the cracks with very good results — no cholera occurred down below."

His family was not always so lucky. His brother and sister died when he was young, and he nearly died of measles when he was ten. His father also died (of pneumonia) when he was young.

During the Civil War, Clemens saw limited service in the Confederate army. After the war, he became a good friend of his onetime enemy Ulysses S. Grant. It was Clemens who later published Grant's memoirs (see page 37).

Clemens remembered his father, John Marshall Clemens, as a stern man who had wanted and tried to be rich but never was. After his death, the Clemens children worked to support the struggling household. Clemens quit school and became a printer's apprentice at the *Hannibal Courier.* In exchange for learning the trade, he fetched water, worked the press, set type, and delivered papers. At night, he and the other apprentices snatched potatoes and onions from the cellar and roasted them over the stove before going to sleep on the floor.

In 1850, Clemens left the *Courier* to work for his older brother, Orion, new owner of the failing *Hannibal Journal.* Together they published the small paper from the Clemens family home but never made a profit. Orion refused to publish articles written by Sam, but when Orion was away, Sam published them anyway — attracting the town's attention "but not its admiration," according to Orion.

At about the same time, Clemens began sending stories about Hannibal to such big-city publications as *The Carpet-Bag* in Boston. Several of his stories were published when he was just sixteen.

Perhaps as a result of this early taste of success, Clemens left Hannibal the following year, 1853. Traveling alone, he found a job in New York City setting type for four dollars a week. "I am not afraid," he wrote his sister. "I shall ask favors from no one."

He visited the World's Fair, saw the Atlantic Ocean, and worked for a while in Philadelphia and Cincinnati. Then he joined his brother Orion in Keokuk,

Iowa. Twice more, they failed in publishing ventures.

In 1857, Clemens journeyed again, this time down the Mississippi River of his boyhood. He was bound for South America, where he hoped to make a fortune, but he never reached his destination. He stayed on the river and trained to be a pilot.

Piloting brought Clemens an excellent wage and a bit of glory, and he might have stayed a pilot all his life. But in January 1861, the Civil War interrupted his happiness. Because traffic on the Mississippi River was uncertain, Clemens joined a local group of irregular volunteers who supported the Confederacy. When news arrived of approaching Union forces, he quit the war and headed west to become a prospector, newspaperman, and author.

A fortuneteller advised him, "You write well, but you are rather out of practice. No matter, you will be in practice some day." Clemens believed that she was right.

STORYTELLING JOURNALIST

by Mary Ann Trevathan

"When I was younger I could remember anything, whether it happened or not, but I am getting old, and soon I shall remember only the latter." Such was Samuel Langhorne Clemens's approach to writing, including news reporting.

As a child, he used to entertain neighbors with astonishing tales of his adventures — tales his family learned not to believe. "I discount him ninety percent," his mother used to say. "The rest is pure gold."

When he was eleven years old, after his father died, he quit school and became a printer's apprentice. He liked his work and became a kind of assistant editor.

Two years later, his older brother, Orion, bought a weekly newspaper called the *Hannibal Journal.* Sam went to work for Orion in 1850. Once, when Orion went out of town, Sam took over as editor. He decided to spice up the news to get more readers, so he took a true story about the editor of a rival newspaper and exaggerated it.

The subject of his tale had been jilted by the woman he loved, had gone down to the river to drown himself, and then had changed his mind. Clemens told the story in great detail and even drew a picture and wrote a poem to go with it. He sold a lot of newspapers, but the poor, lovelorn editor became so embarrassed that he left town and did not come back.

Shortly before his eighteenth birthday, Clemens left the *Hannibal Journal.* He worked for printers in New York, Philadelphia, and Cincinnati before becoming

"When I was younger I could remember anything, whether it happened or not, but I am getting old, and soon I shall remember only the latter."

This photograph of Clemens was taken in 1864 when he worked as a reporter for the Virginia City *Territorial Enterprise.*

lyceum circuit. Traveling around the country on drafty trains, sleeping in musty hotels, and lecturing night after night took its toll on his time and creativity. Yet Twain remained on the lecture circuit until his literary works could support the lifestyle he desired.

AMERICAN FOLK ART

Early American families had to make most of the things they used in their daily lives. Many items they produced we now call folk art. Folk art is handmade, and no two pieces are identical.

Farm families were among the most numerous early American folk artists. Others included sailors, who whittled objects from whalebone; sign makers, who carved and painted images to represent businesses; traveling painters, who produced portraits and other pictures to decorate people's homes; and

stonecutters, who decorated buildings and gravestones.

By the late 1800s, many things that people needed were being made in factories. Old quilts, thick pottery, and the wooden signs that marked village shops were destroyed or put in attics and old barns and forgotten. These objects were rediscovered by the 1920s. Today folk artists no longer need to make objects for daily use, but they still use materials that are readily at hand.

This whirligig (spinning toy) of a soldier dates from 1860–1880. The rocking horse dates from the 1870s.

Hundreds of men and women gave lyceum lectures, but Twain's was unique. Even before he appeared on-stage, his wit preceded him in posters making statements such as "THE CELEBRATED BEARDED WOMAN! is not with this circus" or "A SPLENDID ORCHESTRA is in town, but has not been engaged."

When the performance began, Twain shuffled onto the stage and looked as if he were lost. During the lecture, he spoke in a slow drawl punctuated by intense pauses. All through the lecture, he appeared to be speaking spontaneously, as if addressing friends. He rarely smiled, even while the audience hooted with laughter. What appeared to be a relaxed, informal manner was an effect achieved by memorizing his script and carefully studying his audiences and their reactions. Twain took his lecturing seriously, even though his talks were humorous.

Although Twain left the lecture circuit whenever he could afford to do so, when his publishing company went bankrupt, he was forced to make his last worldwide tour to earn the money he owed his creditors. Beginning in Cleveland, Ohio, on July 15, 1895, Twain circled the globe, stopping in Australia, New Zealand, India, and South Africa before finishing in London in May 1896.

A financial and popular success, this tour established Twain as the premier humorist of the world. He then retired from the lecture circuit, giving only a few paid public performances and after-dinner talks until his death in 1910. "Talking for money is work and that takes the pleasure out of it," he said. His last public lecture was at a girls' school in Maryland ten months before his death.

Mark Twain once wrote that the ability to talk is invaluable, far superior to the ability to put thoughts on paper. The trouble did, indeed, begin at eight, but so did an evening of humor, entertainment, and enlightenment.

PHOTOGRAPHER WITH A DREAM

by Ron Hirschi

The camera shutter clicked, and a group of North American Indians were captured on film. The man taking the picture was Edward Sheriff Curtis. He was a remarkable man with an even more remarkable dream: to photograph American Indian cultures before they disappeared.

To accomplish his dream, Curtis devoted many years, traveled thousands of miles, and endured many hardships. In the end, he completed a set of photographic books that has been called the "most gigantic undertaking in the making of books since the King James edition of the Bible."

Curtis was born in Wisconsin in 1868. In 1887, he moved with his family to Puget Sound, Washington. It was there that he fell in love with the natural beauty of the West and began taking photographs. He took pictures of scenery but focused more on the original inhabitants of the area, the Coast Salish people. One of those early photographs is one of his more famous. It is a portrait of Princess Angeline, daughter of the great Suquamish chief Seattle. (The city of Seattle is named after this chief.)

In 1899, Curtis sailed to Alaska on a major scientific expedition. On the journey, he took many more photos of Native Americans. After he returned home, photographing American Indian people became his life's work.

At first Curtis worked at his own expense, although he soon had many admirers. One was President Theodore Roosevelt. He introduced Curtis to millionaire J. Pierpont Morgan, who helped Curtis raise the $1.5 million necessary to complete his series of books and photos called *The North American Indian.*

The first two volumes of *The North American Indian* were published in 1907 and 1908. The last volume was not published until 1930. But the project took more than time and money. Curtis carried his cameras down rivers, across canyons, and out to sea. He worked for months with little rest. At all times, he knew that he must complete the task of photographing what he thought was a vanishing race of people.

By the time Curtis finished his work, he had visited more than eighty Indian tribes and had taken more than forty thousand photographs. Sometimes he risked his life to get just the right photo.

No matter what tribe he photographed, Curtis got to know his subjects well and gained their respect. He also took part in rituals that were among his greatest adventures. These included his participation in the Hopi Snake Dance. To take part,

Edward Sheriff Curtis

Above: A self-portrait of Curtis, taken in 1899 when he was in his early thirties. Below: Curtis took this photograph of President Theodore Roosevelt, a friend and supporter, in 1904.

In 1905, Curtis photographed Red Cloud, an Oglala Sioux chief. Red Cloud died four years later.

he had to go without food for nine days and have no contact with other members of his photographic team. He also wore a traditional costume and performed a dance with a snake dangling from his mouth. That experience and others allowed him to obtain photos of events that no other white person had ever experienced.

Curtis photographed many great Indian leaders, including Geronimo, Red Cloud, and Chief Joseph. But he spent most of his time photographing common tribal life. He listened to people who remembered bison roaming the prairies. He photographed their homes, recorded their songs, and preserved for future generations the images of Indian children.

Today Curtis photographs are highly valued, and his books are found in major library and museum collections. Entire sets of his books and photos, which once sold for three thousand dollars, are now valued at one hundred thousand dollars. Individual photos sell for several hundred dollars each. But his work is valued more for what money cannot buy. It is a lasting reminder of his dream and a record of a vanishing way of life.

Thanks to Curtis, we can all share in the history of the American Indian. Indian people also are grateful because he provided a very personal record of their families and their cultural traditions. That record also can be seen in Curtis's motion picture *In the Land of the War Canoes.* It shows the sights and sounds of the Kwakiutls, a Northwest Coast seagoing people.

THROUGH THE EYES OF AN ARTIST

by Christina Ashton

Corporal Scott was down, shot in both legs. All around him, his comrades of the Tenth Cavalry lay wounded and dying in this latest encounter with Apaches in the Southwest during the summer of 1886. Suddenly, from behind the boulders on the slope where the rest of the soldiers had retreated, Lieutenant Powhatan H. Clarke dashed out. Crouching low under a hail of bullets, he dragged Scott to safety.

A picture of this incident, signed by Frederic Remington, appeared on the cover of the New York magazine *Harper's Weekly.* It was the young artist's first assignment as a war correspondent.

Remington was born in Canton, New York, in 1861. During his youth, he neglected his studies in favor of drawing. As a young man, he was bored by most jobs and a failure at business. All he ever wanted to do was go west and paint the Indians, Mexicans, outlaws, cowboys, and old frontiersmen who lived there. He began visiting the western territories while he was still in his teens. By then he had become a talented artist and an accomplished horseman.

During the long struggle to capture the Apache leader Geronimo, *Harper's Weekly* was looking for a war correspondent/artist who knew the Southwest well enough to survive a long campaign and could ride well enough to keep up with the U.S. Cavalry. Although only a few of Remington's drawings had been published, many people admired his vivid scenes of men and horses in wild action against the dramatic western landscape. He presented his qualifications to *Harper's* and was sent to Arizona.

On this first assignment, he did not join the battle against the Apaches, but stayed in camp to observe the day-to-day activities of the Tenth Cavalry, a regiment of buffalo soldiers (African Americans assigned to the West). While buying a drink for an African American sergeant, Remington learned about Clarke, who was white, and his heroic rescue of Scott, who was African American. After hearing the story, Remington visited Scott in the hospital, where he was recovering from the incident. He described the corporal as "a fine tall Negro soldier" and listened to the trooper tell his version of the story "in simple soldierly language." After Scott finished, Remington sketched his face. Having sketched Clarke and some of the other soldiers, he composed the picture and sent it to *Harper's.* Remington deeply admired the buffalo soldiers, remarking in his journal that "Negro cavalrymen" were "good style men." Although African American soldiers were generally held in low esteem by many of the officers and had to endure prejudice, poor food and housing, and faulty weapons and gear, Reming-

ton's picture showed valor, loyalty, and the respect African American and white fighting men could have for each other. It also showed that frontier battles were far more brutal than people back east had been led to believe.

In 1888, Remington made a second visit to the Tenth Cavalry to do an article and pictures for *Century Magazine.* This time the soldiers took him on a particularly grueling scouting mission in intense heat over treacherous terrain covered with clumps of cacti and thorny mesquite. Saddle sore and bleeding from thorns, Remington ended each day exhausted and often in low spirits. In his article, he noted that the buffalo soldiers were just as weary as he but never complained. They rose every morning at dawn, he reported, always cheerful and unflinching in the face of whatever the day had in store. "I like the Negro soldiers [sic] character as a soldier in almost every particular," he remarked.

But it was his pictures, more than his words, that best conveyed his impressions of the admirable work and character of the African American soldiers. He made several detailed illustrations to accompany his article.

Remington works on *The Broncho Buster,* his first sculpture, which was cast in bronze on his thirty-fourth birthday.

By the end of this assignment, Remington's fame as an artist was firmly established.

Unfortunately, for decades after the frontier battles were over, the buffalo soldiers were largely forgotten. Remington's pictures help us to remember their contributions to the Old West.

THEATER IN THE GOLD RUSH WEST

by Brandon Marie Miller

For twenty years after the California Gold Rush of 1849, any type of entertainment was welcomed in the mining camps of the Old West. Circus and minstrel acts were applauded as loudly as operas and Shakespearean plays. There were even hand-painted "travelogues" half a mile long, slowly unrolled to music and narration. But the most popular fare was comedies, musicals, and melodramas. Since the miners had to take what they could get, the performances were not always good, and brawls in the aisles sometimes were more interesting than the shows on-stage!

Western theaters were as varied as the entertainment they provided. San Francisco, the greatest Gold Rush boomtown, boasted gilded halls with velvet curtains. Most stages, though, were simply tacked onto the back of a saloon. Out in the mining camps, theaters were constructed from whatever was at hand — rough planks for a stage and a tent canvas or blankets draped as curtains.

Demand for theatrical performances was so high and the chance for reward so great that many acting celebrities found their way west. Famous dramatic actor Junius Brutus Booth and his sons brought their talents to California, but in a land where men outnumbered women more than ten to one, a female on-stage guaranteed a packed house. Following are some of the favored "darlings" of the Gold Rush theater.

In the early 1850s, actress Caroline Chapman arrived in San Francisco. From an acting family that traveled the Mississippi River on a showboat, Chapman was already a success in New York theater. Miners flocked to see "Our Caroline" in Shakespearean and musical extravaganzas. Her greatest role was in the play *She Stoops to Conquer*. Chapman was one of the first accomplished actors to tour the mining towns, riding muleback even through bandit-infested areas. In Sonora, New Mexico, more than a thousand grateful miners escorted her into

The Bella Union Theater in Deadwood, South Dakota, 1877.

town. Everywhere her performances were rewarded with buckskin purses filled with gold and so many silver coins that a shortage resulted. Chapman was secure enough in her own popularity that she dared to poke fun at another stage favorite, Lola Montez.

No one credited Montez with being a good actress. She was a fiery woman with whom many men from Europe to California fell in love. Montez's claim to fame was a notorious dance in which spiders of rubber, whalebone, and cork fell from her skirts. One observer noted that Montez performed such wild dances as an excuse to "kick high and shake her petticoats." After Chapman's parody of her performances, Montez retired (for a while) to Grass Valley, California, where the miners named a mountain peak in her honor.

In Grass Valley, Montez befriended a young girl named Lotta Crabtree, whose father had come to California to mine for riches. He never struck gold, but his daughter certainly did. Crabtree became one of the true stars of the American theater. Her career began in the mid-1850s when she was eight, and by age twelve she was supporting her family. Crabtree's mother traveled with her, oversaw her career, and swept up the coins and nuggets from the stage. A tiny redhead, Crabtree sang and played the banjo. She danced and performed comedy, all with such spirit and enthusiasm that western audiences loved her.

Adah Menken, herself a star, described Crabtree as "a lovely and breathing poem that set the heart to music."

When "La Petite Lotta" retired thirty-seven years later, she had conquered audiences in the East and Europe as well. Unlike some women stars of her day who married many times, Crabtree never wed. When she died, she left her four-million-dollar fortune to charity.

Adah Isaacs Menken was twenty-eight when she met young Lotta Crabtree. A poet who could speak, read, and write four languages, Menken hit San Francisco in 1863 in a turmoil of publicity and excitement. Tom Maguire, who owned many theaters in and around the city, lured her west with the promise of fifteen hundred dollars a week to play her famous role in *Mazeppa*. Critics called her "a dreadful actress," but Menken thrilled her *Mazeppa* audiences when she was strapped to the back of a "wild" horse and carried up a ramp into stage-set mountains. Her costume was scandalous: only a little flowing robe and flesh-colored tights in an age when ladies did not show even an ankle beneath their skirts. In Virginia City, Nevada, the miners built a special stage for Menken at the base of a mountain. Her single performance was greeted with an outpouring of gold, silver, and jewels — more than one hundred thousand dollars' worth — and the men named the mining district Menken in her honor.

These actresses and others like them took full advantage of the fervor and riches of the Gold Rush West. Perhaps only in that environment could they have obtained such fortune and fame.

Lotta Crabtree

Crabtree was a sensation in the West, performing in mining towns throughout California. She also met with great success when she went to New York City in 1867 to appear in Charles Dickens's *Old Curiosity Shop*. When she died in 1924, she left millions to charity.

6

. . . .

'WITH MALICE TOWARD NONE':
RECONSTRUCTION

On March 4, 1865,

Abraham Lincoln stood on the portico of the Capitol Building to take the oath of office as president for the second time.

Thick gray clouds filled the sky as Lincoln stepped forward to deliver his inaugural address.

"With malice toward none," he urged, "with charity for all...let us strive on to finish the work we are in; to bind up the nation's wounds." More than anything else, the war-weary Lincoln wanted "peace among ourselves." As he spoke these hopeful words, the sun broke through dramatically, thrilling the crowd.

But Lincoln did not live to pursue his dream. Five weeks later, he was assassinated. The delicate task of putting the Union back together — Reconstruction, as it came to be known — was left to others.

Unfortunately, Reconstruction divided America almost as bitterly as had slavery. Liberal northerners wanted African Americans to be granted full and equal rights immediately. Conservative southerners resisted all efforts to extend the benefits of citizenship to their former slaves. For a full generation, Americans angrily debated civil rights, voting rights, Black Codes, carpetbagging, and other heated issues.

It was not the peaceful era Lincoln had hoped it would be. But it brought America, slowly but surely, closer than ever to making the American dream a reality for all its people.

RECONSTRUCTION: PUTTING THE UNION BACK TOGETHER

by H.S. Stout and D.H. DeFord

Have you ever built a big house of blocks or a sandcastle on the beach? If so, you know that you can spend hours making it just right, working with great care to balance and support each new part. But watch out! It takes only one

Gilbert Gaul, a northerner who was sympathetic to the southern cause, painted *Return Home*. In this scene, a haggard Confederate soldier returns after the war to find his home in ruins.

swift kick or an unexpected wave to knock down all those hours of careful work. To build it again — to reconstruct it — you have to fix what is left and then slowly repeat the whole process.

In one of his most famous speeches against slavery, Abraham Lincoln stated, "'A house divided against itself cannot stand.'" He was not talking about a real house, though, or a sandcastle. He was taking about the United States. At the time of his speech, the southern states depended on slavery to make their plantations profitable. The northern states wanted to eliminate slavery. North and South disagreed violently, making the United States a "house divided."

Later in that same speech, Lincoln said, "I do not expect the house to *fall*." Tragically, for Lincoln and the American people, the house did fall. North and South went to war, and in the destruction of civil war, more than six hundred thousand Americans lost their lives to battle and disease. More than four hundred thousand were injured. Never before had such a large house fallen with such terrible consequences.

Even before the war ended, though, Lincoln had worked on a plan to reconstruct it as smoothly and peacefully as possible. He knew people would want to be repaid for what they had lost in the war. They would even want revenge. Lincoln's plan for Reconstruction called for the Confederacy (the South) and the Republic (the North) to forgive one another and to get back together quickly.

Lincoln's assassination in April 1865 proved tragic, not only for him but also for the United States. Imagine trying to rebuild your fallen sandcastle with your worst enemy for a helper. That is how it felt in the United States after the Civil War. Under Lincoln's successor, Andrew Johnson, a group of Radical Republicans took charge of Congress. While many of the new congressmen wanted to "bind up the wounds" of the nation (as Lincoln had suggested), a few demanded revenge on the "proud traitors" from the South. Lincoln had wanted to let the Confederates rejoin the Union as soon as they promised to be loyal. Leading congressmen such as Thaddeus Stevens of Pennsylvania and Charles Sumner of Massachusetts pushed to make it difficult and costly for the South to come back.

White southerners felt that Congress was harsh, but the new Republicans did what they thought was necessary to rebuild the country "correctly." Not only did they appoint northern rulers, but they also passed laws to make life better for freed slaves (or freedmen) and allow them the rights of full citizenship. Congress's most important actions were the Thirteenth, Fourteenth, and Fifteenth amendments to the U.S. Constitution. The Thirteenth Amendment (1865) outlawed slavery in the United States; the Fourteenth Amendment (1868) guaranteed freed slaves the status of full citizens of the United States; and the Fifteenth Amendment (1870) guaranteed African American men the right to vote. All these amendments were necessary to give African American men political equality.

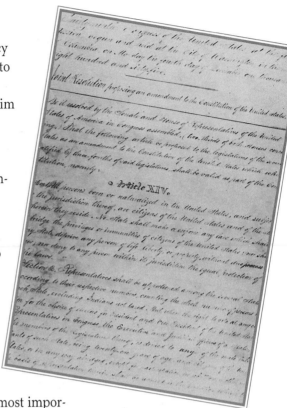

The Fourteenth Amendment (1868) guaranteed freed slaves the status of full citizens of the United States.

Besides having to abide by these national laws, each southern state had to set up a government based on both African American and white voters. The First Reconstruction Act of March 2, 1867, divided the South into five military districts governed by tough northern generals. These generals were required to call the elections, in which former Confederate leaders from the army and government could neither vote nor hold office, while African Americans were encouraged to do so. This infuriated white southerners and fed the resentment that continued between North and South. Even so, these elections did produce a constitutional convention in each southern state. The convention wrote a new constitution, which ensured every male citizen the right to vote, regardless of race. As each southern state ratified its new constitution and chose a new, loyal government, it was approved by Congress to rejoin the Union.

The new state constitutions and the amendments to the U.S. Constitution succeeded in ending slavery and giving freedmen the right to vote. But laws cannot make people stop hating. Racism (hatred for races not your own) continued in both the North and South. The South was determined to keep white men in power and to keep African Americans separate (or segregated). The North was little better.

THE FREEDMEN'S BUREAU OFFICE — MEMPHIS, TENNESSEE

Soon leaders in the South and North grew tired of Reconstruction. It was very expensive, and the temporary governments often were corrupt. In addition, northern leaders were sidetracked by new issues such as tariffs, currency, and expansion in the West. Finally, in the Compromise of 1877, northern Republicans agreed to let the South retain white supremacy if it would support the election of presidential candidate Rutherford B. Hayes.

Reconstruction reunited the North and South and ended slavery by putting the Thirteenth Amendment to work. But Reconstruction failed to bind the races together. Nevertheless, it did take the first step toward overcoming racism. One agency that helped in this process was the Freedmen's Bureau, created by Congress in March 1865.

The Freedmen's Bureau offered economic relief to freed slaves and provided them with hospitals and schools. The bureau maintained more than four thousand schools for African American children, most of which were staffed by northern women who were sent south through the American Missionary Association. By the end of Reconstruction, six hundred thousand southern African Americans were in elementary schools.

Just as important as the elementary schools were the African American colleges founded to train teachers and leaders. The federal government set up Howard University in Washington, D.C., while private foundations in the North set up industrial schools in the South (such as Hampton Institute in Virginia and Fisk University in Tennessee).

Reconstruction's real success is still in the making. Education has given African Americans the chance to take part in building and running the United

States. Over generations, African American schools have produced many leaders, from Booker T. Washington and W.E.B. Du Bois to Reverend Martin Luther King, Jr., and Mary McLeod Bethune. Some of these people led the United States into a "second reconstruction" in the 1950s and 1960s. Not until citizens of the United States can work together without regard to skin color and other racial, religious, and gender differences, however, will "reconstruction" be complete.

GLOSSARY

Black Codes   Series of statutes passed by the ex-Confederate states dealing with the status of newly freed slaves. The codes granted African Americans certain rights — to marry, to own property, to sue and be sued, and to make contracts. They denied them other rights — to bear arms, to serve as jurors, and to hold mass meetings. Black Codes varied from state to state.

Carpetbagger   Derogatory name for a northerner who went south during Reconstruction and made a lot of money or held political office. The name comes from the carpetbags in which such people carried their belongings.

Emancipation Proclamation   Executive order from President Abraham Lincoln abolishing slavery in the Confederacy (which was out of the reach of the federal government). Formally issued on January 1, 1863, it did not affect the legal basis of slavery.

Freedmen's Bureau   Federal agency established to help African Americans make the transition from slavery to freedom. The bureau provided relief to African Americans and whites in war-stricken areas, supported African American education, regulated African American labor, and sought to administer justice in cases involving African Americans.

Impeachment   Charge of misconduct in office against a public official. An impeachment is tried by the U.S. Senate; agreement by two-thirds of those present is needed for conviction.

Ku Klux Klan   Group organized in 1866 by ex-Confederates to oppose the Reconstruction policies of the Radical Republicans and terrorize African Americans and their supporters. The Knights of the White Camelia were another such terrorist group.

Plantation   Large farming estate of a wealthy landowner. Slave laborers worked the plantation without pay and with varying provisions for food and housing.

Radical Republicans   Branch of the Republican party that, during Reconstruction, sought wide-sweeping changes in southern culture in a short period of time. The Radicals were strongly opposed to slavery and believed in the equality of whites and African Americans.

Reconstruction   Period of readjustment following the Civil War, generally recognized as 1865 to 1877. (Some historians believe that Reconstruction began in 1862, when Union troops captured New Orleans and Tennessee at about the same time.) There were many problems to be solved during those years. The status of freed slaves had to be defined, the seceded southern states had to be reincorporated into the federal government, and the economy and social structure of the South had to be reestablished.

Scalawag   Derogatory term describing a white southerner who joined the Republican party and helped carry out Reconstruction policies.

Sharecropping   System of agriculture that arose from the plantation system. Plantations were divided into smaller units and worked by African American families. The white landowner kept a share of the crops instead of paying wages and collecting rent.

Ten percent plan   Plan of Abraham Lincoln stating that if ten percent of the men of any southern state who were eligible to vote in the 1860 presidential election took an oath of allegiance to the Constitution, they would be allowed to organize a new state government. Many historians believe that the plan was not Lincoln's final solution to restoring the Union.

195

★ ★ ★ ★ ★ ★ ★ ★ ★ ★

THE SOUTH AFTER THE WAR
Mrs. Frances Butler Leigh's Account

Frances Butler Leigh describes her travels through the South
after what she calls the "revolution" in these excerpts.*

The year after the war between the North and South, I went to the South with my father to look after our property in Georgia and see what could be done with it.

The whole country had of course undergone a complete revolution. The changes that a four years' war must bring about in any country would alone have been enough to give a different aspect to everything; but at the South, besides the changes brought about by the war, our slaves had been freed; the white population was conquered, ruined, and disheartened, unable for the moment to see anything but ruin before as well as behind, too wedded to the fancied prosperity of the old system to believe in any possible success under the new. And even had the

people desired to begin at once to rebuild their fortunes, it would have been in most cases impossible, for in many families the young men had perished in the war, and the old men, if not too old for the labor and effort it required to set the machinery of peace going again, were beggared, and had not even money enough to buy food for themselves and their families, let alone their negroes, to whom they now had to pay wages as well as feed them....

On March 22, 1866, my father and myself left the North. The Southern railroads were many of them destroyed for miles, not having been rebuilt since the war, and it was very questionable how we were to get as far as Savannah, a matter we did accomplish however, in a week's time.... [We reached] Richmond at

*From Frances Butler Leigh, *Ten Years on a Georgia Plantation. After the War* (London: R. Bentley and Son, 1883). From *The South: A Documentary History,* by Ina Woestemeyer Van Noppen (Princeton, New Jersey: D. Van Nostrand Company, Inc., 1958).

four o'clock on Sunday morning....

I can hardly give a true idea of how crushed and sad the people are. You hear no bitterness towards the North; they are too sad to be bitter; their grief is overwhelming. Nothing can make any difference to them now; the women live in the past, and the men only in the daily present, trying, in a listless sort of way, to repair their ruined fortunes. They are like so many foreigners, whose only interest in the country is their own individual business. Politics are never mentioned, and they know and care less about what is going on in Washington than in London.

...The fine houses have fallen to decay or been burnt down; the grounds neglected and grown over with weeds; the plantations left, with a few exceptions, to the negroes; olive groves choked up with undergrowth; stately date-palms ruthlessly burnt down by negroes to make room for a small patch of corn, where there were hundreds of acres, untilled, close at hand; a few solitary men eking out an existence by growing fruit trees and cabbages, by planting small patches of cotton or corn, by hunting deer, or by selling whiskey to the negroes.

....

Problems of Daily Life

Both white southerners and freed slaves endured tremendous suffering after the war. The following passages describe the problems faced by both races.*

...The general destitution has rendered many kindly disposed people unable to do anything for the negroes who were formerly their slaves, and who might be supposed to have some claims upon them for temporary assistance on that account, and there is much suffering among the aged and infirm, the sick and helpless, of this class of people.... It is a common, and everyday sight in Randolph County, that of women and children, most of whom were formerly in good circumstances, begging for bread from door to door.

Meat of any kind has been a stranger to many of their mouths for months. The drought cut off what little crops they hoped to save, and they must have immediate help or perish....

By far the greatest suffering exists among the whites. Their scanty supplies have been exhausted, and now they look to the government alone for support. Some are without homes of any description. This seems strange and almost unaccountable. Yet on one road leading to Talladega I visited four families, within fifteen minutes' ride of the town, who were living in the woods, with no shelter but pine boughs, and this in mid-winter. Captain Dean, who accompanied me, assured me that upon the other roads leading into town were other families similarly situated. These people have no homes. They were widows, with large families of small children. Other families, as provisions fail, will wander in for supplies, and I am fearful the result will be a camp of widows and orphans. If possible, it should

Before setting out for the war in 1864, Christopher Hughes, a widower, bought a home and a family burial plot for his four children in Boston. This was an unusual achievement for an Irish immigrant laborer. His framed discharge paper from the Union army hangs today in his eighty-seven-year-old granddaughter's home.

*First excerpt, quoted from the *Senate Executive Document* No. 27, Congress, 1 Session. Second excerpt, quoted from the *Senate Executive Document* No. 2, 39 Congress, 1 Session.

be prevented; and yet I saw about thirty persons for whom shelter must be provided, or death will speedily follow their present exposure and suffering....

When the war came to a close, the labor system of the South was already much disturbed. During the progress of military operations large numbers of slaves had left their masters and followed the columns of our armies; others had taken refuge in our camps; many thousands had enlisted in the service of the national government. Extensive settlements of negroes has been formed along the seaboard and the banks of the Mississippi, under the supervision of army officers and treasury agents, and the government was feeding the colored refugees, who could not be advantageously employed, in the contraband camps. Many slaves had been removed by their masters, as our armies penetrated the country, either to Texas or to the interior of Georgia and Alabama.

Thus a considerable portion of the laboring force had been withdrawn from its former employments. But a majority of the slaves remained on the plantations to which they belonged, especially in those parts of the country which were not touched by the war, and where, consequently, the emancipation proclamation was not enforced by the military power. When...the report went...out that their liberation was...a fixed fact, large numbers of colored people left the plantations; many flocked to our military posts and camps to obtain the certainty of their freedom, and others walked away merely for the purpose of leaving the place on which they had been held in slavery, and because they could now go with impunity. Still others, and their number was by no means inconsiderable, remained with their former masters and continued their work on the field, but under new and as yet unsettled conditions, and under the agitating influence of a feeling of restlessness.... The country found itself thrown into that confusion which is naturally inseparable from a change so great and so sudden....

North Western Depot, Charleston, South Carolina, 1865.

[The South] looked for many miles like a broad black streak of ruin and desolation — the fences all gone; lonesome smoke stacks, surrounded by dark heaps of ashes and cinders, marking the spots where human habitations had stood; the fields along the roads wildly overgrown by weeds, with here and there a sickly patch of cotton and corn cultivated by Negro squatters.

Union general Carl Schurz, 1865

Economic Disaster

Historian Walter Lynwood Fleming described the South's desperate economic conditions in the following selections.*

From Harper's [sic] Ferry to New Market, which is about eighty miles...the country was almost a desert.... We had no cattle, hogs, sheep, or horse or anything else. The fences were all gone. Some of the orchards were very much injured, but the fruit trees had not been

*From Walter Lynwood Fleming, *The Sequel of Appomattox: A Chronicle of the Reunion of the States* (New Haven: Yale University Press, 1919).

destroyed. The barns were all burned; chimneys standing without houses, and houses standing without roof, or door, or window.

Much land was thrown on the market at low prices — three to five dollars an acre for land worth fifty dollars. The poorer lands could not be sold at all, and thousands of farms were deserted by their owners. Everywhere recovery from this agricultural depression was slow....

There were few stocks of merchandise in the South when the war ended, and Northern creditors had lost so heavily through the failure of Southern merchants that they were cautious about extending credit again. Long before 1865 all coin had been sent out in contraband trade through the blockade. That there was a great need of supplies from the outside world is shown by the following statement of General Boynton:

"Window-glass has given way to thin boards, in railway coaches and in the cities. Furniture is marred and broken, and none has been replaced for four years. Dishes are cemented in various styles, and half the pitchers have tin handles. A complete set of crockery is never seen, and in very few families is there enough to set a table.... A set of forks with whole tines is a curiosity. Clocks and watches have nearly all stopped.... Hair brushes and tooth brushes have all worn out; combs are broken.... Pins, needles, and thread, and a thousand such articles, which seem indispensable to housekeeping, are very scarce. Even in weaving on the looms, corncobs have been substituted for spindles. Few have pocket knives. In fact, everything that has heretofore been an article of sale at the South is wanting now. At the tables of those who were once esteemed luxurious providers you will find neither tea, coffee, sugar, nor spices of any kind. Even candles, in some cases, have been replaced by a cup of grease in [which] a piece of cloth is plunged for a wick."

This poverty was prolonged and rendered more acute by the lack of transportation. Horses, mules, wagons, and carriages were scarce, the country roads were nearly impassable, and bridges were in bad repair or had been burned or washed away.

Steamboats had almost disappeared from the rivers. Those which had escaped capture as blockade runners had been subsequently destroyed or were worn out. Postal facilities, which had been poor enough during the last year of the Confederacy, were entirely lacking for several months after the surrender....

The South faced the work of reconstruction not only with a shortage of material and greatly hampered in the employment even of that but still more with a shortage of men....

...The poorer whites who had lost all were close to starvation. In the white counties which had sent so large a proportion of men to the army the destitution was most acute. In many families the breadwinner had been killed in war. After 1862 relief systems had been organized in nearly all the Confederate States for the purpose of aiding the poor whites, but these organizations were disbanded in 1865....

Acute distress continued until 1867; after that year there was no further danger of starvation. Some of the poor whites, especially in the remote districts, never again reached a comfortable standard of living; some were demoralized by too much assistance; others were discouraged and left the South for the West or the North. But the mass of the people accepted the discipline of poverty and made the best of their situation.

The difficulties, however, that beset even the courageous and the competent were enormous. The general paralysis of industry, the breaking up of society, and poverty on all sides bore especially hard on those who had not previously been manual laborers. Physicians could get practice enough but no fees; lawyers who had supported the Confederacy found it difficult to get back into the reorganized courts because of the test oaths and the competition of "loyal" attorneys; and for the teachers there were few schools. We read of officers high in the Confederate service selling to Federal soldiers the pies and cakes cooked by their wives, of others selling fish and oysters which they themselves had caught, and of men and women hitching themselves to plows when they had no horse or mule.

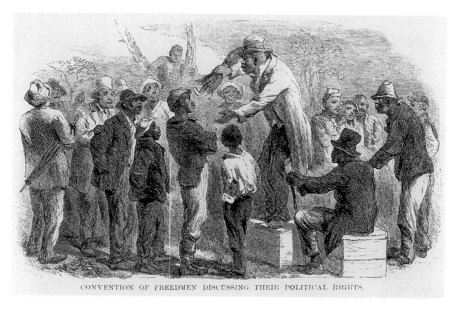

CONVENTION OF FREEDMEN DISCUSSING THEIR POLITICAL RIGHTS.

★ ★ ★ ★ ★ ★ ★ ★ ★

FORMER SLAVES SPEAK OUT

Two former slaves, Toby Jones and John McCoy, describe their lives after
emancipation in the following excerpts.*

Toby Jones

I worked for Massa 'bout four years after freedom,
'cause he forced me to, said he couldn't 'ford to let
me go. His place was near ruint, the fences burnt,
and the house would have been, but it was rock....
When the war was over, Massa come home and
says, "You son of a gun, you's supposed to be free,
but you ain't, 'cause I ain't gwine give you freedom." So I goes on working for him till I gits the
chance to steal a hoss from him. The woman I
wanted to marry, Govie, she 'cides to come to
Texas with me. Me and Govie, we rides that hoss
'most a hundred miles, then we turned him a-loose
and give him a scare back to his house, and come
on foot the rest the way to Texas.

All we had to eat was what we could beg, and
sometimes we went three days without a bite to eat.
Sometimes we'd pick a few berries. When we got

cold we'd crawl in a bushpile and hug up close
together to keep warm. Once in a while we'd come
to a farmhouse, and the man let us sleep on cotton-
seed in his barn, but they was far and few between,
'cause they wasn't many houses in the country
them days like now.

When we gits to Texas, we gits married, but all
they was to our wedding am we just 'grees to live
together as man and wife. I settled on some land,
and we cut some trees and split them open and
stood them on end with the tops together for our
house. Then we deadened some trees, and the land
was ready to farm. There was some wild cattle and
hogs, and that's the way we got our start, caught
some of them and tamed them.

I don't know as I 'spected nothing from freedom,
but they turned us out like a bunch of stray dogs, no
homes, no clothing, no nothing, not 'nough food to last

*From Botkin, ed., *Lay My Burden Down: A Folk History of Slavery* (University of Chicago Press, 1945).

us one meal. After we settles on that place, I never seed man or woman, 'cept Govie, for six years, 'cause it was a long ways to anywhere. All we had to farm with was sharp sticks. We'd stick holes and plant corn, and when it come up we'd punch up the dirt around it. We didn't plant cotton, 'cause we couldn't eat that. I made bows and arrows to kill wild game with, and we never went to a store for nothing. We made our clothes out of animal skins.

John McCoy

Freedom wasn't no different I knows of. I works for Marse John just the same for a long time. He say one morning, "John, you can go out in the field iffen you wants to or you can get out iffen you wants to, 'cause the government say you is free. If you wants to work I'll feed you and give you clothes but can't pay you no money. I ain't got none." Humph, I didn't know nothing what money was, nohow, but I knows I'll git plenty victuals to eat, so I stays till Old Marse die and Old Miss git shut of the place. Then I gits me a job farming, and when I gits too old for that I does this and that for white folks, like fixing yards.

I's black and just a poor old nigger, but I reverence my white folks 'cause they reared me up in the right way. If colored folks pay 'tention and listen to what the white folks tell them, the world would be a heap better off. Us old niggers knows that's the truth, too, 'cause we larns respect and manners from our white folks, and on the great day of judgment my white folks is gwine to meet me and shake hands with me and be glad to see me. Yes, sir, that's the truth!

> Neither slavery nor involuntary servitude, except as a punishment for crime whereof the party shall have been duly convicted, shall exist within the United States, or any place subject to their jurisdiction.
>
> *Thirteenth Amendment to the U.S. Constitution, 1865*

PRESIDENT LINCOLN'S RECONSTRUCTION PLANS

by Maureen Wolfgarth

President Abraham Lincoln, foreseeing an eventual Union victory, planned for the South's restoration to the Union as early as 1862. He rarely used the word "reconstruction," preferring the term "restoration" instead. He looked forward to governing a reunited nation during a time of peace.

Lincoln wanted to get the southern states back into the Union as painlessly and as quickly as possible. The president did not want the South punished. He once remarked, "I do not intend to hurt the hair of a single man in the South if it can possibly be avoided." He strongly supported General Ulysses S. Grant's surrender terms at Appomattox Court House, Virginia, in April 1865. Although the Army of Northern Virginia was to disband, the soldiers were permitted to keep their horses and mules and were given food rations by the Union army. Two days after this surrender, Lincoln spoke of the South's reconstruction. He knew there would be problems "fraught with great difficulty," but he proposed that everyone work together in "restoring the practical relations between these states and the Union."

Lincoln wanted the South to be able to rebuild the homes and cities that had been destroyed in the war. His desire was for government departments, including the U.S. Post Office and the U.S. Treasury, to continue working as though the South had never seceded.

Lincoln first presented his Amnesty Proclamation to Congress on December 8, 1863. Using his executive powers, the president proposed to offer pardons, with some exceptions, to anyone in the Confederacy who would take an oath to support "the Constitution of the United States and the Union of the States thereunder." Also called the ten percent plan, this proposal called for presidential recognition of a state government if only ten percent of the state's voters (those who voted in the 1860 presidential election) would take this oath of allegiance.

Lincoln actually attempted these restoration policies in several Confederate areas that had been recaptured by Federal troops. In early 1862, he appointed a military governor in Tennessee. Soon Louisiana, Arkansas, Florida, and North Carolina followed suit. The president wanted these leaders to establish governments loyal to the U.S. government. They were to grant citizenship to anyone who took an oath of allegiance to the United States.

African American laborers work on a wharf on Virginia's James River.

But things did not run as smoothly as the president had hoped. First, Confederate troops were still active in these areas, and the Union position was not firmly established. Also, there was a question of who should be permitted to take the oath. Could the Confederates be trusted to remain loyal? In addition, political unrest still plagued these states, as politicians disagreed about many of the problems facing the reestablishment of a state's government. Who should be allowed to hold office? How and when should elections be held? Finally, the slavery issue remained unsettled.

Although most of Congress supported the ten percent plan, the opposition drafted the Wade-Davis bill in 1864. Introduced by Senator Benjamin F. Wade and Representative Henry Winter Davis, this bill gave Congress a bigger role in Reconstruction. It further limited those who would be eligible to vote and prohibited slavery in the reconstructed states.

Some support for the Wade-Davis bill came from those congressmen who wanted the legislative, rather than the executive, branch to have the most power in establishing Reconstruction policies. Lincoln, unwilling to be committed to any single formula for Reconstruction and believing that Congress did not have the authority to abolish slavery, pocket-vetoed the bill.

Lincoln was convinced that this restoration policy would form a solid foundation for reunification. He wanted the South to return to the Union. He spoke of forgiveness when he stated, "We must not sully victory with harshness." But Lincoln was unable to carry out his plans. When John Wilkes Booth ended Lincoln's life in April 1865, he harmed the South far more than he helped it. For when Abraham Lincoln died, not only did the North lose a leader, but the South lost a true friend.

By 1867, almost every county in the South had at least one school for African Americans, old and young.

RELIEF AND EDUCATION
Freedmen's Bureau

The federal government created the Freedmen's Bureau to administer emergency assistance to former slaves and white southerners after the war. The Bureau's volunteers set up schools, fed the hungry, found temporary housing for the homeless, and helped the freed slaves adjust to their new lives. Journalist John T. Trowbridge from Massachusetts wrote about his observations of a school run by the Freedmen's Bureau. An excerpt from his work follows.*

There were three thousand pupils in the freedmen's schools. The teachers for these were furnished, here as elsewhere, chiefly by benevolent societies in the North. Such of the citizens as did not oppose the education of the blacks, were generally silent about it. Nobody said of it, "That is freedom! That is what the Yankees are doing for them!"

Visiting these schools in nearly all the Southern States, I did not hear of the white people taking any interest in them. With the exception of here and there a man or woman inspired by Northern principles, I never saw or heard of a Southern citizen, male or female, entering one of those humble school-rooms....

The wonder with me was, how these "best friends" could be so utterly careless of the intellectual and moral interests of the freedmen. For my own part, I could never enter one of those schools without emotion. They were often held in old buildings and sheds good for little else. There was not a school room in Tennessee furnished with appropriate seats and desks. I found a similar condition of things in all the States. The pews of colored churches, or plain benches in the vestries, or old chairs with boards laid across them in some loft over a shop, or out-of-doors on the grass in summer, — such was the usual scene of the freedmen's schools.

...I never visited one of any size in which there were not two or three or half a dozen children so nearly white that no one would have suspected the

From Cheryl Edwards, ed., *Reconstruction: Binding the Wounds,* Perspectives on History Series, pp. 25–27. Copyright © 1995 Discovery Enterprises, Ltd., Carlisle, Massachusetts.

*From *A Picture of the Desolated States and the Work of Restoration* by J.T. Trowbridge (Hartford, Conn., 1868).

A classroom in a Mississippi freedmen's school.

negro taint. From these, the complexion ranges through all the indescribable mixed hues, to the shining iron black of a few pure-blooded Africans, perhaps not more in number than the seemingly pure-blooded whites. The younger the generation, the lighter the average skin; by which curious fact one perceives how fast the race was bleaching under the "peculiar" system or slavery.

· ·

Mary Ames's Diary

As a young woman from Boston, Mary Ames volunteered to become a teacher. In 1865, she went to South Carolina to teach former slaves how to read and write.*

The school was in a building once used as a billiard room, which accommodated a large number of pupils. We often had a hundred and twenty, and when word went forth that supplies had come, the number increased. Indeed, it was so crowded that we told the men and women they must stay away to leave space for the children, as we considered teaching them more important....

When we made out the school report to send to Boston, we were surprised that out of the hundred, only three children knew their age, nor had they the slightest idea of it; one large boy told me he was "Three months old." The next day many of them brought pieces of wood or bits of paper with straight marks made on them to show how many years they had lived. One boy brought a family record written in a small book....

In January smallpox broke out among the soldiers quartered on our place. Many of our scholars took it, and we closed the school for five weeks. We escaped, although in continual danger, for the negroes, even when repulsively sick, were so eager for our gifts of clothing that they forced their way to our very bedrooms, and our carryall, drawn by men, was used to carry the patients to the improvised hospital.... When on Monday, February twenty-sixth, we began school again, we had thirteen pupils. One of them, when asked if there was smallpox at her plantation, answered, "No, the last one died Saturday." On the third day one hundred children had come back.

*From Mary Ames, *From a New England Woman's Diary in Dixie in 1865* (Springfield, 1906).

★ ★ ★ ★ ★ ★ ★ ★ ★

CARPETBAGGERS AND SCALAWAGS

*R*econstruction governments were made up of African Americans, white southerners, and northerners. The northerners who went South to serve in the Reconstruction governments were called carpetbaggers. The term comes from the fact that they carried their belongings in large cloth bags.

Most carpetbaggers were good people who wanted to help both blacks and whites. Some worked for the Freedmen's Bureau, others were businessmen who came to invest their money. Also, many ex-Union soldiers decided to stay and help rebuild the Southern states. Many white southerners resented the carpetbaggers for several reasons. Primarily, the white southerners disliked northerners running their governments, and disapproved of the carpet-baggers' acceptance of African Americans as their equals.

Scalawags were southern natives who worked with African Americans and white southerners for their own personal gain. Most wanted to make fast money and gain political power. They often took advantage of people and gained a reputation of being ruthless.

From Cheryl Edwards, ed., *Reconstruction: Binding the Wounds,* Perspectives on History Series, pp. 43–45. Copyright © 1995 Discovery Enterprises, Ltd., Carlisle, Massachusetts.

Horace Greeley Campaigns

In 1872, the Liberal Republicans nominated
Horace Greeley, a newspaper editor,
to run as their presidential candidate.
Greeley ran against President Grant, a Republican.
During the campaign, Grant was blamed
for the failure of Reconstruction.
Carpetbaggers were also blamed and were
an easy target for critics. In this excerpt from a
speech given by Horace Greeley in 1871,
Greeley attacks carpetbaggers.*

The thieving carpet-baggers are a mournful fact;
they do exist there, and I have seen them. They are
fellows who crawled down South in the track of our
armies, generally at a very safe distance in the rear;

*From the *Chicago Tribune,* which serialized the speech on June 14, July 18, 24, August 14, 26, 1872. From *Those Terrible Carpetbaggers,* by Richard Nelson Current (New York: Oxford University Press, 1988).

From left to right: Senator H.R. Revels of Mississippi; Benjamin S. Turner of Alabama; Robert C. DeLarge of South Carolina; Josiah T. Walls of Florida; Jefferson H. Long of Georgia; Joseph H. Rainey of South Carolina; and R. Brown Elliott of South Carolina.

★ ★ ★ ★ ★ ★ ★ ★ ★

BLACK RECONSTRUCTIONISTS

Blacks in Office

During Reconstruction, African Americans were elected to public office. However, public opinion was not in their favor. Many whites argued that their lack of education and skills prevented them from carrying out their political jobs effectively. Despite the disadvantages of a lack of education and experience, black lawmakers were successful at helping to draft new state constitutions. These constitutions withstood the test of time, and did not need to be rewritten until long after Reconstruction had ended.

The first African American to be elected to the United States Senate was Hiram R. Revels of Mississippi. He was elected by the Mississippi legislature to serve the unexpired term of Jefferson Davis. Many Senators expressed opposition to the seating of Revels. They cited the fact that Revels did not meet the constitutional requirement of being a U.S. citizen for nine years prior to becoming a United States Senator. According to the law, African Americans had just recently attained citizenship, a point used by critics to try to block Revels from being seated.

In the following passages taken from debates in the U.S. Senate and House of Representatives, Senator Garret Davis of Kentucky and Senator James

Nye of Nevada express their opposing opinions on seating a "Negro" in the United States Senate.*

Mr. President, this is certainly a morbid state of affairs. Never before in the history of this government has a colored man been elected to the Senate of the United States. To-day for the first time one presents himself and asks admission to a seat in it. How does he get here? Did he come here by the free voices by the spontaneous choice of the free people of Mississippi? No, sir; no. The sword of a military dictator has opened the way for his easy march to the Senate of the United States....

Senator James Nye of Nevada replies to Davis of Kentucky.

Sir, it seems to me that this is the crowning glory of a long series of measures. It seems to me that this is the day long looked for, when we put into practical effect the theory that has existed as old as man. We say that all the men are brothers; whatever their color all are subject to the same law, and all are eligible to fill any place within the gift of the people.

Is the honorable Senator from Kentucky afraid to enter in the race for future glory with these colored men?...

From Cheryl Edwards, ed., *Reconstruction: Binding the Wounds,* Perspectives on History Series, pp. 40–42. Copyright © 1995 Discovery Enterprises, Ltd., Carlisle, Massachusetts.

*Reprinted with the permission of Simon & Schuster from *Black Reconstructionists: Great Lives Observed,* edited by E.L. Thornborough. Copyright © 1972 by Prentice-Hall, Inc.

An Outsider Considers
Black Reconstructionists

Sometimes an outsider's opinion of a country's political problems gives a more objective view of the situation. This selection offers the viewpoint of Sir George Campbell, an English traveler, who toured the Southern states after the fall of the Republican governments. It presents Campbell's views on black Reconstructionists.*

During the last dozen years the negroes have had a very large share of political education. Considering the troubles and the ups and downs that they have gone through, it is, I think, wonderful how benefi-cial this education has been to them, and how much these people, so lately in the most debased condition of slavery, have acquired independent ideas, and, far from lapsing into anarchy, have become citizens with ideas of law and property and order. The white serfs of European countries took hundreds of years to rise to the level which these negroes have attained in a dozen....

On the whole, then, I am inclined to believe that the period of Carpet-bag rule was rather a scandal than a very permanent injury. The black men used their victory with moderation, although the women were sometimes dangerous, and there was more pil-fering than plunder on a scale permanently to crip-ple the State.

*Reprinted with the permission of Simon & Schuster from *Black Reconstructionists: Great Lives Observed,* edited by E.L. Thornborough. Copyright © 1972 by Prentice-Hall, Inc.

THE FIRST BLACK CONGRESSMEN

by Betty Little

Although President Abraham Lincoln's Emancipation Proclamation of 1863 freed the slaves in the Confederate states, many new laws and other changes were needed to guarantee African Americans full civil rights. One of the impor-tant rights gained by African American men during Reconstruction was the right to vote. This right resulted in African American candidates being elected to posi-tions in the state and federal governments.

Northerners held the majority of seats in Congress during Reconstruction, and they supported laws protecting African Americans' rights. They wanted to prevent the South from becoming as strong as it had been before the Civil War. They believed that southern African American voters would elect politicians who agreed with the policies of northerners and that this would keep the South weak.

Between 1869 and 1901, African Americans were more widely represented in legislative bodies than at any other time up to the 1970s. During those years, twenty-two African Americans served in the U.S. Congress. Twenty were repre-sentatives; two were senators.

Of the twenty African American representatives, twelve were ex-slaves and eight were born free. Many had gained experience in politics by serving in state legislatures, holding appointed political positions, or practicing law. Some were self-educated; others were college graduates. They were ministers, teachers, farmers, and businessmen.

John Willis Menard of Louisiana was the first African American elected to Congress. His election was challenged, however, and he never took his seat. In 1869, Georgia elected Jefferson Long, the first African American to be seated in Congress.

John Mercer Langston

Langston (1829–1897) is considered to be the first African American to hold public office, becoming the town clerk of Brownhelm, Ohio, in 1855. He went on to become inspector general of the Freedmen's Bureau, professor of law and dean at Howard University, and a U.S. representative.

TWO AFRICAN AMERICAN SENATORS

by Betty Little

Hiram Rhoades Revels, the first African American U.S. senator, represented Mississippi from 1870 to 1871. He was elected to finish the term of Jefferson Davis, the former president of the Confederacy.

Born of free parents in North Carolina, Revels studied and was ordained in the African Methodist Episcopal ministry. He served as an army chaplain during the Civil War. In 1868, he won election as a city councilman and two years later as a Mississippi state senator.

As a U.S. senator, Revels helped African American mechanics obtain jobs at a U.S. Navy shipyard, and he favored restoring the rights of former Confederates to vote and to hold office. After his Senate term ended, Revels became a college president.

Blanche Kelso Bruce, the first African American to serve a full term in the Senate, represented Mississippi from 1875 to 1881. He was born a slave in Virginia but escaped to the Northwest when his master joined the Confederate army. There he started schools for African Americans.

Bruce studied for two years at Oberlin College in Ohio and entered Mississippi politics in 1868. He held several offices, including sheriff, tax collector, school superintendent, and sergeant-at-arms in Mississippi's state senate. The Mississippi legislature elected him to the U.S. Senate in 1874.

Senator Bruce worked for American Indians' rights and for improvements in racial harmony and education.

Blanche Kelso Bruce

John R. Lynch of Mississippi and Josiah T. Walls of Florida each served three terms. John Mercer Langston, an Oberlin College graduate and a lawyer, represented Virginia for one term. Charles E. Nash was the only representative elected and seated in Congress from Louisiana.

Alabama sent three representatives to Congress: Jeremiah Haralson, James T. Rapier, and Benjamin Sterling Turner. Each man served one term. James E. O'Hara, a practicing attorney, and Henry P. Cheatham, a school principal, both served two terms for North Carolina. John S. Hyman, also of North Carolina, served one term.

South Carolina elected eight representatives, more than any other state. Richard Cain, Robert Brown Elliott, and George W. Murray each completed three terms. Elected to one term each were Robert DeLarge, Thomas Ezekiel Miller, and Alonzo J. Ransier.

Only two African Americans served more than three terms as representatives. Joseph Hayne Rainey and Robert Smalls, both of South Carolina, each completed five terms in Congress.

These congressmen spoke out on many important issues. Their attempts to create laws seldom reached the voting stage, however, because they lacked the necessary influence within the full House of Representatives.

The African American congressmen concerned themselves not only with civil rights for African Americans but also with civil rights for American Indians and former Confederates, who had had some of their rights taken away as punishment for rebelling against the Union. They spoke out for changes in election policies and education, and they advocated antilynching laws. James G. Blaine, a white Republican leader, praised them highly: "They were, as a rule, studious, earnest, ambitious men, whose public conduct...would be honorable to any race."

RECONSTRUCTION AND THE FIVE CIVILIZED TRIBES

by Otis Hays, Jr.

In September 1865, chiefs of the Cherokee, Creek, Seminole, Choctaw, and Chickasaw nations (known as the Five Civilized Tribes) were called to meet with U.S. Indian affairs commissioners to discuss plans for Reconstruction. Major portions of the five Indian nations had supported the Confederacy during the war. The leaders now would learn what their people could expect for having done so. They feared that the penalties would be harsh, and they were right. Reconstruction would gradually destroy their independence.

A generation earlier, the United States had sought the removal of the tribes from the southeastern states to "Indian country" west of the Mississippi River. Under pressure from the U.S. government, Indian leaders reluctantly signed treaties that surrendered one hundred million acres of Indian land in North Carolina, Georgia, Florida, and Mississippi. In exchange, they received thirty-two million acres in Indian Territory (Oklahoma).

About fifty thousand Indians abandoned their hereditary homes and were herded westward under military guard. The Cherokee ordeal has come to be known as the Trail of Tears. The suffering of the other four tribes was equally great.

Although most of the Indians survived the horrors of relocation, internal conflict arose when they arrived in their new homeland. Those who supported and those who opposed the signing of the removal treaties turned on one another, with bloody results. Eventually, the violence ceased, as the leaders persuaded their people to live together in peace.

Guthrie, Oklahoma, 1893 — "Opening the Cherokee Strip in Oklahoma Territory."

The removal treaties awarded a large tract of land to each tribe, and national boundaries separated the tribes. To govern themselves, the tribes adopted constitutions that combined democratic principles based on U.S. law and Indian traditions. Tribal laws were written and in turn enforced by Indian courts.

Most of the families lived on farm homesteads, while others bought slaves and built large plantations. By 1860, many of the Indians were living comfortably, but their peace was shattered when the Civil War erupted.

Most of the Indian slave owners were members of the Choctaw and Chickasaw nations, and those two tribes quickly gave their support to the Confederacy. In the other three nations, internal conflict raged, as pro-Union and pro-Confederate factions clashed. Regiments of Indian troops fought in several Civil War battles, often on opposing sides, both in Indian Territory and elsewhere.

In 1885, a wagon train leaves Arkansas City after abandoning its plans to invade Indian Territory and settle in Oklahoma. This territory had been divided up among various Indian tribes after they were forced to leave their homelands. Whites were not allowed to settle there.

As the fortunes of the Confederacy declined, so did those of the Indians, regardless of their allegiance. Not only were the Indians killing one another, but their homes were abandoned or burned, fields were untilled, and cattle were scattered and unclaimed. Even before the end of the Civil War, chaos consumed the tribes.

The leaders of the tribes grimly awaited the details of Reconstruction. At the 1865 meeting with the Indian affairs commissioners, they were told that the "Great Father" (President Andrew Johnson) was willing to return his "erring children" to his arms. But the "forgiving father" imposed the following conditions:

☞ The Indians' slaves would be freed.

☞ U.S. Army posts would be built in the midst of the five nations.

☞ Railroads would be granted rights of way through Indian lands.

☞ Some of the western lands given to the tribes by the removal treaties would be surrendered for white settlements and for the use of other Indian tribes.

☞ Measures would be introduced that would eventually lead to U.S. territorial government for Indian Territory.

While the five tribes were adjusting to the Reconstruction edicts, they rebuilt their homes and began to regain their prosperity. The new railroads that crisscrossed Indian lands carried masses of white settlers into the area, however, and soon non-Indians outnumbered Indians by three to one. The non-Indians demanded changes in each tribe's national political structure and legal system. Gradually, these changes occurred.

In 1890, Oklahoma Territory was created in the eastern part of what is now the state of Oklahoma. The five Indian nations still existed outside the new territory but not for long. In 1898, Congress abolished the Indian courts and placed everyone, Indian and non-Indian alike, under U.S. law enforced by U.S. courts. Finally, in 1906, the Five Civilized Tribes agreed to abolish the remnants of their national governments. The following year, Oklahoma entered the Union as the forty-sixth state.

CHIEF RED CLOUD VISITS THE GREAT WHITE FATHER

by Nancy Whitelaw

Red Cloud was a chief of the Oglala Sioux. His tribe lived for a long time in the northwestern part of Nebraska, above the North Platte River, and hunted in the beautiful Powder River country, in what is now Montana and Wyoming. It was to defend that country against white settlers that Chief Red Cloud led a great fight not long after the Civil War. That fight ended in 1868 with the white men signing a treaty that promised to leave the Powder River hunting grounds to the Indians forever. Red Cloud was the only Indian chief ever to win a war with the United States.

But the people who had interpreted the treaty for the Indians had not told them everything that was in it. From 1868 to 1870, Red Cloud's people battled the U.S. Army. The Army was trying to build a road through the Powder River land for pioneers going to Montana. Red Cloud thought that no white people should be in his territory, so his warriors harassed the road builders.

Then in 1870, Ely Parker, President Ulysses S. Grant's commissioner of Indian affairs, asked Red Cloud to come to Washington. Parker was as Iroquois Indian who understood both sides of the conflict, and he hoped that they could agree on the treaty and end the fighting. Red Cloud accepted the invitation.

When Chief Red Cloud and the other nineteen Sioux leaders stepped off the train in Washington, D.C., the June sun was hot — hot on the black suits and derby hats of the white government officials who greeted them and hot on the ill-fitting white man's clothing the Indians wore for the visit. The wide cobble-

Red Cloud came to Washington, D.C., in 1870 to discuss the Fort Laramie Treaty, which had been signed in 1868. He is shown here with President Ulysses S. Grant.

stone streets and large buildings were new and fascinating sights to the Indians. But Red Cloud was not on a sightseeing tour. He had come to Washington to tell President Grant to keep white people away from Sioux land in the West. He wanted them to stop attacking his people; stop killing so many buffalo; stop building forts, roads, and railroads; and stop calling the land their own.

The white people who settled on Sioux land said there was plenty of land for both whites and Indians. "We need to travel on the western road," they said. "We need forts so we won't have to worry about Indian attacks."

Red Cloud had traveled reluctantly from the only land he had ever known. He had come east to settle this matter with the Great White Father once and for all. He spent his first few days in Washington with Ely Parker. Parker wanted to find out what the Sioux wanted so that he could be fair to them. He knew that not many other government officials had asked Red Cloud his side of the story. After Red Cloud had explained the Indians' complaints, Parker arranged a meeting with Jacob Cox, secretary of the interior.

At the meeting, Secretary Cox spoke: "We will be glad to hear what you have to say. We want to be friends with you." He talked on and on about how important it was to have peace. He told them that the Great White Father always acted in the right way.

Red Cloud answered him: "I have come here to tell the Great White Father what I do not like in this country. White people have surrounded me and have left me nothing but an island. When we first had this land, we were strong. Now we are melting like snow on the hillsides, while you are growing like spring grass. Move your forts away from us. Stop making roads through our hunting grounds."

Cox was silent, but Parker said that he would tell President Grant what Red Cloud had said.

The meeting with the president was on June 9. Red Cloud repeated what he had said in the previous meeting. As Grant listened, he realized that the Indians had not been told what the treaty said when they had signed it in 1868. After the meeting, he told Parker and Cox to tell the Indians the truth.

The next morning, Red Cloud and the others were escorted to the Senate gallery. They sat quietly while the strange words floated up to them. After they had heard the real meaning of the treaty, Red Cloud said, "This is the first time I have heard of such a treaty. I have never heard of it and I do not mean to follow it." He and the other Sioux stalked out of the meeting. Back at their hotel, they planned to go home. "Staying here is no use," they agreed.

But Parker kept them from leaving. He knew that the government wanted peace with Red Cloud. He told the Indians that he was sure the treaty could be interpreted in a way that was fairer to them.

The next day, they listened to Secretary Cox explain that there must have been a misunderstanding. He interpreted the treaty the same way they did. After listening to Cox, Red Cloud shook hands with him. The great chief said, "Yesterday when I saw the false treaty, I was angry. Now I am pleased. I do not want to make war with the Great White Father. I want to raise my children on my land. Let the Great White Father keep his children away from me. Now I go away in peace."

Red Cloud's visit to Washington helped to ease the tensions between whites and Indians, but only for a short while. The whites continued to think of the Indians as savages who were controlling land that was not theirs. The Indians continued to believe that the land of their fathers and their fathers' fathers belonged to them.

THE WINTER CAMPAIGN OF 1868–69

by Beth Haverkamp, National Archives

Led by the few white officers who would serve with them, African American troops often were segregated from white troops and assigned the most undesirable, dangerous, and monotonous duties. Yet they performed their missions with great courage and spirit.

Typical assignments for the Tenth Cavalry are detailed in archival documents housed in the National Archives. Records there reveal that in the winter of 1868–69, buffalo soldiers of the Tenth Cavalry were scattered among Forts Cobb and Arbuckle (also spelled Arbukle) in Indian Territory and Fort Lyon in Colorado Territory. Some soldiers guarded captured Indians; others patrolled the Kansas border.

On November 10, 1868, B, F, G, and K companies of the Tenth Cavalry left Fort Lyon under the leadership of Brigadier General W.H. Penrose. Their mission was to patrol the North Canadian River basin for Comanche warriors. When located, those warriors were to be driven south toward masses of waiting U.S. troops, who would then relocate the Comanches to reservations.

The soldiers left Fort Lyon with

THE TENTH CAVALRY

Colonel Grierson and the Tenth Cavalry

by Leonard Weisenberg

Colored troops will hold their place in the army of the United States as long as the government lasts," Colonel Benjamin Grierson wrote to his wife in the spring of 1867.

Grierson, who was white, wrote from Fort Leavenworth, Kansas, where he had taken command of the Tenth Cavalry, one of the first regiments of African American soldiers. Grierson had been a distinguished cavalry officer in the Civil War and had been recommended to the peacetime position by General Ulysses S. Grant.

From the start, Grierson and his raw recruits experienced prejudice from the fort commander, General William Hoffman. The Tenth Cavalry was ordered to camp on low, swampy ground and to keep ten to fifteen yards away from the white troops during inspection. Once, at Mrs. Grierson's suggestion, a Christmas party was planned for the entire garrison at Fort Concho, Texas. Some of the white officers and soldiers refused to share the recreation hall with the African Americans, however, forcing them to hold their celebration in an empty warehouse.

Grierson and his wife shared a genuine concern for and commitment to the men of the Tenth. Grierson fought petty prejudices at every turn and insisted on better treatment for his men. He did all he could to make their hard and lonely life tolerable, including organizing a regimental band.

Grierson commanded the Tenth Cavalry for twenty-two years. His troopers fought and patrolled from Oklahoma to West Texas at a time when the Indian wars were reaching their peak. He predicted that the buffalo soldiers could not "fail — sooner or later — to meet with due recognition and reward." It would not be until 1992 that General Colin Powell, chairman of the Joint Chiefs of Staff, unveiled a monument dedicated to the African American frontier cavalrymen at Fort Leavenworth. In 1994, the U.S. Postal Service issued a special stamp commemorating the buffalo soldiers' legacy of courage and honor.

enough food for forty-three days. Penrose estimated that they would reach their destination in less than a month, but he carried extra supplies as a precaution. Five days into the journey, a blizzard struck. Penrose commanded his troops to make camp, but the land was barren, and they found neither firewood nor buffalo chips (waste from bison) to burn. When the storm subsided, Penrose urged his men onward. Twenty-five horses, suffering under the supply burden and treacherous snow, had to be shot.

The buffalo soldiers trudged toward their rendezvous point as temperatures plummeted below zero. Eventually, the troops could travel no farther. Their half-frozen scouts ventured away from base camp but could find neither Indians nor the troop reinforcements they were supposed to meet, led by General E.A. Carr. Many men suffered from frostbite. Supplies ran so low that the men received only a half ration daily. Penrose gave orders to stop feeding the horses altogether. The soldiers, however, never wavered. They took care of each other, rubbing their comrades' frozen toes and sewing makeshift boots from the pelts of dead animals.

In late December, two scouts encountered "Buffalo Bill" Cody, chief scout for General Carr. Carr established a supply post for the two commands at San Francisco Creek and then took five hundred of the strongest men to North Canadian Creek. In January, the troops learned that the Comanches had been driven to the southeast as planned. There was nothing left for the buffalo soldiers to do but plod patiently back to Fort Lyon. The weary soldiers arrived there on February 19, 1869.

Although the buffalo soldiers' greatest risks during the winter campaign of 1868–69 proved to be lack of food and exposure to freezing weather and howling winds, they served the growing nation with unwavering courage.

Benjamin Henry Grierson

THE LAST CRUSADE OF FREDERICK DOUGLASS

by Abby Arthur Johnson and Ronald Johnson

In 1889, in an address titled "The Nation's Problem," Douglass emphasized the source of racial conflict in the United States.

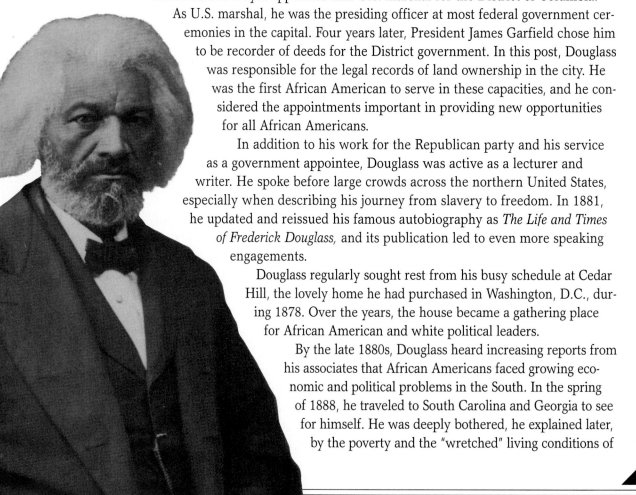

In the final years of his life, Frederick Douglass again became a crusader for racial justice. As he had done before the Civil War, Douglass spoke out forcefully against those Americans who would deny African Americans their civil rights. He talked bluntly about the failure of the federal government to honor its promise to help African Americans achieve political equality. He lamented the passage of laws segregating African Americans and the increased number of lynchings in the South. As his sense of outrage deepened, Douglass committed himself to reversing these unfortunate developments.

This rebirth of Douglass as a moral crusader came about during the late 1880s, as his doubts increased over whether the Republican party would continue to advance the interests of African Americans. Earlier, throughout the 1870s and most of the 1880s, he had regularly praised the Republicans as "the party of Abraham Lincoln." Douglass especially endorsed their efforts to assist former slaves in becoming full and productive citizens. During the 1872, 1876, 1880, and 1884 presidential elections, he worked hard for the party, calling vigorously for northern voters to support Republican policies.

For his efforts on behalf of Republican candidates, party leaders awarded Douglass with a series of federal positions. In 1877, for example, President Rutherford B. Hayes appointed him U.S. marshal for the District of Columbia. As U.S. marshal, he was the presiding officer at most federal government ceremonies in the capital. Four years later, President James Garfield chose him to be recorder of deeds for the District government. In this post, Douglass was responsible for the legal records of land ownership in the city. He was the first African American to serve in these capacities, and he considered the appointments important in providing new opportunities for all African Americans.

In addition to his work for the Republican party and his service as a government appointee, Douglass was active as a lecturer and writer. He spoke before large crowds across the northern United States, especially when describing his journey from slavery to freedom. In 1881, he updated and reissued his famous autobiography as *The Life and Times of Frederick Douglass,* and its publication led to even more speaking engagements.

Douglass regularly sought rest from his busy schedule at Cedar Hill, the lovely home he had purchased in Washington, D.C., during 1878. Over the years, the house became a gathering place for African American and white political leaders.

By the late 1880s, Douglass heard increasing reports from his associates that African Americans faced growing economic and political problems in the South. In the spring of 1888, he traveled to South Carolina and Georgia to see for himself. He was deeply bothered, he explained later, by the poverty and the "wretched" living conditions of

African American sharecroppers and their families.

He initially blamed President Grover Cleveland and the Democrats for these developments. Over the next two years, he came to a different conclusion: Both the Republican and Democratic parties were guilty of turning their backs on the needs of African Americans. He spoke out more and more about the failure of whites, northern and southern alike, to respect the basic rights of African Americans.

Disappointed and angry, Douglass began to talk with his old fire about the right of African Americans to live free from persecution. He wrote a series of speeches and articles denouncing those who were trying to take the vote away from African Americans and make them second-class citizens.

Frederick Douglass is buried in Mount Hope Cemetery in Rochester, New York.

In 1889, in an address titled "The Nation's Problem," Douglass emphasized the source of racial conflict in the United States: the failure of whites to accept African Americans on an equal basis. In so doing, he expressed dissatisfaction with all politicians, both Democrats and Republicans. He was particularly unhappy with African Americans and whites who were urging African Americans to return to Africa in the face of growing racial hostility. He rejected all such proposals and insisted that the United States represented the only home for African Americans.

That same year, the new president, Republican Benjamin Harrison, appointed Douglass consul general to Haiti. Douglass believed it was an honor to represent the United States, and he got along well with the Haitians. Before long, however, the U.S. government was pushing to establish a naval base in Haiti, a plan most Haitians opposed. Douglass refused to exert diplomatic pressure on the Haitian government, which eventually turned down the U.S. request. The press blamed Douglass for this refusal, and, suffering from ill health, he resigned the consulship and returned to the United States in 1891.

In 1894, Douglass issued a pamphlet titled *The Lesson of the Hour: Why the Negro Is Lynched.* He boldly ridiculed the idea of "a Negro problem" as a distortion of the truth. Douglass stated that the facts instead revealed a white problem with racial equality and that this was the cause of brutal acts such as lynchings. In the same essay, he identified the Republicans as "the party of money," a statement indicating his growing differences with the party he had served for so long.

Douglass died on February 20, 1895, from a heart attack. He was seventy-seven years old. After a funeral in Washington, he was buried in Rochester, New York, the city where he had raised his family.

At the time of his death, Douglass was ready to launch a new moral crusade similar to the one he had joined almost fifty years earlier. As he had done in the battle to end slavery, he called on white Americans to search their hearts, to reject racial segregation and the use of violence to enforce it, and to accept African Americans as equals. With these fiery proclamations at the end of his life, Douglass prepared the way for the civil rights movement of the twentieth century.

7

· · · · · · · · · · · · · · · · · · · ·

INDUSTRY AND IMMIGRATION

Some historians argue that America changed more rapidly between 1865 and 1900 than it had during the first eighty years of its existence. Certainly, no one who fought in the American Revolution would have recognized the country that greeted the new century.

Industrial might made the United States stronger, and richer, than ever before. Immigration brought eager new citizens to its shores. But new industries and new immigrants brought with them new problems. Concern grew over the right of workers to a fair wage and reasonable working hours. Meanwhile, some Americans objected to the new wave of "foreigners" flooding our shores.

As this chapter shows, the last three and a half decades of the nineteenth century meant startlingly different things to different people. Some Americans prospered, but others suffered. To a new generation of millionaires, the so-called Gilded Age meant comfort and power.

But to those who immigrated here in search of streets they had heard were paved with gold, the Gilded Age brought good fortune only to others.

THE STORY OF AMERICA'S INDUSTRIAL REVOLUTION

by Kathleen Burke

"To be independent for the comforts of life," wrote Thomas Jefferson in 1816, "we must make them ourselves." He addressed an issue that aroused great concern in the fledgling United States: the need for the young nation to produce its own goods.

Even after the United States won its independence at the close of the Revolutionary War in 1781, the country remained dependent on England in a funda-

Samuel Slater

To understand the genius of Samuel Slater, often called the father of the American Industrial Revolution, visit Slater Mill in Pawtucket, Rhode Island (top). Slater built the first successful water-powered cotton mill in the United States in 1793. Moses Brown gave Slater his start, putting Slater's inventions to use in his mill.

Moses Brown

mental way. Manufactured goods of every description — glass, pottery, tools, woolen cloth, and cotton prints — still arrived in shipments from bustling British ports. In return, Americans traded the raw materials that formed the wealth of the new nation. Manufacturing in America took place on a very small scale, and the major industries (flour milling, lumbering, and shipbuilding) were based on natural resources.

This uneasy relationship with England came to an abrupt end in 1812, when the United States again declared war. The British navy had interfered with American shipping, seizing cargo bound for England's archrival, France, and kidnapping American sailors for service in the Royal Navy. As soon as Congress declared war, all trade with England ceased.

The result was that the articles formerly supplied by Britain had to be produced at home. Fortunately, a handful of farsighted pioneers had paved the way for America's emergence as a great commercial nation. Among them was Samuel Slater, today known as the father of the American Industrial Revolution.

Slater, an immigrant from England, arrived in Pawtucket, Rhode Island, in 1789. He brought with him — stored away in his head, for British law forbade the export of plans detailing inventions — methods for constructing advanced new spinning machines powered by water. He took his designs to the Quaker merchant Moses Brown, and soon laborers at Brown's mill were sitting before the new spinning and weaving machines. Before long, they were turning out cotton goods equal in quality to those produced in England.

The American textile industry had been born — but more important, the factory system had arrived. Laborers gathered in centralized workplaces, in those days known as manufactures. When the War of

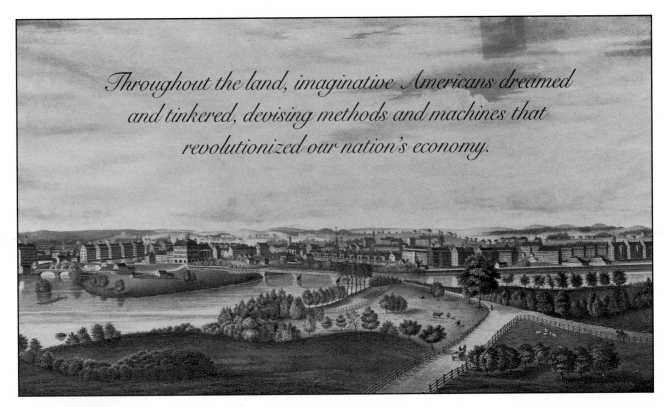

Throughout the land, imaginative Americans dreamed and tinkered, devising methods and machines that revolutionized our nation's economy.

Robert Fulton

1812 ended in 1815, this newfound efficiency in production set the stage for America's becoming a formidable industrial power.

Several inventors had begun to harness the power of steam. As early as 1787, John Fitch built a small steamboat and demonstrated it to the members of the Constitutional Convention in Philadelphia. Robert Fulton's steamboat, the *Clermont,* chugged up the Hudson River from New York City to Albany in 1807. Crowds lining the shore cheered the vessel along the route of its first voyage. In 1832, New Yorker John Stevens established the first steam locomotive company, putting into operation the Camden and Amboy Railroad in New Jersey.

Soon gleaming steel tracks crisscrossed the East and the South. By 1840, the railroad extended across the Mississippi River. A system of canals also cut across the landscape. Steamboats and trains transported raw materials to the factories that were dotting the East.

Eli Whitney, already known for his development of the cotton gin in 1793, introduced his system of interchangeable fittings for guns in 1798. By 1846, another young inventor, Samuel Colt, had improved on Whitney's idea. He instituted the first assembly line, where each worker performed only one or two tasks over and over. An unprecedented and supremely efficient approach

Above: After textile mills were built on the Pawtucket Falls in Rhode Island, the city of Lowell, Massachusetts, located where the Merrimack and Concord rivers meet, became a major textile center.

Left: Fulton built the first commercially successful steamboat, the *Clermont,* in 1807 (see volume 1, page 164).

Eli Whitney

Above: Whitney developed the cotton gin in 1793 and a system of producing interchangeable parts in 1798. Below: McCormick (1809–1884) had a sharp business sense. His mechanical reaper was extremely successful partly because of his decision to mass-produce it.

to production took hold in American industry.

In 1846, Elias Howe invented the sewing machine, and the production of clothing moved from the tailor's shop and the home to the factory.

Another development that propelled America toward industrial prominence was the increased use of iron. As the market for tools, nails, weapons, and utensils grew, more and more smelting furnaces were built. After surveyors discovered vast iron deposits in northern Michigan in 1844, industries producing iron and the refined form of the metal, steel, expanded dramatically. Farsighted investors such as Andrew Carnegie made great fortunes as the demand grew for items such as steel railroad car axles, factory machinery, iron bridges, and metal ships.

Coal mining also was becoming an important industry. Because coal heated more efficiently than wood, companies were quick to convert their iron-smelting furnaces to coal heat.

By 1851, America's growing industrial strength impressed even the prosperous British. At a great exhibition in London in 1851, nations from around the world displayed new machines and intriguing inventions. American machinery and manufactured goods attracted a great deal of interest. In less than fifty years, the nation had moved from dependence on Britain to almost total self-sufficiency in production.

The discovery of oil in Titusville, Pennsylvania, in 1859 opened yet another chapter in the story of America's industrial growth. Oil rigs sprouted up across the Pennsylvania countryside, and inventors began experimenting with uses for the black, sticky liquid. After gasoline was distilled from oil, it was used for the internal combustion engine and eventually for the automobile. Transportation was revolutionized.

The coming of the Civil War in 1861 brought untold tragedy and destruction to the nation. But the war also paved the way for more industrial growth. Factories expanded to meet the need for weapons. The pace of production, particularly in the heavily industrialized North, continued to increase even after the war ended. A new class of businessmen pressed for a national banking system, tax structures that favored large companies, and the extension of railroads to the Pacific Ocean.

Before the beginning of the Industrial Revolution, the average farm family produced enough food to feed two families. After machines, including Cyrus McCormick's mechanical reaper, were introduced to the fields, the same family could grow enough food to feed twelve families. As the demand for agricultural workers decreased, more and more rural laborers flocked to the rapidly growing cities to work in industry.

Of these laborers crowding into the urban workplace, millions were immigrants. From 1869 to 1910, the population of the United States rose from thirty million to about ninety million. As the nation's population increased, so did industrial productivity. By the early 1900s, American manufacturing outranked that of every country in the world.

Cyrus Hall McCormick

Emigrants leave their homes in Ireland for America's promised land.

THE BUILDING OF A CITY

by Mark Travis

In 1822, an Irishman named Hugh Cummiskey led thirty countrymen to a stretch of farmland along the tumbling rapids of a river. In the years to come, those Irishmen and hundreds more who followed dug wide canals and built great brick mills, powered by water from the canals and filled with noisy machines that made cloth. The city that rose along the river, named Lowell, Massachusetts, was America's first great industrial center.

The Irish who came to Lowell were not really welcomed. They seemed wild and rough; they sounded different; and they were Roman Catholic, a religion many New Englanders thought was evil. But when the mill owners realized that they were not leaving, the owners began to help them. They tried to make sure the children attended school and donated land for a church.

In time, the Irish began to seem less like outsiders. The Civil War united northern communities, as men of different ethnicities fought for a common cause. This image is tainted, however, by the fact that many Irishmen were paid to serve as substitutes for wealthy Yankees who did not want to fight in the war.

THE GILDED AGE

by Ellen Hardsog

The American way of life changed dramatically in the years between the end of the Civil War in 1865 and the outbreak of World War I in 1914. Increased industrial productivity and the consequent demand for factory-produced goods shifted the national economy from agriculture to industry and the population from farm to city. Everyone was eager to forget the shame of slavery and civil war and to explore new possibilities for prosperity. America was whole again, and there was no limit to the things Americans could do.

Mark Twain called these years the Gilded Age because of the way the rich tried to imitate the fancy dress, manners, homes, and entertainment of the British upper class. The families of bankers, lawyers, and factory owners enjoyed a fine way of life. The new industries made many millionaires, who drove ornate carriages, attended the opera and theater, and bought expensive toys for their children. They lived in huge mansions and took their vacations at the seashore in even bigger mansions, which they called "summer cottages."

Factory managers, small business owners, and gentlemen farmers also lived well during the Gilded Age. They became known as the middle class because they were neither rich nor poor. They lived in modest homes with new labor-saving devices such as electric lights and telephones. They went to the country for vacations. Many middle-class people traveled by train to visit the Centennial

The Women's Pavilion at the Philadelphia Centennial Exposition in 1876.

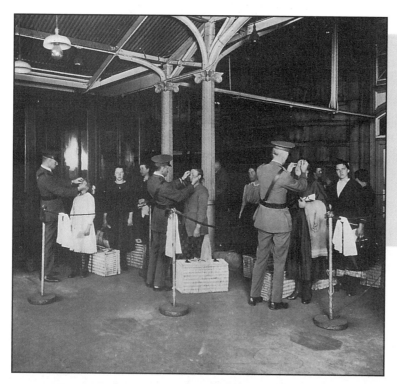

Arriving immigrants are inspected for health problems in 1923 at Ellis Island, a major immigration station that was opened in New York City in 1892.

Officials tried to make sure that immigrants were healthy and that they would be able to support themselves or knew someone.

Runners worked for the owners of boarding houses and businesses. They were paid by the owners to find tenants and workers. The more immigrant tenants and workers a runner brought in, the more the runner was paid. At times, runners would do almost anything to make money, including boarding immigrant ships in the harbor and trying to force the passengers to follow them. Runners were outlawed at Castle Garden.

Later in the 1800s, the federal government began to operate immigration stations. The two major stations were located near the places where most immigrants arrived in this country — New York City on the Atlantic coast and San Francisco on the Pacific. The Ellis Island station in Upper New York Bay opened in 1892. An immigration station on Angel Island in San Francisco Bay opened in 1910.

These stations existed to help immigrants as well as to protect American citizens. Officials at each location tried to make sure that immigrants were healthy and that they would be able to support themselves or knew someone who could help them. In addition, officials were responsible for seeing that immigrants who believed in ideas considered dangerous to the U.S. government did not enter the country.

During the first twenty-five years of the 1900s, federal immigration officials at Ellis Island handled more than twelve million immigrants. Most of these immigrants came from southern and eastern Europe. The Angel Island station served mostly Chinese, Japanese, and Filipino immigrants.

For much of the time the federal immigration stations were in operation, they were the subject of many complaints. People argued that the stations were too isolated, that the buildings were unsafe, that the immigration officials were not treating the immigrants properly, and that the time taken for handling the immigrants was too long. Federal officials responded by saying that the isolation of the islands was one way to prevent problems with runners, even though some officials themselves were working as runners.

The immigrants often complained about the food they received while waiting for their cases to be handled. A sign above the dining hall tables at Angel Island warned the newcomers not to make trouble and not to spill food on the floor. Mealtime protests over the poor quality of the food were not unusual, however.

The buildings at both stations were originally viewed as places that immigrants would pass through quickly, but this was not always the case. They became long-time homes for those who did not meet all of the government's standards at first and for those who were to be sent back to their home country. Also, because security precautions were taken to keep immigrants from leaving the islands, the stations were often used to hold American citizens who were federal prisoners. After several amazing escapes, this use of the stations was discontinued.

Investigations into conditions at the stations continued as long as there were immigrants on Angel and Ellis islands. Nothing was ever resolved. Finally, the Angel Island station was closed after its administration building was destroyed in a large fire in 1940. The Ellis Island station was closed in 1943.

Since the 1940s, both stations have taken on various roles. During World War II, the U.S. Army took over Angel Island and used it as a prisoner of war station. After the war, Angel Island was one of the locations considered as a possible headquarters for the new United Nations. Today it is the headquarters for the California state parks in the San Francisco area.

Between 1943 and 1954, Ellis Island held people being sent out of the country by order of the U.S. government. Starting in 1965, it was considered part of the Statue of Liberty National Monument. Liberty Island, where the Statue of Liberty is located, is near Ellis Island. Since 1976, Ellis Island has been operated by the National Park Service.

Both Angel Island and Ellis Island are now open to tourists. They serve to remind many Americans of their family origins.

Due to the number of immigrants entering California, an immigrant station was built on Angel Island in San Francisco Bay in 1910.

IMMIGRANTS

Even before the final spike was driven into the Utah soil,* the railroads were seeking immigrants for several reasons. First, the settlers would pay the transit fares to their new lands. Second, they would buy land from the railroad, acreage that had been given to the companies by the government as construction incentive. Third, they would purchase freight and goods shipped to them from other areas of the country. Fourth, they would pay to ship their crops to other cities and towns — via the railroad. The companies not only monopolized cross-continental shipment, they controlled the choicest waterfront properties and warehouse locations, extending their influence far beyond the sound of the train's whistle. The companies mounted massive advertising campaigns that stretched or buried the hard truth.

Scandinavians, Germans, Russians, Welshmen, Scots — all were lured to the

From Jeanne Munn Bracken, ed., *Iron Horses Across America: The Transcontinental Railroad,* Perspectives on History Series, pp. 36–37. Copyright © 1995 Discovery Enterprises, Ltd., Carlisle, Massachusetts.

*The transcontinental railroad was built beginning from east and west and met in the middle, in Utah, in 1869.

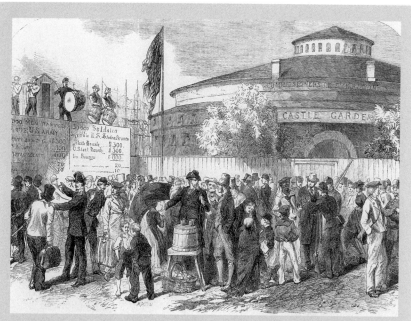

At New York's Castle Garden, Irish and German immigrants are encouraged to enlist in the army in 1864.

GERMAN JEWS:
MAKING A PLACE IN AMERICA

by Brandon Marie Miller

From 1830 to 1880, more than two hundred thousand German Jews immigrated to the United States. In the early years, most were young men from poor villages. Working mostly as peddlers, one of the few jobs Jews had been allowed to do in Europe, they traveled across America. Day after day, Jewish peddlers lugged on their backs items settlers could not make for themselves: pins and needles, buttons, thread, combs, and fabric. Sometimes peddlers were the only link to goods and news from the outside world.

After the 1840s, whole families — sometimes whole villages — of German Jews came to the United States. Many of these immigrants were educated and soon moved into America's middle class as storekeepers, lawyers, and teachers. These Ashkenazic Jews formed strong communities. Proud of their German heritage, they continued to speak German at home, in school, and in the synagogue. Many Jewish weekly newspapers were published in German.

Despite their desire to maintain their German identity, these immigrants were determined to be accepted in their new home. They developed a rich social network; founded hospitals, orphanages, and schools; and raised money to help the poor. Religious reformers called for modernizing some of the old restrictions of their faith. Books on Judaism were translated into English, and German and English versions of a new prayer book, *Minhag America* (The American Custom), was published. This Reform Judaism gathered a large following among German Jewish immigrants.

During the Civil War, Jewish men fought on both sides, but they were not free from anti-Semitism. For instance, in December 1862 General Ulysses S. Grant ordered all Jews to leave his military district in Tennessee within twenty-four hours. Although President Abraham Lincoln revoked the order when Jewish citizens appealed to him for help, the incident was a slap in the face to those who were serving the Union cause.

During this time, some German Jews moved into banking, while others revolutionized the retail trade. Some men, such as Benjamin Bloomingdale and Adam Gimbel, started out as poor peddlers but went on to own some of the world's largest department stores. The decades following the Civil War were the golden age for German-Jewish Americans, as their power and influence helped establish a strong Jewish community in America.

American interior by agents who targeted the poorest of European peasants. Here, they were promised, was the true "Land of Milk and Honey." No mention was made of blizzards, dust storms, insect plagues, periodic droughts, prairie fires and the multitude of other challenges the settlers would face.

The agents outdid themselves with wild assurances. There might not be, they acknowledged, enough wood for fuel, but the settlers could always dig for coal — in Kansas! The fertile soil would yield twenty-pound radishes, four-pound potatoes, massive crops of wheat per acre.

Those worried about vast arid stretches of wilderness were assured that it had been scientifically proven: plowing the land would draw more rain, and locomotives and the railroads themselves would cause more rain to fall. Changing the climate of the great plains was just a masterful stroke of the pen for these corporate liars.

European governments saw an opportunity here. While they were often reluctant to see their citizens leaving their homelands, they also saw a golden opportunity to send some of their less productive folks somewhere else. So paupers and convicts had their passage paid to the New World.

Like the Chinese and Irish before them, these Europeans proved to be made of sturdy stock. Place names all across North America bear reminders even today of those early settlers who may not have found coal in Kansas, but who came and stayed anyway.

The Union Pacific Railroad between Ogden, Utah, and Evanston, Wyoming.

ACROSS THE PLAINS

by Robert Louis Stevenson

Robert Louis Stevenson (1850–1894) was born in Scotland, died in Samoa, and lived for a time in the United States. Although *Across the Plains* wasn't published until 1892, it was written some fifteen years earlier, relating the poet/novelist's experiences riding the immigrant train from the Missouri to San Francisco. After completion of the first section of the transcontinental railroad in 1869, the ride across the country was faster than by wagon train or stagecoach, but it was not necessarily more comfortable. Those who could afford it rode in relative style; a second group of passengers (mostly those traveling from one inland city to another rather than the entire cross-country trip) had some comforts, but those usually poorer folks relocating from the east to the west coast's Promised Land used special cars. These were sparsely furnished, as Stevenson describes, and were often shuttled aside for faster trains to pass. While they were not the fastest trains, they were the cheapest. Stevenson, on his way to the Pacific, was not planning to settle in America, as were many of his fellow travelers.*

It was about two in the afternoon of Friday that I found myself in front of the Emigrant House (near Council Bluffs, Iowa), with more than a hundred others, to be sorted and boxed for the journey. A white-haired official, with a stick under one arm, and a list in the other hand, stood apart in front of us, and called name after name in the tone of a command. At each name you would see a family gather up its brats and bundles and run for the hindmost of the three cars that stood awaiting us, and I soon concluded that this was to be set apart for the women and children. The second or central car, it turned out, was devoted to men travelling alone, and the third to the Chinese.

...I suppose the reader has some notion of an American railroad-car, that long, narrow wooden box, like a flat-roofed Noah's ark, with a stove and a convenience (toilet), one at either end, a passage down the middle, and transverse benches upon either hand. Those destined for emigrants on the Union Pacific are only remarkable for their extreme plainness, nothing but wood entering in any part into their constitution, and for the usual inefficacy of the lamps, which often went out and shed but a dying glimmer even while they burned. The benches are too short for anything but a young child. Where there is scarce elbow-room for two to sit, there will not be space enough for one to lie.... Hence the company...prevail upon every two to chum together. To each of the chums they sell a board and three square cushions stuffed with straw, and covered with thin cotton. The benches can be made to face each other in pairs, for the backs are reversible. On the approach of night the boards are laid from bench to bench, making a couch wide enough for two, and long enough for a man of the middle height; and the chums lie down side by side upon the cushions with the head to the conductor's van and the feet to the engine. When the train is full, of course this plan is impossible, for there must not be more than one to every bench....

...A great personage on an American train is the newsboy. He sells books (such books!), papers, fruit, lollipops, and cigars; and on emigrant journeys, soap, towels, tin washing dishes, tin coffee pitchers, coffee, tea, sugar, and tinned eatables, mostly hash or beans and bacon....

There were meals to be had, however, by the wayside: a breakfast in the morning, a dinner somewhere between eleven and two, and supper from five to eight or nine at night. We rarely had less

than twenty minutes for each; and if we had not spent many another twenty minutes waiting for some express upon a side track among miles of desert, we might have taken an hour to each repast and arrived at San Francisco up to time. For haste is not the foible of an emigrant train. It gets through on sufferance, running the gauntlet among its more considerable brethren; should there be a block, it is unhesitatingly sacrificed; and they cannot, in consequence, predict the length of the passage within a day or so. Civility is the main comfort that you miss. Equality, though conceived very largely in America, does not extend so low down as to an emigrant. Thus in all other trains, a warning cry of "All aboard!" recalls the passengers to take their seats; but as soon as I was alone with emigrants, and from the Transfer all the way to San Francisco, I found this ceremony was pretermitted; the train stole from the station without note of warning, and you had to keep an eye upon it even while you ate. The annoyance is considerable, and the disrespect both wanton and petty.

Many conductors, again, will hold no communication with an emigrant. I asked a conductor one day at what time the train would stop for dinner; as he made no answer I repeated the question, with a like result; a third time I returned to the charge, and then Jack-in-office looked me coolly in the face for several seconds and turned ostentatiously away. I believe he was half ashamed of his brutality; for when another person made the same inquiry, although he still refused the information, he condescended to answer, and even to justify his reticence in a voice loud enough for me to hear. It was, he said, his principle not to tell people where they were to dine; for one question led to many other questions, as what o'clock it was? or, how soon should we be there? and he could not afford to be eternally worried.

...It had thundered on the Friday night, but the sun rose on Saturday without a cloud. We were at sea — there is no other adequate expression — on the plains of Nebraska.... It was a world almost without a feature; an empty sky, an empty earth; front and back, the line of railway stretched from

Artist Augustus Saint-Gaudens (1848–1907) portrayed Robert Louis Stevenson reclining and writing. The words are from his poem "Underwoods." Stevenson fought tuberculosis all his life and had to be especially careful about his health.

horizon to horizon, like a cue across a billiard-board; on either hand, the green plain ran till it touched the skirts of heaven. Along the track innumerable wild sunflowers, no bigger than a crown-piece, bloomed in a continuous flower-bed; grazing beasts were seen upon the prairie at all degrees of distance and diminution; and, now and again we might perceive a few dots beside the railroad which grew more and more distinct as we drew nearer till they turned into wooden cabins, and then dwindled and dwindled in our wake until they melted into their surroundings, and we were once more alone upon the billiard-board....

At Ogden we changed cars from the Union Pacific to the Central Pacific line of railroad. The change was doubly welcome; for, first, we had better cars on the new line; and, second, those in which we had been cooped for more than ninety hours had begun to stink abominably.... But one thing I must say, the car of the Chinese was notably the least offensive.

The cars on the Central Pacific were nearly twice as high, and so proportionally airier; they were freshly varnished, which gave us all a sense of cleanliness as though we had bathed; the seats drew out and joined in the centre, so that there was no more need for bedboards; and there was an upper tier of berths which could be closed by day and opened at night.

...Of all stupid ill-feelings, the sentiment of my fellow-Caucasians towards our companions in the Chinese car was the most stupid and the worst. They seemed never to have looked at them, listened to them, or thought of them, but hated them a priori.... They could work better and cheaper in half a hundred industries, and hence there was no calumny too idle for the Caucasians to repeat, and even to believe. ...my emigrants declared that the Chinese were dirty. I cannot say they were clean, for that was impossible upon the journey; but in their efforts after cleanliness they put the rest of us to shame. We all pigged and stewed in one infamy, wet our hands and faces for half a minute daily on the platform, and were unashamed. But the Chinese never lost an opportunity, and you would see them washing their feet — an act not dreamed of among ourselves — and going as far as decency permitted to wash their whole bodies....

...The Chinese are considered stupid, because they are imperfectly acquainted with English. They are held to be base, because their dexterity and frugality enable them to underbid the lazy, luxurious Caucasian.... A while ago it was the Irish, now it is the Chinese that must go. Such is the cry....

THE GEORGE EASTMAN STORY

by Alyce Mitchem Jenkins

"You press the button; we do the rest." These words seemed exciting in 1888 when they appeared in magazine advertisements. Up until that time, the complicated tasks of preparing photographic materials and developing pictures discouraged amateur photographers. Today anyone, child or adult, can use a camera to take pictures, because a man named George Eastman helped make photography easy.

Early in the 1850s, photographers began using the wet collodion process, which produced negatives on glass plates. The photographer had to make the plates light sensitive immediately before he took the picture. After he developed and fixed the negative, it was printed on paper to produce a positive image. This process allowed the photographer to make duplicates. Although the wet collodion process was easier than the daguerreotype, photography was still complex. Mathew Brady and other war photographers using the wet collodion process traveled with heavy wagons to carry the necessary glass plates, chemicals, and darkroom.

In the late 1870s, the introduction of factory-produced gelatin-glass plates freed photographers from preparing light-sensitive plates. But they still had to develop and print their own pictures. The average person did not have the skills or materials to take pictures.

In 1880, George Eastman, a serious amateur photographer, gained the financial help of Henry A. Strong, a buggy whip manufacturer, to produce and sell gelatin plates. Eastman had invented a machine for coating the glass plates. But Eastman also was anxious to find a replacement for the heavy, bulky, breakable glass.

In 1884, Eastman and camera maker William Hall Walker created a roll-film system that included the film, the film-holder mechanism, and the film-making machinery. Eastman waited for photographers to buy his new products, but they still preferred the glass plates. He had created a failure. But he had an idea to solve his problem. Why not make a camera so lightweight, simple, and inexpensive that anyone could take pictures and then use his service department to develop and print the pictures? The camera, using the roll-film system he had invented, would be small enough to hold in the hand. Eastman then created the trade name Kodak, using his mother's maiden initial, K, and tested his camera on his partner Strong in 1888.

"I gave one of these cameras to Mr. Strong," Eastman said. "It was the first time he had ever carried a camera, and he was tickled with it as a boy over a new top.... He apparently never realized that it was a possible thing to take pictures himself."

Like Strong, the general public, both young and old, liked the camera. For twenty-five dollars, anyone could buy a Kodak camera already loaded with a one-hundred-exposure roll of film. Turning a key brought fresh film in place for each picture, pulling a cord cocked the shutter, and pressing a button made the exposure. After taking all one hundred pictures, the amateur photographer sent the entire camera to the Eastman factory to be unloaded. After the film was processed, circular negatives, prints, and the reloaded camera were returned to the photographer. This service cost ten dollars.

Because of Eastman's idea, many people became photographers. Later, Eastman renamed his company the Eastman Kodak Company and began producing various models of the Kodak camera. The cameras became prized possessions of young and old alike.

Today it is fun to take pictures as well as collect old cameras from garage sales and flea markets. You might even find one of the original Kodak cameras produced in 1888. It is a leather-covered box, 6 1/2 by 3 1/4 by 3 3/4 inches, with the lens in a rotating cylinder. Surprisingly, it has no viewfinder; photographers had to aim at their subjects by guessing. In 1976, a visitor to New York City purchased one of these cameras from an antique dealer who did not know what a treasure he owned. Today that camera is worth thousands of dollars.

Whether you take pictures or collect cameras, the pleasure of amateur photography came about because George Eastman turned his failure into a success with the words "You press the button; we do the rest."

The New York *World* building in the 1870s, about ten years before Pulitzer bought it.

THE WORLD OF JOSEPH PULITZER

by Peter Roop

In 1864, a penniless Hungarian boy jumped from a ship into the chilly waters of Boston harbor. Within twenty years, he would become the wealthy and powerful owner of two successful American newspapers. His energy and opinions shaped the news Americans read and made a lasting impact on the history of newspapers.

Joseph Pulitzer arrived in America during the last year of the Civil War. His first job as a soldier in the Union army was short-lived when the war ended within a year. Like so many other veterans, Pulitzer found himself searching for a job, so he took a train to St. Louis, Missouri, to look for work.

In St. Louis, Pulitzer worked as a mule keeper, hack driver, waiter, construction worker, and law clerk. He eventually became a lawyer, although he practiced the profession only briefly. Pulitzer had discovered the newspaper.

St. Louis had a large German-speaking population. They supported the German-language newspaper *Westliche Post.*

The Statue of Liberty, complete with its pedestal, was front-page news on August 11, 1885.

Pulitzer, fluent in German, impressed the owners of the paper with his intelligence and zeal. They hired him as a reporter.

At one point, Pulitzer left the *Westliche Post* to enter politics. However, his fling in politics was brief; he returned to the paper and bought stock in it. Eventually, the owners of the paper made him a partner.

Charged with energy, brimming with knowledge, and possessing self-assurance almost to a fault, Pulitzer proved to be a difficult partner. When the opportunity came, he sold his share of the paper back to the original owners for a handsome profit. With this money, he traveled extensively, unable to settle down at any job. Newsprint was still in his blood.

In 1878, Pulitzer returned to St. Louis and bought the *Dispatch,* an ailing newspaper with a shrinking circulation. Joining forces with the rival *Post,* Pulitzer created a new, vibrant newspaper, the *St. Louis Post-Dispatch.* The paper featured accurate, thorough news and clear, concise writing.

"Never be satisfied with merely printing news" was Pulitzer's policy. He urged his reporters to dig below the surface of the news to find the "original, distinctive, dramatic, romantic, thrilling, unique, curious, quaint, humorous, odd, apt to be talked about" stories. Pulitzer's quest for the sensational, combined with his own compelling editorials, proved to be a successful formula. The *Post-Dispatch* quickly became the leading St. Louis newspaper.

In 1883, Pulitzer entered the influential New York newspaper business when he purchased the struggling *World.* After two years under Pulitzer's command, the *World*'s sales rocketed to 150,000 copies a day, or ten times its previous circulation. Between 1883 and 1887, the *World* broke every publishing record in America.

One of Pulitzer's earliest and lasting triumphs was his drive to raise one hundred thousand dollars for the pedestal for the Statue of Liberty. Using the pages of the *World* for this crusade, he wrote, "The people's paper now appeals to the people to come forward and raise this money." Pennies, nickels, and dimes flowed in from around America in support of Miss Liberty's base. Pulitzer was doubly pleased: Miss Liberty received her pedestal, and the *World*'s circulation rose significantly.

Pulitzer used other techniques to reach the public. Dramatic headlines such as "Death Rides the Blast," "Love and Cold Poison," and "A Heroine or a Criminal?" captured readers. He introduced the first color comics in his Sunday *World.* He spoke out against corrupt politicians, urged reforms, and fought monopolies. His editorial page, championing the underdog — whether male or female, worker or unemployed, native or immigrant — was called a "million-candle-power torch of liberty and intelligence." Pulitzer's crusades for the public interest were among his vital contributions to American journalism. Other newspapers quickly imitated his techniques.

Pulitzer's drive for success was not without its price. Years of poring over newsprint aggravated an eye problem that eventually made him go blind. His struggle for perfection also wore his nerves to the point that the striking of a match sounded like the explosion of a gun next to his ears.

Pulitzer's doctors urged him to rest. For the remainder of his life, he pursued peace, building soundproof homes and living aboard a soundproof yacht. Yet he remained in constant communication with his newspapers, checking up on his editors, advising, cajoling, and pushing his staff to the limits of their abilities. Pulitzer maintained control of his newspapers even though he could not read them himself.

Pulitzer died in October 1911 at age sixty-four. He left money to found the world's first school of journalism at Columbia University in New York City. He also established the annual Pulitzer Prizes.

A poll of newspaper editors in 1934 selected Pulitzer the leading American editor of modern times. This is a fitting tribute to the man who fought for journalistic excellence and the betterment of life for all Americans.

'A GIFT OF THE WHOLE PEOPLE'

by Kathleen Keenan

"One Hundred Thousand Dollars!" The *World,* a New York newspaper, printed this victorious headline on August 11, 1885. Patriotic Americans of all ages had contributed enough pennies, nickels, and dimes to help a dream come true. The Statue of Liberty would have a pedestal, a base on which to stand.

The Statue of Liberty was designed by a young French sculptor named Frédéric Auguste Bartholdi. A friend of Bartholdi's suggested the idea of a monument to "liberty, equality, and fraternity" (the motto of the French Revolution) built by French and American craftsmen. *Liberty Enlightening the World* would represent a shared love of democracy and the friendship between the two countries.

Bartholdi traveled to the United States eager to explain the project to officials. He arrived in 1871, wide-eyed at the vast size of the country. If everything in America was so big, the people would surely appreciate his 151-foot statue! The men Bartholdi met, including President Ulysses S. Grant, were polite but wanted to see the work in progress before giving their enthusiastic approval.

Back in Paris, Bartholdi rented the spacious studio of Gaget, Gauthier, and Company. The air was filled with the rhythm of mallets pounding sheets of copper as talented craftsmen labored to complete the project. Visitors who crowded into the workshop thought of "the Lady" as a friend.

Money was scarce. In Paris, the Franco-American Union, which managed the Statue of Liberty project, planned numerous fundraising activities. Dinners and musicals featured liberty themes. Miniature terra-cotta (clay) copies of the

"*Miss Liberty*"

statue, engraved with the buyer's name, were sold. Despite his hectic schedule, Bartholdi made many speeches, and audiences contributed generously. Schoolchildren, merchants, and descendants of Revolutionary War heroes were among the supporters.

The French expected such an important project to be a combined effort, with Americans supplying the pedestal for the statue. But few U.S. funds were donated. Many Americans mistakenly believed that the statue was a gift only to New York, since Bartholdi had chosen Bedloe's Island in New York harbor as the site for his statue. Millionaires preferred to spend their money on luxuries. The Statue of Liberty was ready to be shipped. Would the pedestal be ready in time?

This lack of interest angered Joseph Pulitzer, owner of the *World*. A Hungarian immigrant, Pulitzer wholeheartedly believed in the freedom symbolized by the statue. His editorial of March 16, 1885, changed America's mind.

Pulitzer wrote that the Statue of Liberty was "a gift of the whole people of France to the whole people of America." He challenged his readers to give as the French had done and promised to print the name of every donor, regardless of the amount offered. The response was incredible.

Soon the daily list of contributors occupied a full page in the *World*. Pulitzer also published letters he received, especially from the poor, the elderly, and schoolchildren. Some students wrote of class projects in which they collected money. Although most people could give less than a dollar, through determination and sacrifice, 120,000 Americans raised $100,000 in only five months.

Work on the pedestal, which had been halted, could now resume. Into the mortar of the last stone, a workman tossed a handful of coins as a "thank you" to all who had made it possible.

OUR MOST FAMOUS IMMIGRANT

by Nancy Whitelaw

It is April 1876. Frédéric Auguste Bartholdi, a French sculptor, has a problem. He has been commissioned to complete a statue as a birthday gift from France to the United States for its one-hundredth birthday. "It can't be done," he mutters over and over to himself. Then an idea comes to him: "I'll finish the arm and torch and send them in time for the Fourth of July so that the Americans can at least imagine the whole statue." This is no small present; the hand alone is sixteen feet high.

Workers construct wooden molds for the twenty-one pieces that will be sent. Then they hammer sheets of copper over the molds, making exact replicas. When the arm and torch are completed, Bartholdi has them shipped to the Philadelphia World's Fair. The Americans are delighted, but the sculptor still has a great deal of work to do on the world's largest statue.

Finally, in 1884, she stands tall and proud, looking over the rooftops of Paris, France. She stays there until January 1885, while the Americans build a pedestal for her. Then Bartholdi orders his crew to dismantle the statue and pack her into boxes. That June, two hundred fourteen boxes arrive at Bedloe's Island in New York harbor. A little over a year later, on October 28, 1886, Bartholdi, positioned high in the torch, pulls a cord to unveil the face of the statue called *Liberty Enlightening the World*. Thousands cheer, wave banners, sound sirens, and ring bells in tribute to the artist.

The Statue of Liberty as it appeared after its dedication in 1886. This photograph was taken by Edward Bierstadt, the brother of the famous Hudson River School painter Albert Bierstadt.

The dedication date was set for October 28, 1886. Because of heavy fog, even Bartholdi was unable to view his masterpiece ahead of time. He counted the minutes until he would have the honor of introducing "Miss Liberty" to her people.

Bartholdi tugged at a cord, releasing the red, white, and blue French flag that had covered the statue's face. Thousands of onlookers clapped, cheered, and shouted. Together, the United States and France had created an inspiring monument for people everywhere and a reminder of their love of democracy and their abiding friendship.

MILL CHILDREN

by Hilda Brucker

At 5:00 A.M., the mill whistle blew, its shrill blast waking the town's children from a deep sleep. There was just time enough for them to wash and dress quickly before hurrying through the darkness to their jobs at the textile mill. Anyone not at work when the whistle sounded again at six would be locked out of the mill and lose much-needed wages. For the next twelve hours, children as young as six years old would toil at the machines, often with only a fifteen-minute break for lunch.

The textile mills of the early 1800s were cold, dark, and noisy. Children labored as bobbin boys who fed yarn into the looms, at the spinning machines, at keeping machines greased and oiled, and at moving supplies from room to room. Many stood all day, their heads throbbing from the continuous roar of the machines. Although their eyes tired quickly, they dared not let their concentration wander, for they had seen others lose fingers in the whirling gears of the machines. Strands of long hair also could get caught in the metal jaws, pulling out not only the hair but a piece of the scalp as well. Older children tried their best to watch over their younger brothers and sisters, but accidents were common. Any child could easily fall prey to pneumonia or other illnesses due to the dampness of the mill and lack of rest.

For six days out of every week, this nightmare continued. How could parents who loved their children allow them to live with such misery? They saw no other choice.

The grandparents and great-grandparents of these New England mill children had been farmers. Their families had made up a complete work force, with everyone from youngest to oldest pitching in to get the crops planted and harvested. But the geography would not cooperate. The soil in most of the New England states is stony, difficult to cultivate, and not very fertile. The climate is cool, making the growing season short. Families could raise just enough food to live on, but with nothing left over to sell, they never seemed to get ahead.

Then the Industrial Revolution arrived. The first patented looms, which ran on waterpower, provided a much quicker method of producing woven cloth, and the textile industry became a profitable one. Businessmen quickly set up mills along the many streams, rivers, and waterfalls that dotted the New England countryside. Men went to work at the mills, leaving the farm chores to women and children. As more and more workers flocked to the mills, towns

This young spinner worked in a North Pownal, Vermont, cotton mill in 1910.

Breaker boys at a South Pittston, Pennsylvania, mine in 1911.

sprang up around them. Upon the invention of the steam engine, factories were no longer dependent on waterpower, and even more mills were built.

Machines also became simpler to operate, and that gave mill owners an idea as to how they could increase profits. They began to hire women and children to work at machines, paying them less money than men because, they reasoned, they were less capable. Soon mill owners began firing men and hiring children for all but the most skilled positions. Grown men could not find work, and desperate families, living off their children's wages, began to send younger and younger children to work in an effort to make ends meet.

While the situation rapidly worsened, the plight of the mill children did not go unnoticed. Their misery attracted the attention of social reformers who were willing to fight for the rights of the poor. Newly founded organizations held meetings in mill towns and petitioned the state governments to set fourteen as the minimum age for children working in factories. They met with little success.

In 1904, key leaders from each state met in New York City to form the National Child Labor Committee. They represented not only the mill children of New England but also the children who toiled in southern mines and midwestern steel mills. Their goal was to educate the public to want reform, but little progress was made until the children and their parents joined the struggle.

On the morning of January 12, 1912, twenty-five thousand men, women, and children walked off their jobs at the American Woolen Company in Lawrence, Massachusetts. For sixty-three days, the wheels stopped turning and the mill shut down. During that time, parents with no means of feeding their children sent them off to stay with relatives or in temporary homes set up by the reformers. Violence also occurred. The mill owners called in troops to keep order among the strikers, and in the chaos at least one child was killed. During the ensuing congressional investigation, sixteen children from the Lawrence mill were brought to Washington to testify before the House of Representatives.

The result was the Palmer-Owen bill, adopted in 1916. The law that resulted from this bill was the first federal law to regulate child labor. It set the minimum working age at fourteen, set the maximum working day at eight hours, and prohibited the employment of children on night shifts.

No sooner was this victory won, however, than the Supreme Court, under pressure from powerful manufacturers, declared it unconstitutional. Reformers went back to work on their state governments, this time changing their tactics slightly, and succeeded in having compulsory education laws passed. If the children were in school, they could not go to work.

By 1932, only half the states in the Union had child labor laws in effect. Not until 1938 was a federal law, the Fair Labor Standards Act, passed by Congress. By this time, children had been in the mills for more than a hundred years, inadvertently making a significant contribution to U.S. history. The children who toiled so miserably in the mills not only paved the way for today's stringent child labor laws but also demonstrated that the basic rights of childhood should not be denied.

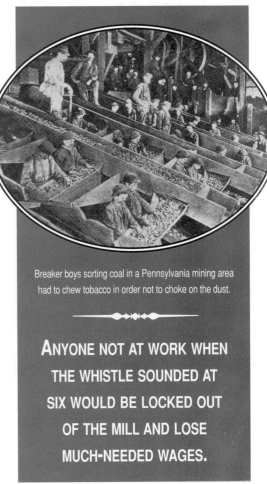

Breaker boys sorting coal in a Pennsylvania mining area had to chew tobacco in order not to choke on the dust.

ANYONE NOT AT WORK WHEN THE WHISTLE SOUNDED AT SIX WOULD BE LOCKED OUT OF THE MILL AND LOSE MUCH-NEEDED WAGES.

CRUSADER WITH A CAMERA

by Tedd Levy

Jacob Riis was one of the few outsiders who came to Mulberry Street. The others were usually policemen or undertakers. The heart of Mulberry Street, known as "The Bend," was the center of New York City's slums in the 1880s. It was not the kind of place people visited, but hundreds lived there. Many of the residents of Mulberry Street were immigrants, as Jacob Riis himself had been.

As a boy in Denmark, Riis had been apprenticed to a carpenter in Copenhagen. Unable to find a job as a carpenter and unable to marry the girl he loved because her father objected, he sailed for America in 1870, when he was twenty-one years old.

Times were hard in the United States, and the victims of these difficult times were often the jobless, hungry, and homeless immigrants. Riis arrived without much money, without a place to live, and with no job. He did chores for meals. He slept in barns and alleys. He once walked from New York to Philadelphia in hopes of finding work with a Danish family he knew there. During the next three years,

Jacob A. Riis

....

Riis (1849–1914), a newspaper reporter, was concerned about conditions in New York City's tenements. He taught himself to be a photographer and used his photographs to bring the problems of "the other half" to the attention of people who could help. Riis wrote the book *How the Other Half Lives*, which was published in 1890, and founded the Jacob Riis Neighborhood House in 1888.

Riis found employment in Philadelphia as a carpenter, farm hand, lumberjack, laborer, railroad worker, and salesman.

Finally, Riis managed to find a job as a newspaper reporter. He worked hard at this and earned a reputation as a good reporter. With the money he earned, Riis traveled to Denmark for the girl he loved. They were married and returned to live in New York City.

Long before Riis and his wife returned to New York, many large, comfortable houses had dotted the countryside in the vicinity of Mulberry Street. Seeing an opportunity to make money, the owners of the old houses began renting rooms. Later, as more people came, the landlords divided the large rooms into smaller ones. Many of these rooms had no windows, so the air became very stale. Soon every available space, from the clammy cellar to the stuffy attic, was divided and rented. These once-lovely houses had become tenement buildings and the homes of many immigrants.

The tenements were usually four to six stories high. There was often a store on the first floor. At least four families lived on each of the floors above. An apartment had one or two dark, closet-size spaces, which were used as bedrooms, and a tiny living room. Only partitions separated families or groups of people from each other.

An energetic police reporter, Riis covered the life and crimes on Mulberry Street and knew the poor people who lived there in the tenements. By himself or with a policeman, he often went through the slum district between two and four o'clock in the morning to "see it off its guard." What he saw were people sleeping in alleys and in the filthy, crowded buildings. He saw lodging houses that rented sleeping space on their dirty floors to thieves, beggars, and drunks. By day, he saw many homeless children living in the streets, begging or stealing food from pushcarts.

The people of Mulberry Street spent most of their time outside. They stayed inside only when they were sick or sleeping. Inside the tenements, the heat was nearly unbearable, and there was no fresh air. Heaps of straw and rags served as beds. Broken stoves leaked smoke at every turn of their stacks, and there was no place to throw out rubbish. The smell alone drove people to the street.

"The sight I saw there," Riis said of the slums, "gripped my heart until I felt that I must tell of them or burst. One half of the world does not know how the other half lives." Riis believed that the world did not care about its poor, and he set out to change that.

Several years earlier, in 1873, the *New York Daily Graphic* had published the first photograph in a newspaper. By 1888, a flash had been developed that allowed photographs to be taken in dark areas. Cartridges had to be fired from a revolver to ignite the flash. It was noisy and clumsy, but it meant that photographs could be taken to show life in the tenements. Riis bought a camera and taught himself how to use it.

His photos and newspaper stories brought slum life to everyone's attention. Working late at night, often after giving illustrated lectures, he wrote about the slums. In 1890, he published *How the Other Half Lives,* a book of writings and photographs portraying life in the slums. It was the first time the terrible conditions were revealed in photographs. His book was a success.

In 1901, Riis left his job as a newspaper reporter. He worked on several books, including *The Battle With the Slum,* which told of inadequate schools and play-grounds. His writings and photographs helped to close run-down lodging houses, open playgrounds and small parks, and improve health and safety in tenements.

"Our country has grown great," he said, "our cities wealthy — but in their slums lurk poverty and bitterness — bitterness because the promise has not been kept that every man should have an even chance to start with."

Jacob Riis waged a lifelong battle to eliminate slums and to improve life for the poor. President Theodore Roosevelt once called him "the best American I ever knew."

STREET ARABS
by Heather Mitchell Amey

Jacob Riis revealed many shocking problems of tenement life. Another problem that concerned him was the existence of thousands of homeless children who lived as vagabonds in the streets. Immigrant and native children alike, they were known as "street arabs."

They could be found on every street corner of New York City in the early years of this century. Many were newsboys, selling their papers with cries of "Extra! Get your extra edition!" Others were bootblacks, armed with shoeshine kits and a strong sales pitch. A few gambled for a living, and some could pick a pocket as deftly as the Artful Dodger* himself.

These street arabs fended for themselves and claimed no place as home. They might use a warm steam vent in winter, an abandoned shed, a sheltered spot under a bridge, or even a barrel in an alley for shelter.

With names like The Snitcher, Slobbery Jack, and The King of Bums, street arabs were known for their spunky good humor and their generosity toward fellow street rats who were down on their luck. They often ignored the law, but they strictly obeyed their own code of fair play and swift justice. They were tough, independent, and clever. But they also were very poor and un-educated, and because of this they stood little chance of rising up from their way of life.

To combat this army of vagabonds, a group of citizens established the Children's Aid Society. The purpose of the society was to help the street arabs to help themselves. Newsboys' Lodging Houses — "hotels" for homeless boys — cropped up here and there across the city. One of the few rules of the houses was posted on a sign outside the door: "Boys who swear or chew tobacco cannot sleep here."

If a boy lacked the eighteen cents for his room and board, he was given credit. If he wished to go into an honest business selling newspapers or shining shoes, the Children's Aid Society loaned him the money to get started. Evening classes were held so that street arabs could learn to read and write, giving them a fair chance at steady jobs when they grew older. The society also provided many street arabs with a great opportunity by sending some three thousand boys a year to host families in the West, where they could begin a new life away from the city.

Street arabs were proud of their independence and did not want anyone's charity. The Children's Aid Society did not give charity. Rather, it offered a fair deal, and the street arabs respected and appreciated this. Thanks to the society and to concerned individuals such as Jacob Riis, many street arabs were able to become honest, hard-working citizens.

*A character in Charles Dickens's novel *Oliver Twist.*

THE CIVIL WAR ERA   A NEW NATION

AMERICAN TECHNOLOGY

The Civil War

*has been called America's first modern war,
in part because it introduced awesome new
weapons that had never before been used.*

Ironclad warships, the first submarines, and vastly improved artillery were only some of the innovations inspired by the war.

America continued its steady march toward higher technology after the war ended. The transcontinental railroad conquered the wide continent. A "wizard" in Menlo Park, New Jersey, lit the world with his electric lamp. And in the South, two brothers proved that man could really fly.

This chapter recalls not only the best known of these American geniuses, such as Thomas Alva Edison and Orville and Wilbur Wright, but also some others whose stories are far less well-known. Together, they helped make America the most scientifically advanced nation in the world.

Thomas Edison and his first dynamo.

Time Line of Ideas and Inventions

1612

John Rolfe improves the method for curing tobacco, America's first export crop.

1752

Benjamin Franklin helps discover the properties of electricity and invents the lightning rod.

1790

Samuel Slater founds the American factory system with his water-powered cotton mill.

1793

Cotton becomes the South's leading crop when Eli Whitney invents the cotton gin.

1798

Eli Whitney develops a system of interchangeable parts in the manufacture of guns.

1807

Robert Fulton perfects the steamboat for commercial use.

1830

Peter Cooper races his steam-powered locomotive against a horse.

The Boott Cotton Mills in Lowell, Massachusetts.

1834

Cyrus McCormick patents his horse-drawn wheat reaper.

1844

An early model of Samuel Morse's telegraph is put into operation.

1846

Samuel Colt uses the assembly line system to make the Colt revolver.

1854

In England, Henry Bessemer patents a cheap and efficient process for manufacturing steel.

1859

The first oil well is drilled by Edwin Drake.

1870

John D. Rockefeller organizes his refineries, forming the Standard Oil Company.

1873

Andrew Carnegie invests in the production of Bessemer steel.

1876

The first public demonstration of the telephone is given by its inventor, Alexander Graham Bell.

1882

Thomas A. Edison opens the first electric-generating station to power the incandescent light.

1903

Orville and Wilbur Wright fly the first manned airplane.

1909

Henry Ford manufactures his Model T automobile on an assembly line.

SUBMARINES IN THE CIVIL WAR

by James McCaffrey

Submarines. When we see this word, most of us think of sleek underwater ships driven by nuclear power and capable of firing guided missiles. This image is of submarines as they exist today. But what about the submarines of long ago? What about the submarines of the Civil War? Indeed, the first submarine ever to sink an enemy ship did so during the Civil War.

Both the North and the South developed submarines during the war. The North, with greater industrial capacity and a long-established naval tradition, had a submarine by the time the war was only a year old.

In the summer of 1861, Brutus de Villeroy of Philadelphia sought a government contract to build a submarine. He had experimented with such craft in his native France for a number of years. Naval officers inspected a submarine that he had already built and recommended that he be given a chance to build another one for military use. The resulting ship, known as the *Alligator,* was launched six months later.

The *Alligator* looked like a long, dark green, iron cigar. Of course, it did not have a nuclear power plant to push it through the waves, as do its modern descendants. In fact, it did not have an engine at all. It was propelled by eight sets of oars. These oars passed through watertight openings in the side of the ship. In operation, the oars folded up as they swung forward and flattened out again on the backstroke. In this way, the *Alligator* slowly paddled through the water like a giant reptile.

The weapons used on the *Alligator* also were unlike today's missiles and torpedoes. This early submarine was expected to approach very near its intended target and stop. Then two divers would leave through the bottom of the vessel and swim to the enemy ship, where they would attach explosives beneath the water line. After the divers were safely back inside the *Alligator,* the explosives would be set off by an electric signal.

This photograph of a model of the *Alligator* is in the collection of the Submarine Force Library and Museum in Groton, Connecticut.

Late in June 1862, the *Alligator* was sent south, where it was to operate along the Virginia shore. Its first assignment was to travel up the James River and remove some underwater obstructions so that large surface ships could sail the river. It seemed like an easy task until someone realized that the *Alligator* required seven and a half feet of water in which to operate and the James River was much shallower than that. The plan was abandoned, and the submarine was sent to the Washington Navy Yard for more testing.

Modifications made to the small craft increased its speed a little, although it was still very slow. On April 1, 1863, another ship took the *Alligator* in tow and started south again. This time, the destination was Port Royal, South Carolina.

A bad storm hit the next day, and one of the towlines broke. The weather got worse, and the submarine was rapidly becoming unmanageable. Several times, it nearly ran into the vessel that was towing it. Finally, on April 2, the *Alligator* was cast adrift in an effort to save the larger ship. The little submarine sank.

The loss made little difference to the Union. At the start of the war, Union warships had anchored just outside Confederate seaports and blockaded the ports to prevent war supplies from reaching the South. The main problem for the Union navy was capturing the South's swift "blockade runners," a job that could not be done underwater. Thus, the North had little use for submarines and did not try to replace the *Alligator.*

The Confederate government was far from idle during the short life of the *Alligator.* Efforts were under way early in the war to develop some sort of craft that would be capable of defeating the Union ships that blocked southern ports. Conventional wooden ships were not helpful, and because iron was scarce in the South, it was difficult for the Confederates to build the ironclads that the North

was using. Perhaps an underwater ship could be used to solve the problem.

The South's first submarine was the *Pioneer,* designed by J.R. McClintock and built in New Orleans. The Confederate government did not actually own the *Pioneer,* and it was agreed that if the submarine was successful against Union warships, the Confederate government would have to reward the ship's owners. The ship was undergoing tests when Union forces captured the city, and the *Pioneer* was purposely sunk to keep it from falling into the hands of Federal troops.

The second Confederate submarine was built in Mobile, Alabama, and was designed by McClintock, Baxter Watson, and H.L. Hunley. Hunley provided all the money to build the craft. Though unnamed, the ship is often called the *Pioneer II.* It was lost while being towed to attack the Union fleet off Fort Morgan, Alabama.

The *H.L. Hunley* was the third Confederate submarine, again designed by McClintock, Watson, and Hunley. It was intended to tow a floating bomb behind it. After passing beneath the enemy craft, the submarine would surface and continue on course until the bomb struck the enemy ship and exploded. The idea of the towed explosives had to be given up when the Confederates decided to use the *H.L. Hunley* off Charleston. The water was not deep enough for the submarine to pass under the large Union warship that had been chosen as a target. A bomb on the end of a long pole, called a spar torpedo, was substituted.

Another change had to be made before the planned attack could take place. Several accidents had occurred during test runs, and thirteen men, including Hunley, had lost their lives. Due to these mishaps, it was decided not to let the submarine completely submerge during the attack.

On the night of February 17, 1864, the small, clumsy submarine moved slowly through the waters off Charleston, headed for the USS *Housatonic*. The crewmen of the *Housatonic* discovered the approach of the submarine too late. The violent explosion of the spar torpedo ripped a huge hole in the Federal ship, which sank in a matter of minutes.

Naval history was written that night as the *H.L. Hunley* became the first submarine to sink an enemy ship. This feat would not be duplicated for another fifty years. Unfortunately for the Confederate sailors, they were not able to realize their fame. The *H.L. Hunley* failed to surface after its historic clash. It may have been damaged by the explosion of the spar torpedo and sunk along with the *Housatonic*.

THE FIRST TRANSCONTINENTAL RAILROAD

It was shortly past noon, May 10, 1869. The place was Promontory Point, a tiny settlement on the shores of the Great Salt Lake in Utah. A large crowd had gathered to witness a very important ceremony. Telegraph wires waited to carry the news across the nation. Two locomotives idled on their tracks nose to nose — one from the east, the other from the west.

Leland Stanford of the Central Pacific Railroad got ready to hammer in the spike that would finally connect East and West. He swung and missed.

NEWSPAPER

tered according to the Act of Congress in the year 1865, by FRANK LESLIE, in the Clerk's Office of the District Court for the Southern District of New York.

VIII.] NEW YORK, JUNE 5, 1869. [PRICE

On June 5, 1869, *Frank Leslie's Illustrated Newspaper* covered the "completion of the Union Pacific Rail Road. Dr. Durant and Governor Standford [sic] drive the last spikes, connecting the Union and Central Pacific Rail Roads, at Promontory Point, Utah, at 5 minutes past 3 pm, New York time, May 10, 1869."

Thomas Clark Durant of the Union Pacific Railroad also missed. But the crowd cheered, and other important people took their turns. The spikes, of silver, iron, and gold, were hammered in place. The first transcontinental railroad had been completed! The telegraph wires hummed their message.

The Union Pacific locomotive from the east, called the *119*, crossed over onto Central Pacific tracks. Then it backed up to allow the *Jupiter*, the locomotive from the west, to chug across onto Union Pacific tracks. Everyone cheered again and celebrated all afternoon.

The next day, Promontory Point was practically deserted. It was hard to picture the elaborate ceremony that had taken place the day before. Why was a transcontinental railroad so important? The answer to that question is more easily understood if we begin with the story of the railroad.

The Story of the Railroad

The idea of a railroad, or any roadway with rails that both guide and support a set of wheels, began long ago when it was discovered that a heavy cart rolled much better when the wheels were on a hard surface.

In Roman times, stone-paved roads with deep foundations were built for hard-wheeled carts and chariots. This was a major improvement over dirt roads because the hard road surface allowed the carts to roll much more easily and to carry much heavier loads. However, the road had to be more than twice the width of the vehicles and was very expensive and difficult to construct.

Later, during the Middle Ages, miners had to push heavy loads through tunnels. Because tunnels were very difficult and expensive to build, they were only as wide as the cart itself. Carts were guided through the tunnels on pulley-like wheels, which ran on a track. The track was made from wooden rails nailed to crossties. Like the stone-paved Roman roads, the wooden tracks provided a hard surface for easy rolling. However, unlike the Roman roads, they were much easier to build. Tracks later were extended outside the mines.

During the eighteenth century, in South Wales, tramways carrying coal used a special kind of track. A flange, or collar, was mounted on the inside edge of the cast-iron rail. This flange helped to keep the plain-wheeled carts on the track. The track itself was mounted on stone blocks. Some of these tracks were twenty miles long. They were very useful but difficult to keep clear of debris. If a branch or rock lay on the tracks, the tramway was easily derailed.

After much experimenting, an important improvement was made, placing the flange on the wheel instead of the track. The track itself was shaped like an I or T, and the wheel's flange ran along its head. The rails were held firmly parallel by wooden crossties. This was an improvement because the rails were self-cleaning, were easily crossed by other roadways, and were not too expensive to build. The rails were even cushioned by the flexibility of the wooden crossties.

Once the carts were rolling easily, people began hitching several of them together. This was exciting because a much larger load could be moved in one trip. But the horses or oxen that were used to pull the wagons could move only a few at a time. Much more power was needed to pull a train.

When James Watt invented a motor that was powered by steam, people began to work on the idea of a steam-powered locomotive. After forty-four years of experimenting, a locomotive was used to haul a train loaded with iron. The experiment took place in Wales. Even though this first locomotive did not work very well, the idea caught on. Improvements were made, and the steam-powered locomotive was hauling other things as well.

At the same time that railroads were being developed, canals also were used to transport large loads of material. Many people felt that railroads would never work and that more canals should be built. In America, the Erie Canal was opened in 1825. That same year, a man in England had built a locomotive that was safe enough to carry passengers. For a time, people in America argued over whether

Tracklayers building the Union Pacific Railroad christened this the 1,000-mile tree in mid-January 1869. It marked the 1,000th mile completed from Omaha, Nebraska. This group posed beneath the tree's branches during an excursion following the completion of the railroad.

they should spend money on canals or railroads, but railroads soon won out.

In 1827, construction began on the Baltimore & Ohio Railroad. At first, the company planned to use horses to pull the wagons. But then a famous race between the steam-powered locomotive *Tom Thumb* and a horse-drawn wagon convinced the owners that they should become the first steam-powered line. (Actually, the horse won the race because the *Tom Thumb* broke down in the middle of it. Even so, people were convinced that in the future, the engines would improve and be a much better way to pull a train.)

The growth of railroads in America was amazing. In 1830, only twenty-three miles of tracks had been laid. By 1840, the network of tracks had grown a hundred times. And by 1870, the tracks looked like a spider web across the continent.

Speed had increased as well. The *Tom Thumb* had traveled from twelve to eighteen miles per hour. In 1848, a train called the *Antelope* ran a twenty-six-mile race in twenty-six minutes. The train pulled one small coach and carried several passengers. The passengers were so scared that they lay down on the floor of the coach and prayed. No one knew that it was possible to travel so fast.

The dining car on the Great Western Railroad, 1879.

A Transcontinental Railroad

The idea of a transcontinental railroad came into being when large groups of people began to settle in California and the western territories. A group of businessmen predicted that a railroad connecting the East Coast with the West Coast would make a good deal of money in trade. They even expected to transport goods brought to California from China.

At first, the building of a transcontinental railroad seemed an impossible task. In 1862, President Abraham Lincoln signed a bill giving the railroad companies special land grants and government bonds to help pay for the job. Even so, the owners of the companies had to find ways to raise more money.

The Central Pacific Railroad began construction in Sacramento, California, in 1863. The Union Pacific began in Omaha, Nebraska, in December of the same year. In less than four years, 1,776 miles of tracks were laid across the wilderness.

Both companies had tremendous difficulty getting their supplies. The Central Pacific had to ship its equipment from the Atlantic coast. The only way to do this was to send it across the Isthmus of Panama (in Central America) or around Cape Horn (at the southern tip of South America) to San Francisco. This was very expensive and took a long time.

The Union Pacific had its own problems. At first, it had to ship its supplies and equipment up the Missouri River by steamboat, then carry them overland by stagecoach and wagon. Later the railroad was able to send supplies along the tracks it had laid, but this was slow and hardly an improvement. All the digging and carrying, pushing and pulling had to be done by men with picks and shovels, wheelbarrows, wagons, and mules. It took the labor of hundreds of men, and the lives of many, to complete this incredible task. Work continued for many years after 1869. Even though the tracks were laid, there was still work to be done grading and banking along the way.

Ten years after the Golden Spike Ceremony, Robert Louis Stevenson traveled across America by train. His journal shows that trains were still far from comfortable. (See page 237.) But over the years, they did improve. For a time, they were the most popular way to travel and to ship many things.

Railroad companies began losing money when the automobile and the truck were developed. Many companies were forced out of business. Today it is just as common to see an abandoned railroad track as to see one that is still used. But the story of the railroad does not end here. Perhaps when we no longer have enough fuel to run our automobiles and trucks the way we would like to, we will turn to the rails again.

Alfred Waud's sketch illustrates European and Asian laborers working side by side on the last mile of the railroad.

THE BUILDERS OF THE FIRST TRANSCONTINENTAL RAILROAD

by Charlotte Gemmell

The newly formed Union Pacific Railroad was moving west from Omaha, Nebraska. It had all the workers it could use. Twelve thousand men had drifted there from the North and South. The Civil War was over, and soldiers from both sides needed work. Former slaves also needed work. The biggest group of workers, however, were the Irish. Some had fought in the war, but many were fresh off the boat from Ireland.

Blue and gray army uniforms mingled with checked shirts, broad-brimmed hats, and high boots. Each man received a revolver or rifle, which he would need.

The Native Americans were friendly until they realized that their survival depended on stopping the "iron horse." They attacked constantly. The workers would drop their shovels, grab their guns, and start shooting. They had learned through the hard years of war how to protect themselves.

Living conditions were difficult. The men lived either in tents or in converted boxcars. But the food was always good, and there was plenty of it. A good cook was the most important person in camp. A bad cook might be run out at gunpoint! Every day started with a huge breakfast. There were platters of meat, fried potatoes and other vegetables, canned fruit, several kinds of pie, and cup after cup of coffee. At noon, the workers would come roaring in for more of the same.

They were strong, hard-working, tough men. They lived for the weekend at the "hell-on-wheels" towns that sprang up at the end of the line. These towns were portable. When about fifty miles of new track had been laid, the gamblers, saloonkeepers, swindlers, and dance-hall girls raced on up the track to set up a new town. The flimsy buildings, often with canvas roofs, were taken down, piled on wagons, and erected at the new spot.

The workers may have lived for the weekend, but they died for it, too. The combination of whiskey and gambling usually meant brawling and shooting. Bodies were constantly dragged from the saloons. For every man killed in a work accident, four were murdered in fights. Others died later from diseases they had picked up there. As each "hell-on-wheels" town packed up for its next location, it left a brand-new cemetery behind.

As the Union Pacific and Central Pacific crews came together, their dislike for each other grew. There were frequent fistfights and "accidental" blastings.

Finally, on May 10, 1869,
six Irishmen laid the last rail from the east;
six Chinese laid the last rail from the west.
Then the golden spike was to be hammered in place.

Leland Stanford of the Central Pacific swung and missed. Thomas Clark Durant of the Union Pacific swung and missed. All the railroad workers roared with laughter. Eventually, the spike was driven home, and the telegraph operator sent the message "Done" to all parts of the country. Church bells rang, parades began, and people from east to west celebrated. The Native Americans did not.

The Chinese had come to California in 1849 looking for gold. When they wanted to work on the railroads, the railroad bosses would not hire them. In 1865, one out of every three people on the West Coast was Chinese, but they were often discriminated against.

The Central Pacific Railroad was laying track from Sacramento, California, to meet the Union Pacific Railroad crawling out from Omaha. The railroad bosses were having a hard time finding reliable workers. Many would quit after a week or two. They worked only long enough to earn money to go prospecting for gold. Finally, Charles Crocker, the big boss, ordered, "Hire Chinese!" The other railroad bosses were not happy, but they did it.

The other workers made fun of the Chinese, calling them "monkeys" and "little yellow midgets." But at the end of the first day, the Irish bosses knew that the small size of these men did not matter. The Chinese roadbed was straighter, smoother, and longer than that of any other crew.

Thomas Clark
Durant

Leland
Stanford

. . . .

Durant (1820–1885) was discharged from the Union Pacific after the railroad was completed. Stanford (1824–1893) remained president of the Central Pacific Railroad and from 1885 to 1890 served as president of the Southern Pacific Railroad. From 1885 until his death, he was a U.S. senator. He also founded Stanford University as a memorial to his son.

The Chinese worked without stopping. Their cooks would come among them with steaming buckets of tea hung from long rods across their shoulders. That was enough to get them through the day.

After work, behind the tents, each worker had a barrel filled with hot water. He washed himself, then relaxed in the sweet-smelling water. While he soaked, clean clothes were laid out for him. After that, the cooks would have a meal ready.

As the railroad bosses realized how well the Chinese worked, they asked Chinese companies to bring in more workers from China. They agreed, and special food was brought in as well. A shipment might have included dried cuttlefish, bamboo sprouts, sweet rice crackers, dried abalone, Chinese bacon, tea, and rice.

The weekends were their own. They quietly gambled, smoked their opium pipes, and dreamed of home. Each knew that this weekend could be his last. The Chinese were always given the most dangerous jobs. Every ship going back to China carried bodies for burial near their ancestors. As the railroad tracks crept into the Sierra Nevada, some froze to death in tents in the fierce mountain winter. Camps were sometimes swept away by avalanches.

When a railroad bed was needed halfway up the precipice of the American River gorge, construction seemed impossible. The Chinese offered to try. They asked for reeds, then wove waist-high baskets with eyelets for inserting ropes. The baskets, with one or two men in each, were lowered halfway down the cliff. The men used their tiny hand drills and inserted blasting powder. They were *usually* pulled to safety before the explosion.

When the two railroads met at Promontory Point, Utah, on May 10, 1869, a photograph was taken. Not one of the thirteen thousand Chinese workers was in it. The Central Pacific could not have laid its tracks without the Chinese, but their only memorial is the graves that line the route of the first transcontinental railroad.

THE REAL MR. MCCOY

by Anne E. Schraff

Elijah McCoy was born in Colchester, Canada, in 1843, the son of slaves who had fled Kentucky to save their children from slavery. As a small boy, he loved machines and tools and hoped to be an engineer someday. After the Civil War, his family moved back to the United States, settling in Ypsilanti, Michigan. McCoy was determined to study engineering and get a good job.

Unfortunately, in those days many people thought that African Americans were suited only for menial jobs. "A black boy wanting to study engineering?" some people exclaimed. "Not likely!"

McCoy would not give up his dream, so he went to Scotland to get an education. Then he returned to Michigan to find an engineering job.

"A black fella wanting work as an engineer?" people asked, shaking their heads. "Not likely."

McCoy took a job as a railroad fireman, shoveling coal into the firebox on the Michigan Central Railroad. It was hard, dull work — no job for a young man with a head full of mechanical dreams and a heart full of ambition. When the train stopped, he had to pour oil on the machinery to keep it lubricated.

"This is really stupid," McCoy said one day.

"What's stupid?" asked the railroad engineer.

"How we have to stop the train engine just to oil the parts. It seems like a big waste of time."

The engineer laughed. "You don't understand, Elijah," he explained patiently. "You have to stop the engine to oil the parts! You can't oil moving parts!"

"Why not?" McCoy asked.

The engineer just threw back his head and laughed again. "Poor Elijah. You just don't know much, do you?"

McCoy laughed, too. But that very night, he began working on an invention to oil an engine without stopping it. He worked in an old shed, using crude machinery. He worked every spare minute he had. He was happy when he was working on his invention because that is what he had wanted to do all his life.

McCoy found out that not only train engines had to be stopped to be oiled. Even the big machines in factories had to be stopped. Men ran around with little oilcans pouring oil on silent machines. It seemed an incredible waste of time and money.

"I've got it!" McCoy shouted one day. "I've found a way to oil machinery without having to stop it!" And so the twenty-eight-year-old inventor changed American industry.

McCoy's invention was called a lubricating or drip cup. It had tubes and valves, and it let oil ooze onto a machine when the machine needed it. The machine never had to be stopped to be oiled. McCoy received a patent from the U.S. government for his invention, and factories adopted the idea quickly. "Why

Elijah H. McCoy

> ## "A BLACK BOY WANTING TO STUDY ENGINEERING?" SOME PEOPLE EXCLAIMED. "NOT LIKELY!"

McCoy (1843–1929) is best known as the inventor of several locomotive lubricators. The phrase "the real McCoy" came about when customers wanted to be sure that they were buying the real thing, not an imitation.

didn't somebody come up with this before?" factory owners cried. "This will save us a fortune in lost time and production!"

Soon McCoy had no time to be a railroad fireman. He had to invent other things. He perfected twenty-three devices just for oiling different kinds of engines. He kept American industry moving twenty-four hours a day.

Other inventors tried to imitate McCoy's lubricating devices, but the imitations were not as good as the original. So when people bought a lubricating device for an engine, they would ask, "Is this the real McCoy?" That meant did Elijah McCoy really make this, or is it an imitation? The "real McCoy" came to mean something good and trustworthy. If it was not the "real McCoy," it was not acceptable.

McCoy's ambitions kept on growing. He invented a special ironing table and a lawn sprinkler. He started his own company, the Elijah McCoy Manufacturing Company, in Detroit, Michigan. His marvelous inventions spread across America, but he was never a well-known person. Today when somebody says, "It's the real McCoy!" chances are he or she never even heard of Elijah McCoy.

THE WIZARD OF MENLO PARK

Have you ever had trouble with something and thought, "If only they would invent a thingamajig that could make this easier!" You have probably heard the saying "Necessity is the mother of invention." The truth is, we invent things because we feel a need for them.

All of us will probably invent at least one thing in our lifetime, no matter how simple it might be. The clothespin, for example, was invented because people were tired of their clothes falling off the line.

The electric light was invented because people wanted something other than gaslight and kerosene lamps to read by. And today people are working on inventions that do not need gasoline or oil to make them run.

Thomas Alva Edison was an inventor. You probably know that he invented the electric light. But do you know that he also invented the phonograph, motion pictures, an electric locomotive, and the first central power plant to generate the electricity needed for the electric light? In fact, Edison has more patents registered in his name than any other person in the world — 1,093, to be exact. It does not seem possible for one person to have done so much.

But Edison was in the business of inventing. He began experimenting with things when he was a boy. During and just after the Civil War, Edison traveled from city to city as a telegraph operator. He learned a lot about electricity and electric equipment. As he grew older and more experienced, he needed a place to read and study, where he could experiment without bothering anyone.

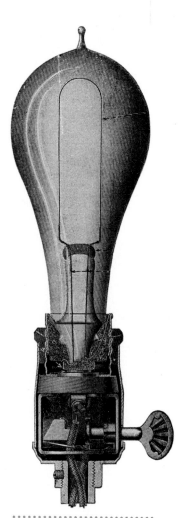

The Edison lamp and socket appeared on the frontispiece of Lewis Howard Latimer's book *Incandescent Electric Lighting*, published in 1890.

When he was twenty-nine years old, Edison moved all his laboratory equipment to a small town in New Jersey called Menlo Park. He started with one building and then built others for different purposes. Everything he needed for his inventions, from the moment he thought of them to the day they were sold to the public, was housed in these buildings. It was the first time anyone had done such a thing. The Menlo Park Compound became the world's first industrial research complex, and Edison became known as the "Wizard of Menlo Park."

Edison also was an organizer. Many engineers, scientists, and craftspeople came to work with him. When Francis Upton came to Menlo Park, he already had some ideas of his own about how to make an electric light work. He and Edison put their heads together and, after many months of experimenting, came up with the carbon filament. It burned brighter and longer than anything else they had tried. Others, like Charles Batchelor, also were coinventors with Edison. Edison is remembered as the inventor because the laboratory and most of the ideas were his.

Edison worked very hard all his life. He was so busy experimenting that he almost never went to bed. He took short naps instead, sometimes lying down on a table. You can imagine how little time he had for family or friends.

Think for a moment what your life would be like if Edison had never lived. How many of Edison's inventions can you name? How many do you use at home? What would it be like if you had to do without them? Is there something else you could use instead? Edison devoted his life to improving everyone else's. The same is true of most inventors.

AN ELECTRIFYING GENIUS

by Shari Lyn Zuber

The bright world of the electric lamp's inventor, Thomas Edison, seemed to be darkening. Bombarded by lawsuits filed by inventors who claimed that new ideas in the world of electric lighting were theirs and not his, he sought the help of a man who knew about the lighting industry and patent law and could provide expert testimony in court. That man was Lewis Howard Latimer.

Latimer, the son of fugitive slaves, was born in Chelsea, Massachusetts, on September 4, 1848. Although he went to work at a young age and could not attend school regularly, he was an excellent student.

When Latimer was ten, his father disappeared, and his mother had to break up the family. He and his older brothers were sent to a farm school, where they worked in exchange for food and lodging. His sister went to live with a friend, and his mother went to work on a ship.

When the Civil War broke out, Latimer wanted to enlist, but he was too young. Finally, in 1864, he joined the Union navy, serving aboard the USS *Massasoit*, a gunboat that was part of the North Atlantic Blockading Squadron protecting other ships from Confederate attack.

After his discharge, Latimer went to work as a clerk for Crosby and Gould, a firm of patent lawyers. There he became interested in the work of the draftsmen who prepared invention drawings. Saving enough

Thomas Alva Edison

Incandescent Electric Lighting (below) was the first book on electric lighting published in the United States. As its subtitle states, it is a "practical description of the Edison system."

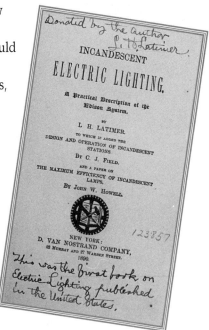

Lewis Howard Latimer

Latimer's home in Queens, New York, shown here in 1920, is being converted into a museum dedicated to the contributions of African Americans to the fields of science and technology.

money to buy used drafting instruments and books, he taught himself how to duplicate their drawings. When he felt he had mastered the technique, he asked if he could present his work.

To his boss's amazement, Latimer's drawings were quite good. In time, he was promoted to junior draftsman and eventually chief draftsman.

Although Latimer's work was a great help to other inventors, he wanted to use his talent to create his own inventions. In 1874, with the assistance of W.C. Brown, he received his first patent for coinventing an improved water closet (bathroom) that was used on trains.

While employed by Crosby and Gould, Latimer became friends with a young teacher from a nearby school for the deaf. He helped the teacher with the patent application and sketches for a machine he had developed that allowed voices to travel long distances through wires. With Latimer's assistance, Alexander Graham Bell's telephone changed the world of communication.

Latimer's work with Bell introduced him to the fascinating world of electricity. In 1880, he joined inventor Hiram Maxim's United States Electric Lighting Company.

At Maxim's company, Latimer tried to eliminate the main problem with Edison's electric light bulb. The filament (the material within a light bulb that glows when an electric current passes through it) lasted only a few days. A long-lasting filament had to be created to make electric lights practical. In 1881, one year after joining Maxim, Latimer and a coworker patented an improved method for bonding carbon filaments. The next year, Latimer received a patent for the less expensive and longer-lasting filament that revolutionized the world of electric lighting.

While at United States Electric, Latimer also patented an improved electric lamp, named the Maxim electric lamp, and a globe supporter (electric lamp socket). Unfortunately, Latimer had to assign his patents to the company for which he worked, so the money that was due him went to Maxim.

Latimer continued to work for Maxim, installing the first electric plants in New York City, Philadelphia, and Montreal. In London, he set up the first Maxim-Weston Electric Light Company and taught workers the entire process for light bulb production, from making filaments to glass blowing.

In 1884, Latimer went to work for Maxim's chief competitor, Thomas Edison. The competition between Edison and Maxim spilled over into the courts. Maxim questioned whether Edison was the first to have patented the light bulb and its improvements. Latimer's expert testimony in these legal battles often resulted in an Edison victory.

In 1890, Latimer wrote and illustrated the book *Incandescent Electric Lighting: A Practical Description of the Edison System,* which became the guidebook for electrical engineers worldwide. His clear and brief explanations made this complicated subject easy to understand.

While he worked with Edison, Latimer continued to develop his own inventions.

Among them were a safety elevator; electric fireworks; a locking rack for hats, coats, and umbrellas that prevented people from taking the wrong belongings in a restaurant; a book supporter, which kept books from tipping over on a shelf; and an "Apparatus for Cooling and Disinfecting," which cooled rooms and killed germs.

In 1892, Edison's Electric Company became the General Electric Company. Four years later, General Electric and the Westinghouse Company established the Board of Patent Control. The board's job was to prevent any more patent lawsuits. Latimer served as the board's chief draftsman and expert witness until its dissolution in 1911.

The Edison Pioneers, formed in 1918, included the original twenty-eight men who had worked with Edison before 1885. Being a member was one of the highest honors in the electric industry. Latimer was included.

Latimer's contributions to the world went beyond his work in electricity and his inventions. In 1925, a book of his poetry, *Poems of Life and Love,* was published. He used his talent as a writer and poet to promote equality for African Americans. He also taught courses at the Henry Street Settlement in New York City to help prepare immigrants for life in the United States.

Latimer continued to work in the electrical field until 1924. He died at his home in Flushing, New York, in 1928. Sixty years later, in 1988, the Queens Historical Society saved Latimer's home from demolition. It is currently being converted into a museum to display his and other African Americans' contributions to the world of science and technology.

THE WRIGHTS AS YOUNG BUSINESSMEN

by Richard Sassaman

Many people think of Orville and Wilbur Wright as only backyard builders. They do not realize that the brothers performed many scientific experiments before inventing the airplane or that the airplane was not their first creation. As long as anyone in Dayton, Ohio, could remember, the Wright boys had worked with mechanical projects.

Luckily, the two had parents who encouraged their love of science. Their mother, Susan, who had trained in college as a mathematician, taught them to draw plans and think out experiments. Their father, Milton, a church official who traveled a great deal, brought back presents that aroused their interest.

Orville and Wilbur long remembered their favorite gift, a toy helicopter made from cork, bamboo, and tissue paper. They called it "the Bat." Powered by two rubber bands attached to two propellers, the helicopter soared into the air when they let it loose.

Wilbur and Orville Wright

The Wright brothers drew on the knowledge and prior experiments of many great inventors to come up with their original designs.

Orville probably thought of "the Bat" when at age ten he started making kites to sell to his friends. Wilbur was not involved that much with the kites. He joined forces with Orville a short time later on their first complicated project, building a seven-foot wood lathe.

When Orville turned twelve, he became interested in carving woodcuts and printing them. This led to his fascination with printing presses. When he discovered that his good friend Ed Sines already owned a small toy press, the two became partners.

Bishop Wright, recognizing his son's interest, arranged for Orville and Ed to get a larger press. Still relatively small, this press was enough for them to start printing *The Midget,* a paper for their eighth-grade class.

Local merchants also started hiring Sines & Wright for printing work. Orville loved printing so much that he persuaded his friends to put on a local circus so that he could print the posters advertising it. As time passed, he bought out Ed's half of the business and worked during the summers at a printing shop in Dayton. He also built a larger press that could print eleven-by sixteen-inch pages.

In 1915, Orville Wright and his sister, Katherine, were photographed in a passenger-carrying model of the Wrights' airplane.

These printing presses operated much like the original press developed in Germany by Johann Gutenberg in the 1450s, more than four hundred years earlier. Orville set words in type, placed the type on a flat stone "bed," and inked it. Placing a piece of paper on top of the type, he worked a roller that pressed the ink onto the paper. (While building his second press, Orville had trouble finding a suitable bed. He finally bought an old gravestone that worked perfectly.)

In 1888, when Orville was almost seventeen, he decided to build an even bigger press. He had problems with this ambitious project and welcomed the help of his older brother, Wilbur.

Constructing the press took almost a year. With it completed in the spring of 1889, the brothers decided to begin a weekly newspaper, *The West Side News.* Orville served as publisher and Wilbur as editor. One friend who wrote for the paper was Paul Laurence Dunbar, who later became a world-famous poet.

In two years, *The West Side News* turned into a daily, *The Evening Item.* Before long, Orville bought his first bicycle and found a new interest.

Bicycles enjoyed great popularity in the mid-1890s for several reasons. The development of air-filled rubber tires and equal-size wheels made bike riding more comfortable. Many women started cycling alongside men, too.

Orville and Wilbur opened a series of four bicycle shops in Dayton, in which they sold and repaired bicycles. Each shop was larger than the one before, as the brothers became more experienced and more popular. In 1896, the Wrights started building their own brands of bicycles, the Van Cleve and the St. Clair.

They manufactured their bicycle parts themselves.

Despite their success, greater challenges attracted their attention after a few years. Hiring other people to run the bike shop, the two began experimenting with gliders and kites, hoping that they could invent the world's first practical airplane.

In fact, the first airplane included many bicycle parts. More important, the money from their cycle shops enabled the Wrights to support their own experiments and remain independent.

One day a customer saw Wilbur working with airplane wing designs using a wind tunnel. "What does that have to do with making Van Cleves?" he asked.

"Nothing at all," Wilbur replied, "but our bicycles paid for it."

A Pioneer Who Believed in Human Flight

by George Beshore

A hush came over the group that had gathered beside the Potomac River on a spot just south of our nation's capital. Then they cheered as a small, unmanned aircraft took to the sky and flew for more than half a mile.

The inventor of the aircraft was Samuel Pierpont Langley, secretary of the Smithsonian Institution in Washington, D.C. The date, May 6, 1896, was seven years before the Wright brothers' first manned flight.

Important connections link the two events. Langley's belief in the possibility of human flight encouraged Orville and Wilbur Wright to go ahead with their work. His attitude also made their own beliefs seem more credible. "When America's leading scientist said that flight was possible, it became harder for others to ridicule the idea," said Tom D. Crouch, chairman of aeronautics at the National Air and Space Museum in Washington and a modern authority on Langley's life and work.

Who was this pioneer who believed in human flight at a time when most people regarded it as a foolish dream? Langley was a self-taught engineer and architect who had become interested in science at the close of the Civil War, when he was past thirty. Although he would later receive several honorary degrees, including a doctorate from Oxford University in England, Langley had only a high school education.

By 1886, when he was already widely known for his work in meteorology and astronomy, Langley became interested in the possibility of human flight. He began to experiment. The next year, he was appointed secretary of the Smithsonian Institution and continued his work there.

Using two 30-foot arms that whirled at speeds up to seventy miles per hour, Langley tested different surfaces to find the proper curvature to give lift to the wings. Then he built model planes and tested them on an indoor track.

After ten years of such tests, Langley was ready for outdoor trials. He built a fifteen-foot-long model that weighed only twenty-six pounds. He called it an "aerodrome," from the Greek words meaning "air runner."

The crowd that watched on May 6, 1896, included the inventor of the telephone, Alexander Graham Bell, and other distinguished people of science. They saw Langley's aerodrome take off and fly for more than half a mile. Later the

Langley's belief in the possibility of human flight encouraged Orville and Wilbur Wright to go ahead with their work.

Dr. Samuel P. Langley

same year, on November 28, a larger model flew for three-quarters of a mile. Satisfied that his theories were correct, Langley expected others to take up where he left off and develop a practical flying machine.

He had an opportunity the same year to share his knowledge and enthusiasm about flying with two bicycle mechanics named Orville and Wilbur Wright. They had read of his work and wrote to the Smithsonian Institution to find out about this and any other experiments being conducted in the world.

The Wright brothers went ahead with their work, first in Ohio and later in North Carolina. Meanwhile, in 1898, the U.S. government provided Langley with fifty thousand dollars to develop a manned aircraft. The Smithsonian added twenty thousand dollars more, and he built a plane that was fifty-five feet long with a wingspan of forty-eight feet.

Twice, first on October 7 and again on December 8, 1903, Langley launched this craft along the Potomac River with an engineer named Charles Manly at the controls. Both times, it crashed into the water. The design of the plane was all wrong. It was never capable of flight.

Along the coast in North Carolina, Orville and Wilbur Wright had been testing their own flying machine. On December 17, 1903 — just nine days after Langley's second unsuccessful attempt — they took off on flat, level ground near the base of a large sand dune near Kitty Hawk, and the aviation age was born.

The Wrights' glider of 1902.

"The knowledge that the head of the most prominent scientific institution of America believed in the possibility of human flight was one of the influences that led us to undertake the primary investigation that preceded our active work.... It was a helping hand at a critical time, and we shall always be grateful."

The Wright brothers did not forget the pioneer who had helped them get their start. When Langley died in 1906 at the age of seventy-one, Wilbur Wright wrote to Octave Chanute, another pioneer in aeronautics. He said, "The knowledge that the head of the most prominent scientific institution of America believed in the possibility of human flight was one of the influences that led us to undertake the primary investigation that preceded our active work.... It was a helping hand at a critical time, and we shall always be grateful."

Langley was a theoretical scientist dedicated to discovering the basic principles on which others could build. As such, he would have been proud of these words of praise.

THE FIRST 1,000 INVENTIONS

by Richard L. Mattis

In 1903, a man running for Congress in Maryland made a speech. He told his audience that African Americans should not be permitted to vote because they were not smart enough. As proof, the man claimed that no African American had ever invented anything.

Henry E. Baker knew better. He was an assistant patent examiner for the U.S. Patent Office and was himself an African American. He had already published a list of three hundred seventy inventions by about two hundred African Americans through the year 1900. In that year, the Patent Office had conducted a survey to gather information about African American inventors and their inventions.

Commissioner of Patents Charles H. Duell had signed the survey letters, but Baker had done most of the work. The survey was necessary because nearly all the official Patent Office records said nothing about the race of the inventors. Only Henry Blair was identified in the records as "a colored man." He patented a corn planter in 1834 and a cotton planter in 1836.

Blair must have been a "free person of color" rather than a slave because a slave could not obtain a patent. It is likely that slaves did invent things to make their daily work easier, but the records of these inventions are lost. Some masters may have taken their slaves' ideas and patented them themselves.

The first African American who we know obtained a patent was Thomas L. Jennings, a tailor in New York City. In 1821, he developed a method for dry-cleaning clothing. Several other African Americans obtained patents before the Civil War. Sometime before he died in 1842, James Forten patented a device for handling sails. In 1846, Norbert Rillieux invented a vacuum evaporator for refining sugar. Sugar makers still use his process for removing the water from sugar cane juice.

After the Civil War and the freeing of the slaves, the number of inventions by African Americans increased. Jan Matzeliger's lasting machine attached the upper portion of a shoe to its sole, a task that had always been done by hand. The savings in labor cut the cost of shoes in half. Granville Woods's many inventions included a brake system for trains, a telegraph between moving trains, and a train for an amusement park. (See volume 1, page 198 for more information on Woods and other African American inventors who specialized in railroad improvements.)

Henry Baker's survey also identified several African American women inventors. Judy W. Reed probably could not write her name, but she patented a hand-operated machine for kneading and rolling dough in 1884. The following year, Sarah E. Goode patented a bed that folded into a cabinet that could serve as a desk.

In 1888, Miriam E. Benjamin patented a chair with a signaling device on it. When the person seated pressed a button, a bell sounded and a red signal appeared on the back of the chair. The House of Representatives adopted her invention. Congressmen could get the attention of their pages without calling to them or clapping their hands.

In 1892, Sarah Boone patented an ironing board that was especially suited to ironing women's clothes. In 1898, Lyda D. Newman patented a hairbrush that came apart for easy cleaning.

Baker was pleased to discover so much talent. But he also realized that many African American inventors would never be known. Some people who answered the survey had not kept accurate records. Some African Americans did not get patents because they could not afford an attorney. Some kept their race a secret, fearing that they would make less money if people knew that the idea had come from an African American. Baker knew that there was some truth to this.

The Patent Office conducted a second survey in 1913. The new information raised the number of known patents by African Americans to more than a thousand. Baker compiled a four-volume book on patents by African American inventors.

Granville T. Woods

Woods's many electrical creations led people to compare him to Thomas Edison.

Andrew Carnegie

In a letter to his uncle in Scotland, Andrew described his new life in America: "Although I sometimes think I would like to be back in Dunfermline, I am sure it is far better for me that I came here. If I had been in Dunfermline working at the loom it is very likely I would have been a poor weaver all my days, but here I can surely do something better than that, if I don't it will be my own fault, for anyone can get along in this Country."

THE KING OF STEEL

by Laurel Sherman

Andrew Carnegie watched as the Abbey Tower disappeared in the distance. He had known that leaving his native Dunfermline, Scotland, would be hard, but the twelve-year-old boy cried anyway. His father was one of the many Scots who had been put out of work by the coming of large, automated weaving mills. These mills left hand weavers like William Carnegie unemployed. With letters from relatives in the United States describing the opportunities there, the Carnegie family left Scotland from the port of Glasgow in May 1848. For young Andrew, it was the beginning of an adventure that would make him one of the most powerful and wealthy American industrialists.

The Carnegies settled in Allegheny, Pennsylvania, a town just outside Pittsburgh. Andrew's father tried to adjust to factory work, but eventually he went back to hand weaving. This meant that the rest of the family had to work to support themselves. Andrew's first job was as a bobbin boy in the cotton mill at $1.20 a week. His next job, which paid the grand sum of $1.65 a week, was in the cellar of a bobbin manufacturer. By this time he was fourteen, and he spent twelve hours a day making bobbins for the cloth-weaving industry.

Because he was so unhappy in his job, he was constantly on the lookout for something better. The new job that came along was the first in a series of lucky breaks that turned the bobbin boy into America's first "steel king." Andrew learned that telegraph messengers were needed in Pittsburgh. The telegraph was only ten years old at this time and was used especially by businesses to relay messages. As a runner for the company, he met many influential businessmen. One of these men hired him to work at the Pennsylvania Railroad Company as a telegraph clerk.

Andrew was a bright and energetic young man. Mr. Scott of the Pennsylvania Railroad grew very fond of him, appointing him as a personal secretary. Then in 1859, when Andrew Carnegie was only twenty-four, Scott made him superintendent of the Western Division of the railroad. Carnegie was not afraid to make quick decisions. When an accident left cars strewn all over the tracks, completely shutting down the railroad, he sent out an order under Scott's name that the cars blocking the line should be burned and traffic started up again right away. He knew he was taking a risk, but when Scott found out that this decisive action had saved the railroad from the expensive business of removing cars from the line, he praised his young assistant.

Carnegie's good judgment worked in his favor in other ways, too. Most of his wealth came from wise financial investments. He made the investment that began his fortune when a stranger named Woodruff approached him with a model of the first railroad sleeping car, something Woodruff had just patented. By the time Carnegie was twenty-five, his investment in the Woodruff Company was bringing him five thousand dollars a year. In the next few years, he continued to work for the railroad but also made other small investments. By the time he was twenty-seven, he had an annual income of almost fifty thousand dollars. At the age of thirty, he decided to leave the railroad and move into the manufacture of iron.

While railroads were expanding west, Carnegie realized that they would need iron bridges and iron rails to reach the Pacific. His first factories were devoted to producing iron. But in the 1870s, a new steelmaking process gained popularity. Steel was less brittle than iron, and steel rails proved more durable.

Henry Bessemer, an Englishman, had discovered that blowing cold air over hot pig iron could drive out almost all the impurities, creating steel that was strong and malleable. The only problem with the process was that it worked only with ore that was low in phosphorus. Many manufacturers had given up trying to use the new process because low-phosphorus ore was not always easy to obtain. But Carnegie opened a Bessemer steel plant near Pittsburgh and rapidly became the most successful competitor in the steel trade.

He owed his success to several things. He equipped his plant with modern, efficient equipment. Then he found and bought his own sources of raw materials and his own railroad and steamship lines to transport the materials and the finished steel. Soon he was independent and could produce steel rails more cheaply than other manufacturers.

But as much as Carnegie depended on his supplies of raw materials and his new Bessemer plant, he depended most heavily on his workers. Some of these workers were beginning to demand that they be allowed to form associations that could bargain with the company over wages, hours, and working conditions. Carnegie was a firm man, but he also tried to be fair with his workers. Despite this, one of America's most violent strikes occurred at his steel plant, the Homestead Works.

The plant was being managed by his partner, Henry Clay Frick, while Carnegie was out of the country. Frick hired Pinkerton guards and brought in outside workers to replace the strikers. These outsiders were met by the striking workers with guns and violence. Many men were killed before the guards fled, leaving the workers in possession of their plant.

The strike was settled at last, and the workers agreed to Carnegie's "sliding scale" of wages — a system in which a worker's wage would never fall below a minimum level but would rise only as the price of steel went up. Some people have blamed Carnegie for the excesses of the Homestead Strike because he backed up Frick and did not return to settle the strike himself.

Carnegie became wealthy beyond most people's dreams. He depended on the labor of thousands of men who were paid only a fraction of his earnings. Yet he was seldom criticized for the difference. Americans viewed their country as a place of opportunity for all. That the son of a poor weaver could rise to become one of the richest men of the century was proof, they thought, that America offered unlimited opportunity.

Carnegie felt that it was the responsibility of the rich to use their money to make life better for others. Many cities and towns across America have Carnegie libraries, art museums, performance halls, and research foundations.

In the summer of 1892, the twenty-eight hundred steelworkers at the Carnegie Steel Company mill in Homestead, Pennsylvania, went on strike. Pinkerton detectives were hired as guards to protect the mill while replacement workers were hired. A riot eventually broke out among the strikers, new workers, and Pinkerton guards. Although the strikers were able to overcome the Pinkertons, they were not as successful when the Pennsylvania Militia was sent in.

9

· ·

THE NEW AMERICAN WEST

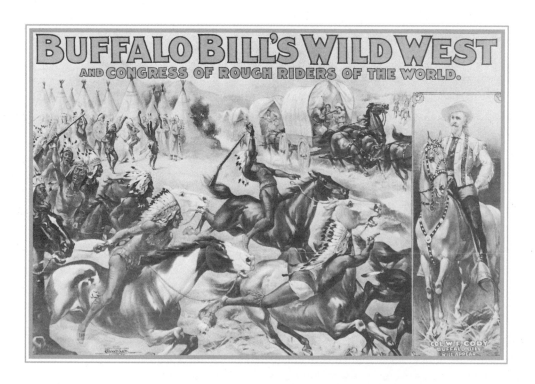

"Go west, young man"

was the famous advice that New York newspaper
editor Horace Greeley offered young Americans.
They took it seriously.

Long before the Civil War, the nation began its migration toward the Pacific Ocean, first into the uncharted territory of the Louisiana Purchase, then into the Great Northwest and Old Southwest, and finally reaching the ocean in time to dig into the earth and find gold.

After the war, more than ever, the West seemed to hold for Americans the promise of a better life in a better future. Just as important, once Americans had established settlements in every territory between the Mississippi River and the Pacific Ocean, the country finally seemed not only reunited but also grander than ever.

On the Red River, Fargo, Dakota Territory, 1878.

The Dalrymple farm, west of Fargo, Dakota Territory, 1878.

26,000–8000 B.C.

Indians cross land bridge from Asia to the Americas.

1500s

Mexican Indians are trained by Spanish conquerors to be *vaqueros*, or cowboys.

1777

Cherokee Indians cede their lands in the South to the United States.

1803

President Thomas Jefferson acquires the Louisiana Purchase.

1804

Sauk and Fox Indians cede fifty million acres in the Midwest to the United States.

1825

Erie Canal opens, providing fast, cheap passage west of the Appalachian Mountains.

1830–1842

Indians east of the Mississippi River surrender lands to the United States.

1833

First U.S. cavalry unit is organized.

1840s

Large-scale migration west on the Oregon Trail begins.

1866

Long cattle drives begin, passing through some Indian lands.

1869

First transcontinental railroad is completed.

1874

Barbed wire is invented.

1885–1887

Era of the long cattle drives ends.

1889

Defeated Sioux Indians cede nine million acres to the United States.

RECLAIMING THE WEST

by Karen E. Hong

Many people seemed to know about the West. Some said it was the "Great American Desert" — a land so forbidding that only fools dared to settle there. Others proclaimed the West the "Garden of the World." As the area was settled, the amount of rainfall coincidentally increased for a while, giving rise to the saying "Rain follows the plow." According to this theory, settlers actually increased the fertility of an area by farming it.

Still, to most people, the West was a mystery. It was a space marked "unknown" on maps. In 1869, John Wesley Powell set out to explore it.

Coming to know the West intimately, Powell worked to change the way the West was viewed and cared for.

Largely self-educated, Powell was a professor of geology and curator of the Illinois Natural History Society Museum. Although he had lost his right arm at the Battle of Shiloh during the Civil War, in 1869 Powell led a group down the Green and Colorado rivers through the Grand Canyon, until then unexplored. The group, formed to collect specimens for the Illinois museum, suffered blistering heat, chilling rain, physical exhaustion, and food shortages. Frequently, the river was unnavigable, causing the men to carry their boats and supplies overland.

Despite newspaper accounts of their deaths, Powell and five others completed the expedition. But Powell did more than simply gather samples. He recorded valuable scientific observations, explored the Grand Canyon, and drew geological sketches of the riverbanks and surrounding plateaus. He computed the height of the canyon walls and measured the flow of its streams. He recorded the barometric pressure, temperature, and mileage.

The American people proclaimed him a hero. Congress, recognizing his efforts, supported his work by granting him money for a geological and geographical survey of the Colorado River and its tributaries. From 1871 to 1879, Powell's surveys explored the adjoining canyon regions of what are now western Colorado, eastern Utah, northern Arizona, and northwestern New Mexico. Mapping and naming canyons, valleys, and streams whose existence had been unknown to white people, Powell's surveys also reported on the plants, animals, fossils, soil, water, and peoples of those areas. Within ten years, Powell had made more than thirty trips through much of the territory that would become Colorado, Utah, Arizona, New Mexico, Idaho, and Nevada. In 1879, he persuaded Congress to combine his work with other government surveys to form the U.S. Geological Survey to oversee western development.

Powell valued knowledge, especially when it was used for the good of humanity. Using his surveys, he studied the land and classified it by precipitation and usage. On this basis, Powell developed proposals for land reform, which he described in his 1878 *Report on the Lands of the Arid Region of the United States.*

In *Arid Lands,* as it came to be called, Powell sought to correct two widespread misunderstandings. The West, Powell explained, was not the Great American Desert. Although the forty percent of the continent west of the one-hundredth meridian received less than twenty inches of rain annually, this area was fertile when irrigated. But neither, Powell emphasized, was the West the Garden of the World. Although the West was then experiencing a period of increased rainfall, Powell knew from his studies that there had been periods of drought that were sure to recur.

Because of this, Powell saw water as the West's critical resource. Homesteaders moving west were doomed to failure unless they could be guaranteed water for irrigation. Since only water could make the land valuable, water monopolies should be prevented and water rights linked to the land by law.

Settlement of the West would require new water-rights laws and forms of cooperation. Although the development of dams and canals would depend on assistance from the federal government, settlers should join together to form cooperative irrigation districts, sharing water because it was scarce. Settlers interested in livestock should receive larger homesteads than customary and band together to form pasturage districts. Careful management of the common pasturage would help prevent the overgrazing that led to soil erosion.

John Wesley Powell

Many consider Powell the originator of conservation in the United States.

John Wesley Powell's expeditions to the Grand Canyon included a photographer who captured the ancient dwellings and writings of the Indians who had lived in the cliffs. Here Powell meets with the Ute chief Tau-gu.

Powell's conservation plan ignited controversy.

Many Americans believed in "rugged individualism," a lone person or family working hard and succeeding, not the cooperation Powell advocated. Many viewed modifying the Homestead Act, which gave a citizen one hundred sixty acres of free land if he or she was willing to work it, as almost sacrilegious (disrespectful toward something sacred). In a time of abundance, Powell spoke of shortages.

Congress failed to pass Powell's land-use program. Over the next ten years, drought and wind changed the West from America's land of promise to a dust bowl. Winters and springs of blizzards and storms passed into summers and autumns of droughts and prairie fires. Wagons returned from the West with "In God we trusted, in the West we busted" painted on their sides.

To solve the West's crisis, Congress put Powell in charge of the Irrigation Survey, designed to select reservoir sites and determine irrigation projects. But in 1890, Congress stopped the survey.

Although many consider Powell the originator of conservation in the United States, it was years before his ideas were widely accepted. Even today, conservation issues are often controversial.

In 1902, President Theodore Roosevelt signed the Reclamation Act, designed to reclaim the arid West by a series of dams and irrigation projects. Following this act, Utah passed an act placing ownership of water with the state. Legal disputes over the possession of water, especially where streams and rivers cross state boundaries and where water has been diverted from its natural course, have continued through the years. In 1963, for example, the U.S. Supreme Court agreed that Arizona had rights to specific amounts of water each year from the Colorado River and all water from the Gila River.

In conservation, the issue is frequently a question of whether to develop an area or preserve it. The completion of the Coolidge Dam on the Gila River in 1930 ended fifty-five years of opposition by Apache Indians who feared the destruction of their tribal burial grounds. To prevent this destruction, an eleven-thousand-dollar concrete slab was laid over the site.

In 1964, Glen Canyon, an area that captivated Powell on his Grand Canyon journey, was flooded to create Glen Canyon Dam. The canyon itself was renamed and is now Lake Powell. Only John Wesley Powell could say whether this development was what he had in mind when he advocated reclaiming the West.

AMERICA'S COWBOYS

Between the end of the Civil War and the end of the nineteenth century, cowboys were cattle herders on ranches in America's Southwest and, toward the end of the cowboy era, the Northwest. They brought new meaning to the word "cowboy." A century earlier, "cowboys" had been the name given to Tory bandits who vandalized areas of Westchester County in New York and who were not well liked.

The legend of the American cowboy dates back to a period of about twenty-five years beginning shortly after the Civil War. During that short period, a special set of circumstances made it possible for cowboys and their way of life to flourish. Then, as progress changed those circumstances, the cowboy era ended almost as suddenly as it had begun.

The cowboy legend tells of great open ranges, thousand-mile trail drives, and the cowboy — that mysterious person who lived in the saddle and cherished the freedom of the untamed West. In the period following the Civil War, America's Southwest was, for the most part, unsettled. Ranchers in the region lived on vast tracts of open land that were sometimes as large as five hundred thousand acres. Before barbed wire made it possible to fence in the land, great herds of longhorn cattle roamed freely there. These cattle were descendants of cattle that had traveled from Spain with the first Spanish explorers in the sixteenth century. Over the centuries, stray longhorns had formed herds, and by the middle of the nineteenth century, thousands lived in the Southwest.

Cattle ranching was not a new idea, but it did not become an important industry in the Southwest until the 1870s. Cattle ranching dates from Mexico in the sixteenth century, when Spanish settlers trained their Mexican Indian slaves to tend their cattle. These Indians became known as *vaqueros* (cow herders) and were America's first cowboys. They were very good at their trade, and our southwestern cowboys learned many skills from them. Their influence was so strong that many of the trade words they used, such as *corral, rancho* (ranch), *la reata* (lariat), and *bronco,* are still used in the cowboy trade today.

Southwestern cattle ranching began when ranchers rounded up some of the wild longhorns and then sold them to manufacturers in the North. The manufacturers used the cattle's hides, horns, hoofs, and tallow (fat). The idea of selling the cattle for their meat did not become popular until years later, when Philip Armour changed the meat industry with his new meatpacking plant in Chicago. He built his plant after the Civil War, and his new ideas made selling beef profitable. The demand for beef became so great that a head of Texas cattle sold for as much as forty dollars. Texas ranchers built up their herds and hired cowboys for the long drives north.

The ranchers' plan was to drive the cattle north to the nearest railhead, or place where the railroad tracks ended. In 1866, the railhead nearest to Texas was Sedalia, Missouri. That year, ranchers planned to drive their herds to Sedalia and load them onto railroad cars. From there, the herd would be transported to markets in the North. The trail drive ended in failure, however, because the farmers along the Missouri section of the trail refused to let the cattle cross their land. The farmers were afraid that the cattle

Nat Love earned the name "Deadwood Dick" after winning a marksmanship competition in Deadwood, South Dakota. Love, one of the most famous African American cowboys, wrote his autobiography in 1907.

would trample their crops and infect their cows with strange diseases. The Texas herds never reached Sedalia and had to be sold elsewhere for very low prices.

In spite of their losses, the ranchers tried again the next year. This time, however, they drove their herds to a railhead that was west of Missouri farm country. That railhead was Abilene, the first cattle town in Kansas. Records show that more than thirty-six thousand head of cattle were loaded onto railroad cars in Abilene that year.

As word of the successful trail drives spread, ranchers were encouraged to ship their herds north from Kansas railheads. Cattle towns, called boomtowns because they appeared to spring up overnight, were created at several locations, one after the other. Towns such as Ellsworth, Caldwell, Wichita, and, the most famous of all, Dodge City, flourished during the years of the cattle drives.

In summer and early fall, at the end of the long trail drives, the cowboys brought business to the boomtowns. They stayed in the hotels and boarding houses, ate in the restaurants, and amused themselves in the saloons, dance halls, and theaters. Once the cattle had been shipped, the cowboys headed south once again to find work and to prepare for another long drive the following year.

Cowboys came from many backgrounds. They were drawn to the trade because jobs in many other fields were scarce. They also may have thought that the life of a cowboy sounded exciting. Some had served as soldiers in the Civil War; others had not been successful back east. Most hoped for an opportunity to start over again, and the cowboy life offered them the chance. No one asked questions about a cowboy's past, and the cowboy's success depended on his skills. Approximately five thousand African American men became cowboys because there was little discrimination in the cowboy business. Many African Americans, including Ben Hodges, Isom Dart, and Bill Pickett, became famous in the West for their riding and roping skills.

People have chosen many heroes from the cowboy era — sheriffs tracking rustlers and bringing them to justice, cowboys single-handedly trying to tame the evils of an untamed West. Such characters have been made popular by movies and advertisements, books and songs. But the life of the cowboy was not an easy one, and it is important to remember that most of the stories we hear about cowboys are legendary.

Progress brought an end to the cowboy era. By the 1890s, railroads reached all the way to Texas, making the trail drives unnecessary. The meatpacking industry made it possible for ranchers to ship just the meat, not the live cattle. And fences made of barbed wire brought an end to the open range.

There are still cattle herders in America, and for them a sturdy cow pony, the annual roundup, and brandings continue to be a way of life. Some of the people who hold these jobs say that they would rather be cowboys than anything else in the world. They speak of the freedom of the wide-open spaces and a comfortable life, even though most of their ranches are fenced in and their work is difficult. Through them, the legend of the American cowboy lives on.

The cowboy's broad hat protected him from the sun and sometimes served as a pillow or a cup for him or his horse.

THE REAL TRUE GRITTERS

by Edward Carr

A federal marshal tracking cattle rustlers, a sheriff on a dusty cow town street shooting it out with a gunslinger — these are familiar images of the Old West and its heroes. They have been made popular in films, books, and even advertisements. Brave lawmen and daring outlaws did play a role in the history of the Old West, but a smaller one than is usually portrayed. A much larger role — and one every bit as adventurous and dangerous — was played by the cowhands who drove herds of cattle hundreds of miles through dangerous territory to the cattle chutes in Dodge City and other Kansas railheads.

These cowpokes, often young men still in their teens, accepted grueling twelve-hour days in the saddle with remarkable good humor and endurance. They rode with only the barest necessities — one change of clothing, stuffed in a tarpaulin, and a "sougan," or patchwork sleeping quilt, which was stored in the back of the chuck wagon. Their diet was monotonous — beef, sourdough biscuits, beans, and dried fruit. If provisions were spoiled or lost in a river crossing, there might be even less variety.

Following the ways of the Indians, a cowboy drags a buffalo hide to stop a prairie fire from spreading.

The longhorns the cowpokes drove were themselves a constant threat to life and limb. Many of the cattle in the herds were called *cimarrones,* which means "wild" in Spanish. They had run uncontrolled over the range during the Civil War years when many of the Texas ranchers were at war. These longhorns did not take kindly to their loss of freedom. Mature steers had horns that often measured four to six feet across. These horns had sharp tips and were used as weapons.

In Charlie Siringo's book *A Texas Cowboy,* he tells of an extreme measure drovers took with particularly unmanageable steers: "Sometimes we had to sew up the eyelids of these old mossy-horn steers to prevent them from running for the timbers every chance they got. It required about two weeks time to rot the thread, allowing the eyes to open. By this time the animal was 'broke in.'"

Two of the main cattle drive trails, the Chisholm and Shawnee, were dotted with stretches of quicksand in the riverbeds and bog holes around watering places. Cowboys sometimes spent entire days pulling cattle out of these death-traps. It took two men to free an animal that was mired — one on horseback with his lariat slung under the stuck steer, the other right down in the quicksand or mud pulling on the animal's forelegs. After the longhorn had been dragged to firm ground, it usually showed its gratitude by charging the men who had rescued it.

Thunder and lightning often caused stampedes, which could last for days. One of the worst recorded stampedes cost the lives of two thousand cattle.

As dangerous as the longhorns were ordinarily, they were even more deadly during a stampede. And stampedes were commonplace. Some journals record as many as four per week. A flash of lightning, the howl of a coyote, the scent of a mountain lion, a bolting jackrabbit, and a loud sneeze were among the dozens of causes of stampedes. Sometimes no apparent cause at all would panic a herd and trigger it into wild flight. A herd might bolt at any time of the day or night, and riders would have to take off after it, riding just out of reach of the steers' tossing horns, trying to turn the leaders and put the herd into a milling circle.

Picture yourself riding in night blackness on a half-wild mustang alongside a thundering herd in an electrical storm, badger and prairie dog holes hidden in the darkness ready to catch your horse's leg and throw you under the hoofs of the stampeding longhorns. The danger was increased by the constant tiredness of the riders, who spent twelve hours a day or more in the saddle and a two-hour shift of night guard circling the herd. Here is drover Teddy Blue's firsthand account of such an experience:

"And that night it come up an awful storm. It took all four of us to hold the cattle and we didn't hold them, and when morning come there was one man missing. We went back to look for him, and we found him among the prairie dog holes beside his horse.... The only thing you could recognize was the handle of his six-shooter."

Even more dangerous than the stampedes were the river crossings. Since the drives were made mostly in the spring, after the thawing of winter snow, the rivers were raging torrents. The banks of the Brazos, Red, Washita, and Cimarron rivers were scarred with the graves of riders who lost their lives in those turbulent waters. There was always the danger of a herd panicking and milling in midstream. A submerged log or a head of cattle being washed downstream might crash into a rider. Diaries speak of disturbed hornets swarming out from thickets on the riverbanks and dropping on riders and their mounts, creating havoc. In their rush to get their cattle to the railheads as early as possible in order to get higher prices, riders were forced to risk many a dangerous crossing.

George Duffield made this diary entry in 1866: "My back is blistered badly from exposure while in the river and I with two others are suffering very much. I was attacked by a beefer in the river and had a very narrow escape by diving [underwater]."

Once the herds had crossed the Red River at the Texas border, they ran into Indian Territory. The Indians, annoyed by these trespassers, often asked to be given cattle or tobacco, and they sometimes stole from the herds. On the Shawnee Trail, the Chickasaws, Creeks, Choctaws, and Cherokees demanded that the trail bosses pay tolls as high as $1.75 a head. Rather than pay the high tolls, trail bosses often chose confrontation.

On the Goodnight Loving Trail, the Comanches and their allies the Kiowas sometimes attacked the herds. For them, the cattle were only of secondary interest. They were more intent on running off the horses in the *remudas*. A remuda was a herd of extra horses taken on a cattle drive to make sure that the drovers had fresh mounts when they needed them. Usually there were three or more extra horses for each cowboy. The ranchers suffered some losses in both men and animals in these attacks, even with the advantage of new repeating rifles. The Comanches, superb horsemen and proud of their reputation as warriors, fought the cowhands with courage and skill.

Outlaw bands were another form of trouble drovers faced, although this happened only rarely. These rustlers waited along the trails to hijack herds and take them to market themselves.

Through it all — short rations, mud, choking dust, rustlers, stampedes, Indian raids, and raging rivers — the young cowboys driving the herds were the real true gritters of the Old West.

WILLIAM TEMPLE HORNADAY

by Shari Lyn Zuber

With a heavy heart, young William Hornaday looked at the gray squirrel lying on the ground, the first animal he had ever shot. There was no fun in this, he thought. The squirrel had not stood a chance. The seed for Hornaday's future dedication to wildlife had been planted.

Born on December 1, 1854, on a farm near Plainfield, Indiana, William Temple Hornaday grew up on another farm in Eddyville, Iowa. Hornaday learned early about animals and soon developed a respect for wildlife.

In college, he studied zoology and taxidermy, hoping to become a naturalist. He was appointed taxidermist of the school museum and taught himself the art of stuffing and displaying animals for public viewing.

To further his skills, in 1873 he became an assistant at Professor Henry A. Ward's Natural Science Establishment in Rochester, New York. At the facility, animals were prepared for display in museums and wildlife exhibitions. Satisfied with the specimens Hornaday collected on his first field trip to Florida and the Caribbean, Ward sent him on a three-year European and Asian expedition in 1876.

In 1880, Hornaday helped found the Society of American Taxidermists to promote his ideas about posing stuffed animals in lifelike positions and making their display settings natural. Professor George Brown Goode, assistant secretary of the Smithsonian Institution in Washington, D.C., agreed with Hornaday's views and offered him the job of chief taxidermist for the United States National Museum, which he accepted in 1882.

Hornaday's interest in animals led him from taking their lives for taxidermy to preserving their existence by creating new homes for them.

William Temple Hornaday

THEY SAW THE FUTURE

by Jean McLeod

In 1881, two years after Scotty and Sarah Philip were married, the last big buffalo hunt took place on the Grand River. During that hunt, Pete Dupree, a neighbor of theirs in Dakota Territory, captured five buffalo calves and turned them loose to graze with his cattle. When Dupree died eight years later, the buffalo had increased to more than fifty.

The Philips knew that they could not change what had happened to the buffalo, but they did want to see the buffalo survive. They purchased the entire Dupree herd, creating a fenced pasture for them on their land. In 1901, the buffalo were moved to their new home.

In 1906, Scotty went to Washington to request that thirty-five hundred acres of government land be added to the Philips' private landholdings "exclusively for the pasturing of native buffalo." Congress passed an act to that effect. Once the pasture was established, many of the buffalo were shipped to other locations to start new herds. Later, South Dakota bought thirty-six of the Philips' buffalo to start the Custer State Park herd.

While working at the museum, Hornaday became aware of the impending extinction of the American bison, whose numbers had dwindled from six million to six hundred within twenty years. Feeling that the species would not survive, he went west to try to obtain specimens for the museum, even though he regretted killing any more buffalo. The display at the National Museum drew much praise and inspired Hornaday to try to preserve the surviving bison. To do this, he wished to create a national zoo in which they could be protected.

Hornaday's 1887 proposal for a national zoo was enthusiastically received by Dr. Goode, who created the Department of Living Animals at the National Museum, with Hornaday as its curator. This "little try-out zoo" was opened on Smithsonian Institution grounds to "test the interest of the American public in collections of living animals."

Hornaday went west again, this time for mule deer, prairie dogs, lynx, and other live animals. Washingtonians flocked to the small exhibit. Its success spurred the creation of a full-size zoological park in Washington's Rock Creek Valley area. While he and Goode were planning the layout of the zoo, Hornaday also was lobbying to get legislators to accept a bill designating this land as the sight of the zoo. A paper he had written, "The Extermination of the American Bison," convinced Congress of the zoo's necessity, and construction began in 1889.

Differences of opinion over the design of the zoo between Hornaday and Professor S.P. Langley, the new secretary of the Smithsonian, forced Hornaday to resign the following year. Disillusioned, he retired to Buffalo, New York, and went into private business. He also wrote two books during this time, one on taxidermy and zoological collecting and the other a novel, *The Man Who Became a Savage.*

In 1896, the members of the year-old New York Zoological Society asked Hornaday to supervise the creation of the society's zoological park. Before accepting, Hornaday made certain that he would have control over the project.

Hornaday began in April, seeking a location for "New York's Splendid Zoo." In time, City Hall approved the 264-acre Bronx Park, with its untouched forests, meadows, and lakes. After a trip to study European zoos, Hornaday completed his final design in 1897. On August 15, 1898, ground was broken for the first building, the Winter House for the Birds.

By November 8, 1899, the official opening of the zoo, 843 animals of 157 species were housed there. Although the zoo was not completed (nor would it be for many years), there was much to see for the three thousand guests who attended opening-day festivities on that overcast afternoon. Hornaday wished to place animals in settings most like their natural habitats and give them as much space as possible to roam free. Cages were designed to blend into the landscape and not overshadow the beauty of the park.

Hornaday served the Bronx Zoo for thirty years, until 1926, overseeing the completion of his dream. During his directorship, he wrote many books about vanishing wildlife and the need for legislation to prevent the extinction of endangered species. His lobbying resulted in the enactment of conservation laws in many states and a ban on hunting species threatened with extinction. Hornaday was the first president of the American Bison Society, which is credited with preserving the bison from extinction in the United States.

Hornaday's interest in animals led him from taking their lives for taxidermy to preserving their existence by creating new homes for them. In the eleven years from his retirement until his death in 1937, Hornaday continued that work, raising money for the Permanent Wild Life Protection Fund he had helped to found.

JOHN MUIR: FRIEND AND PROTECTOR OF NATURE

by Helen Wieman Bledsoe

"In wilderness lies the hope of the world," wrote John Muir. A sequoia grove, glacier, mountain peak, and lake are all named for this woodsman and naturalist who so deeply loved the outdoors that he devoted his life to preserving America's wild beauty for following generations.

Muir was born in Scotland in 1838. When he was only eleven years old, his family set sail for the United States. They settled on a farm in Wisconsin, where hard work left little time for the children's schooling. Muir loved books, however, and despite discouragement from his father, he studied on his own. He was mechanically gifted, inventing things such as a huge outdoor thermometer, an automatic horse feeder, and a wooden pendulum clock.

A neighbor advised him to display his inventions at the state fair, where they won a prize. As a result, Muir was encouraged to apply to the University of Wisconsin, where he was admitted despite his lack of formal education. While a student at the university, he created more unique inventions: a bed that the sunrise caused to tip up and send him sprawling and a desk that toppled one book on the floor and shoved the next one under his nose according to his own timed study schedule.

After college, Muir took a job in a machine shop. One day a piece of metal pierced his eye. While he was hospitalized in darkness, Muir realized how much he loved the bright outdoors, and he resolved never to work in a factory again. As soon as he recovered, he set off on a one-thousand-mile walk from Indiana to

John Muir

"He who gains the blessing of one mountain day is rich forever."

Florida, then continued on to Cuba by ship. Next he traveled to New York and from there by ship to California, where he found his lifework.

Muir was thirty years old when he left San Francisco and climbed up into the Sierra Nevada. He spent the next five years learning about the mountains. He would set off with his blanket roll and a rubber bag containing a little tea and flour and maybe some oatmeal and be gone for days or even weeks. He considered a fifty-mile hike in the rugged mountains a good "two day saunter."

He liked to stand at the top of a waterfall and sing aloud for pure joy. Once he lashed himself to the top of a hundred-foot-high Douglas fir during a storm so that he could experience how a tree withstands the wind's buffeting. During another storm, his feet were frostbitten when he was trapped overnight. He learned more about the Sierra Nevada than anyone had ever known. For instance, he was the first to realize how glaciers had carved out the valleys.

Muir Woods National Monument in Mill Valley, California, was founded in 1908 in honor of John Muir's work as a conservationist, naturalist, and supporter of national parks and reservations. The park features coastal redwood trees.

Muir began writing essays and delivering speeches describing the glories of the wilderness. When he was about fifty years old, he met Robert Underwood Johnson, editor of *Century Magazine*, who persuaded him to write two articles for the magazine. Muir's "Treasures of the Yosemite" and "Features of the Proposed Yosemite National Park" were published in 1890.

With the help of these articles, Johnson convinced a group of powerful people to lobby Congress in support of a bill saving Yosemite as a national park. The articles also caused a greater portion of the American public to see the value of unspoiled forests and mountain meadows. Some, however, still thought that the federal government should be in the business of developing and selling wilderness land, not preserving it.

Congress did pass the Yosemite bill in 1890, and it was written into law, creating a national park. But the lovely Yosemite Valley, still under state control, was not included in the park until fifteen years later, when President Theodore Roosevelt signed a measure including it in the park's boundaries. (Two years earlier, the president had camped with Muir in Yosemite for four days.) Later, Roosevelt and Congress extended the boundaries of the national forest reserves in all states to include a total of 148 million acres. Roosevelt said that the sequoia trees in California needed protection "simply because it would be a shame to our civilization to let them disappear. They are monuments to themselves."

Muir continued his conservation efforts as the first president of the Sierra Club, founded in 1892. The original goal of the club was "to preserve forests and other features of the Sierra Nevada Mountains," but the club's mission is much broader today.

The grandeur and solitude of mountains was necessary to John Muir's spirit. He wrote, "He who gains the blessing of one mountain day is rich forever." Muir's writings spurred the U.S. Congress to set aside areas of unspoiled natural beauty for all Americans to enjoy.

WHERE THE GHOSTS WALK IN DAYLIGHT

by Kenneth P. Czech

Gunfire and war whoops filled the hot June air. Bullets whined, and arrows thumped into the baked ground. Dust swirled in choking clouds. A small band of U.S. Seventh Cavalry troopers, cut off from their company, scrambled along the sloping terrain, hoping to find their commander, Lieutenant Colonel George Armstrong Custer. Pausing only to fire their Springfield carbines or Colt revolvers at Indian warriors looming in the dust, the four soldiers (a sergeant and three privates) could hear the urgent notes of a bugle calling them to assemble. They did not, however, know that most of their blue-coated comrades had already fallen under the guns, arrows, and war clubs of the mighty Cheyenne and Sioux nations.

A slight breeze momentarily cleared the dust and rifle smoke. The sergeant glimpsed the remnants of Custer's troops knotted in a desperate stand at the crest of a nearby hill. Corpses of men and horses littered the ground as far as he could see. Hunkpapa, Brulé, and Minneconjou warriors dashed ferociously about, leaning from horseback to strike the soldiers with lances and clubs. Others fired bows and arrows, ancient muskets, and a few modern repeating rifles.

The sergeant thumbed the hammer of his revolver. A veteran of many campaigns, he realized that the battle was lost. Even if he and the three young privates reached Custer, there was no stopping the Indian attack. Warriors filled the ravines below the hill. Beyond the sparkling ribbon of the Little Bighorn River in the distance, he could see more Cheyennes racing to the fight.

With a sudden whoop of triumph, a Sioux chief thundered down upon the troopers. The sergeant lifted his pistol as the Sioux swung his war club. More Indians followed. The soldiers emptied their guns, then engaged in hand-to-hand combat. In moments, their struggle was over.

The Plains Indians had been pushed from their traditional hunting grounds for generations by white settlers moving west. The discovery of gold in South Dakota's Black Hills brought more whites. They moved onto the land and slaughtered the great herds of buffalo, the Indians' primary source of food, clothing, and shelter. U.S. Army forts were established to protect the new settlers, and many of the tribes were forced to move to reservations in the 1870s. The Lakota, or western, Sioux and the Cheyennes refused to live on reservations. Thousands gathered in a village on the banks of the Little Bighorn in southeastern Montana in June 1876. U.S. soldiers were sent to defeat them.

An experienced Civil War and frontier soldier, Custer had hoped for a stunning victory that would enhance his reputation. Custer undoubtedly underestimated the Indians' strength. He divided his 600-man force into three segments. One wing, under Captain Frederick Benteen, scouted to the south. Another, under Major Marcus Reno, attacked the southern end of the sprawling Indian village but was quickly driven back with heavy losses. Custer and his remaining 225 troopers rode to attack the village near its northern end.

As many as two thousand Indian warriors rode out to meet him. "The smoke was like a great cloud, and everywhere the Sioux went the dust rose up like

George Armstrong Custer

During the Civil War, while fighting for the Union, Custer was cited for gallantry at Gettysburg.

smoke," recalled Cheyenne chief Two Moons, who fought in the battle. "We circled all around him [Custer] — swirling like water around a stone. We shoot, we ride fast, we shoot again. Soldiers drop, and horses fall on them." Custer's entire command was wiped out.

The Indians removed most of their dead from the battlefield and broke camp. Knowing the Army would be looking for revenge, some tribes traveled south, while others went to Canada. Many returned to their reservations.

A relief column of soldiers found Custer's bloody battleground and hastily dug graves for the dead. The telegraph flashed news of Custer's defeat across a shocked nation. Within months, many of the Sioux and Cheyennes surrendered as the army pursued them. Many were killed or sent to prison as well.

The great Sioux chief Crazy Horse surrendered in 1877 and was reportedly killed in a jail in Fort Robinson, Nebraska. Chief Sitting Bull, leader of the Cheyennes and Sioux at the Little Bighorn, returned from Canada and lived in South Dakota until he was murdered in 1890. The strength of the Indians had finally been broken.

A year after the battle, the remains of several officers were uncovered and reburied in the eastern United States. Custer's body was buried in the cemetery at West Point, New York. In 1881, the remains of Custer's troopers were dug up and placed in a mass grave marked by a large granite memorial.

Today marble markers dot the grassy slopes of the Little Bighorn Valley, showing the approximate places where soldiers fell. Markers also indicate the bluff where Reno's and Benteen's men survived continued Indian attacks. Aside from the markers, the battle site looks much as it did on that sweltering June day in 1876. Daisies and yellow mariposa lilies add color to the tall grasses. The Little Bighorn River sparkles in the distance. It is a place, say the Sioux, "where ghosts still walk in broad daylight."

BUFFALO BILL'S WILD WEST AND PIONEER EXHIBITION

by Karen E. Hong

The passengers clambered aboard, settling themselves in the Deadwood stagecoach. After listening to the stage agent's warnings, the driver hoisted himself onto the seat and urged the six mules forward. The stage was rolling on its way, when a band of Indians burst forth from their hiding place. Yelling ferociously, the Indians pursued the coach. The driver whipped the mules and charged ahead, but the Indians quickly surrounded the stage. Shots rang out as the small group of passengers tried to defend themselves against the overwhelming rush of Indians. All seemed lost — the Indians were about to seize the stage!

Just at the moment of capture, Buffalo Bill, leading a group of scouts, burst upon the scene. Shooting began and grew louder and faster as Buffalo Bill and the

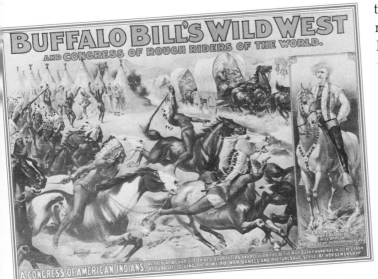

Buffalo Bill's Wild West promised Buffalo Bill at every performance as well as "congresses" of American Indians and rough riders.

scouts drove back the Indians. Thanks to Buffalo Bill and his scouts, the Deadwood stage and its passengers had survived another Indian attack.

Wild with excitement, the audience rose in the grandstand and cheered. The Wild West, Hon. W.F. Cody and Dr. W.F. Carver's Rocky Mountain and Prairie Exhibition was a success. So popular was the Indian attack on the Deadwood stage that it became a permanent part of Buffalo Bill's program, running from the first show in 1883 to the last in 1917.

The Wild West show toured the United States during the summer of 1883. The outdoor extravaganza

offered horseracing by Indians, a reenactment of the Pony Express, the attack on the Deadwood stagecoach, shooting exhibitions, bucking broncos, and a display of steer lassoing. In the final act, "Buffalo Chase," buffalo were turned loose to be roped and ridden by cowboys. Although the show was a popular success, the partnership of Cody and Carver was riddled with conflict. At the end of the first season, they divided the show's property and separated.

Cody joined forces with Nate Salsbury, an author and comedian, in 1884 to organize a new show. Under Salsbury and Cody, Buffalo Bill's Wild West — America's National Entertainment expanded to include more displays of horsemanship and marksmanship.

In 1884, the show was in New Orleans at the same time that the Sells Brothers Circus, which featured the sharpshooting of Frank Butler and Annie Oakley, was in town. In between performances, the couple went to visit the competing show. As they walked around the grounds, they were impressed with what they saw. The performers and animals were treated with kindness; Buffalo Bill seemed to care about every member of his troupe, something Butler and Oakley felt was missing in the Sells brothers' organization. They decided to find out about joining Buffalo Bill.

Oakley joined the show the next year, billed as "The Peerless Wing and Rifle Shot." Her husband had decided that she should be the star and he would help her by planning her act, releasing targets, and taking care of her guns.

Oakley appeared first on the program after the "Grand Review," the opening parade. Petite and feminine, Oakley put the audience at ease with her skill with firearms, preparing them for the almost continual shooting that would follow. For seventeen years, she entertained audiences with her sharpshooting.

The Sioux chief and medicine man Sitting Bull also joined the show in 1885. Although many spectators booed him for defeating George Armstrong Custer at the Battle of the Little Bighorn (see page 285), Sitting Bull displayed a quiet

THE OUTDOOR EXTRAVAGANZA OFFERED HORSERACING BY INDIANS, A REENACTMENT OF THE PONY EXPRESS, THE ATTACK ON THE DEADWOOD STAGECOACH, SHOOTING EXHIBITIONS, BUCKING BRONCOS, AND A DISPLAY OF STEER LASSOING.

Buffalo Bill in the Limelight, an illustration by Frederic Remington, is on permanent display at the Whitney Gallery of Western Art and at the Buffalo Bill Historical Center.

BUFFALO BILL

by Alison T. Kelley

A long-haired, bearded man on a white horse proudly led the long parade of human and animal performers. He doffed his big white Stetson to the excited crowd lining the streets. To the townspeople's delight, Buffalo Bill's Wild West had come to town.

All dressed in white, Buffalo Bill appeared to be a man of dignity and gentility. In reality, he was a rootin' tootin' roughrider who sought adventure and danger in everything he tried.

William Frederick Cody was born in Scott County, Iowa, in 1846. Young Will was always looking for adventure. If he could not find it, he play-acted it. Dressed in a colorful feather headdress, he let out a war whoop at his three sisters, who were riding an imaginary wagon train.

"When I'm grown up, I'm going to be a showman," Will said. "I'm going to run my own show." And he did just that.

Will's father, Isaac, died when Will was eleven. To support his mother and sisters, he got a job after school as a delivery boy for Russell, Majors & Waddell, a freight wagon company. He stayed in school just long enough to learn to read and write a bit, but he never learned his numbers.

Will then took a job away from home as a driver for a wagon-train horse herd. He kept all the extra oxen and horses together and out of the wagons' way. One day a herd of buffalo stampeded the train, overturning wagons and ripping the canvas tops. One buffalo started to charge Will, but the thirteen-year-old quickly shot him dead. That was Will's first buffalo.

By 1860, many people had moved west to start new settlements. That year, a mail delivery service called the Pony Express was started. In 1861, at fourteen, Will Cody was big and strong and an excellent rider. He convinced Captain Jack Slade to let him try the mail route.

High-speed galloping for 75-mile shifts was the rule for Pony Express riders. That was just Will's speed. He loved changing ponies every 10 to 15 miles and throwing a *mochila* (satchel) bulging with mail over the saddle. It is said that on one unusual nonstop ride, Will logged 322 miles and used 21 ponies. Will also welcomed the danger posed by hostile Indians, who were a constant threat to a lone rider on the plains.

Later Cody became an Indian scout for the U.S. Army. He married and had a child. He soon found, however, that he needed more money than his scout's pay could provide. At age twenty-two, Cody took another dangerous job with Goddard Brothers hunting buffalo to supply meat for railroad workers laying track for the Kansas-Pacific line. Cody was the best buffalo hunter the company had. He shot a total of 4,280 buffalo in eight months. From that time on, Cody was known as "Buffalo Bill."

Annie Oakley

Annie Oakley became one of the biggest stars of the Wild West shows. She had an incredible talent as a markswoman and rarely missed her target.

dignity. Souvenir photographs of Buffalo Bill and Sitting Bull, captioned "Enemies in '76, Friends in '85," sold by the thousands.

In 1887, Buffalo Bill's show toured England, playing in London for Queen Victoria's Golden Jubilee, her fiftieth anniversary as queen. To the delight of the British audience, Indians danced and fought, a prairie fire threatened a wagon train, wild animals stampeded, sharpshooters displayed their skills, Custer's last stand at the Little Bighorn was reenacted, and Deadwood City was destroyed by a cyclone. London's *Daily Telegraph* said that the show "was not acting or imitation of Western life, but an exact reproduction of the scenes of fierce frontier life vividly illustrated by the real people."

Back in the United States, thousands saw Buffalo Bill's Wild West at the World's Columbian Exposition in Chicago in 1893. Although the grandstand seated eighteen thousand people, the show was so popular that people sometimes had to be turned away.

Over the years, Buffalo Bill updated the show. Favorite acts such as Annie Oakley and the Indian attack on the Deadwood stagecoach remained mostly unchanged, but 1886 saw the addition of a western cyclone of dry leaves and underbrush created by a huge blower. Featuring horsemen from around the world and the U.S. Cavalry, the Wild West's name was changed to Buffalo Bill's Wild

West and Congress of Rough Riders of the World in 1893. In 1899, a reenactment of the Spanish-American War's Battle of San Juan Hill was added to the program.

The show toured the United States and Canada, sometimes spending whole summers at places such as the 1893 World's Columbian Exposition and Ambrose Park in Brooklyn, New York. Other years, the troupe toured more than one hundred cities in a season, traveling by train across the continent. Annie Oakley stayed with the show through 1901, when she was seriously injured in a train wreck.

By 1908, Buffalo Bill found himself in debt, so he combined his show with Pawnee Bill's Far East show. They intended to tour every town and city in the United States and Canada, but the show had to be auctioned in 1913 to pay Buffalo Bill's debts. In 1916, Buffalo Bill toured with the Miller Bros. 101 Ranch Real Wild West.

After Buffalo Bill's death on January 10, 1917, Johnny Baker, a former sharpshooter with him, tried to reorganize the show. He used the name Buffalo Bill Wild West Show Co., Inc., and many acts that had made Buffalo Bill famous, but after a few months on the road, the show closed. That ended more than thirty years in which Buffalo Bill's Wild West shows had brought the American West and its way of life to the rest of the world.

WILLA CATHER: NEBRASKA'S PIONEER

by Charlotte Van Vleck

Willa Cather was the eyes and ears of an era. With words, she sketched pictures of the 1880s, 1890s, and early 1900s. Through her work, we are able to feel what it was like when Nebraska's prairies were first being settled. We can sense the homesickness, the courage, and even the occasional hopelessness of those new pioneers. She drew not the earlier ones in their covered wagons, but the pioneers who came later in railroad cars with their bundles and odd-looking clothing and strange languages.

Cather knew about these pioneers because she was one of them. Toward the end of her life, she looked back at those first years she spent in Nebraska and said that they were the most important years of her life because they gave her so much to write about.

Willa had been living on a large estate in Virginia before her family decided to move to the prairie farm near Red Cloud, Nebraska. In Virginia, she lived in a large, comfortable, three-story brick mansion surrounded by beautiful, rolling green hills. Her family had servants in the house and many hired people to help her father raise sheep. Willa must have wondered why her father decided to leave it all behind and move to a part of the country where few people had settled.

But Charles Cather was not alone in his decision to move west. Not only had Willa's grandparents and aunt and uncle already moved to Nebraska, but many other southerners also had looked west for a fresh start after the terrible destruction of the Civil War. But why Nebraska?

They went to Nebraska because of the Homestead Act, a law that made large tracts of land available for purchase at a very small cost. In fact, the Homestead Act offered one hundred sixty acres free to anyone who filed a claim, improved

"There was nothing but land; not a country at all, but the material out of which countries are made."

Willa Cather

Quotes are from the book *My Ántonia* by Willa Cather.

Although Cather looks more like a stylish New Yorker in this photograph, she carried the prairie with her throughout her life. She not only wrote about the prairie and the West, but she also visited there often.

the land a little, and lived there for five years. Imagine one hundred sixty acres of what appeared to be good farmland that did not even need to be cleared because there were almost no trees. When Charles Cather's big barn in Virginia burned to the ground, he made up his mind to start over in Nebraska, where good land was available in the early 1880s.

In the spring of 1883, during apple blossom time, the Cather family packed their belongings, wrapping their fine china in useless old Confederate money. Willa and her family boarded the train that would take them to their new home. Willa's dog, which had been given to a neighbor, broke his rope in an attempt to follow them.

How lonesome Willa must have felt when she had her first glimpse of the vast stretches of prairie that were to be her home. We have some idea of her feelings because many years later, she gave those feelings to the characters in her books. In *My Ántonia,* Cather speaks through the character Jim Burden. Like Cather, Jim left Virginia to move to Nebraska. He was to join his grandparents and was met at the train station by their hired hand late at night. This is what he remembers about that first night:

"There seemed to be nothing to see; no fences, no creeks or trees, no hills or fields. If there was a road, I could not make it out in the faint starlight. There was nothing but land; not a country at all, but the material out of which countries are made. No, there was nothing but land.... I had the feeling that the world was left behind, that we had got over the edge of it, and were outside man's jurisdiction. I had never before looked up at the sky when there was not a familiar mountain ridge against it. But this was the complete dome of heaven, all there was.... Between that earth and that sky I felt erased, blotted out."

For Willa, the new land in Nebraska took some getting used to. She rode her horse day after day over the prairie, wandering, exploring, getting the feel of the strange, bleak land so different from the green hills of Virginia. From her initial hatred of it, she grew to love the plains with an intensity that kept her tied to them no matter where she went.

Sod houses were beginning to appear, and there were dugouts wherever there was a small rise in the ground. (A dugout was part cave and part house.) Again Jim, in *My Ántonia,* speaks for Willa when he goes with his grandmother to visit their Bohemian neighbors:

"As we approached the Shimerdas' dwelling, I could still see nothing but rough red hillocks, and draws with shelving banks and long roots hanging out where the earth had crumbled away. Presently, against one of those banks, I saw a sort of shed, thatched with the same wine-coloured grass that grew every-where...and then I saw a door and window sunk deep in the drawbank."

The two Shimerda girls, Ántonia and Yulka, slept in a cave dug into the rear wall. There were some advantages to these caves but not many. If a baby was born, a small hole just big enough for the new baby to sleep in could be dug in the side of the cave. And no one worried about dirt on the floors. But the sod houses and dugouts were mostly uncomfortable, and the settlers replaced them with wooden houses as soon as they could afford them. Willa's family could afford a wooden house right away.

When they first arrived in Nebraska, the Cathers lived in a farmhouse, and Willa's father tried to begin farming this broad, open land. Like many others, he imagined that farming would be easy, for there were no trees to cut down. All he had to do was plow the fields, and the crops would grow. But the ground was packed hard from years of weathering and entangled roots of prairie grasses. It resisted the plow and refused to be cultivated. And the weather itself was brutal. There were blizzards in winter when a person could freeze to death ten feet from his front door and not even know his house was nearby.

Summers could be just as harsh. In one of her stories, Cather tells about the heat. One afternoon on the Fourth of July, a man returned from his fields and asked his wife to prepare a nice picnic for the family. He asked for fried chicken especially, and then he went down to the watering tank by the windmill. He and his two sons went for a swim in the tank. Then they all went to the orchard for their picnic. When they were finishing their meal, his wife asked about the corn in the fields.

"'Corn,' he says, 'there ain't no corn.'

"'What you talkin' about?... Ain't we got forty acres?'

"'We ain't got an ear,' he says, 'nor nobody else ain't got none. All the corn in this country was cooked by three o'clock today, like you roasted it in an oven.'

"'You mean you won't get no crop at all?'

"'No crops this year,' he says. 'That's why we're havin' a picnic. We might as well enjoy what we got.'"

Charles Cather struggled with his farm for a year. During that time, Willa made friends with her neighbors, many of whom came from foreign countries — Bohemia, Germany, Norway, Russia, Poland, and others in northern and central Europe. But the stubbornness of the land discouraged Charles, and he decided to move the family to Red Cloud, a town only fourteen years old that already had twenty-five hundred people. He found a small white house, and Willa fixed up a room for herself by blocking off part of the attic.

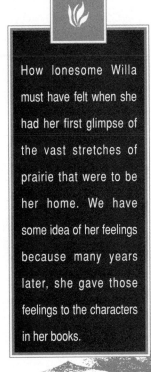

How lonesome Willa must have felt when she had her first glimpse of the vast stretches of prairie that were to be her home. We have some idea of her feelings because many years later, she gave those feelings to the characters in her books.

Town life brought new experiences into Willa's life. She had spunk and imagination. She enjoyed giving speeches, speaking pieces, and putting on plays. In her teens, she had her hair cut shorter than a boy's, at a time when long hair was the rule for girls and women. She wore a man's hat, sometimes even a Civil War cap, and shirts and skirts that were as plain as possible. There would be no ruffles, lace, or embroidery on *her* clothes. Sometimes she even signed her name "William Cather, Jr."

LAURA INGALLS WILDER

Born in 1867, Laura Ingalls Wilder saw our country change from a land of opportunity and adventure, preoccupied with westward expansion, to a modern nation, preoccupied with industrial and technological growth. Wilder grew up on the prairie, moving from place to place and living a rugged pioneer life. Encouraged by her daughter, Rose, Wilder, in her sixties, began to write books based on her childhood. The success of her first book, *Little House in the Big Woods*, published in 1932, motivated her to plan an eight-volume frontier novel. As the books became more complicated, Rose offered sug-

gestions on plot, characterization, and expression. She also dealt with agents and publishers, edited all the manuscripts, and in a sense launched the books into the world.

As a writer, Wilder was interested not only in recounting her childhood but also in using her life to paint a broad historical picture. In reading her works, we not only get to know her characters and share in their experiences, but we also realize their place in our country's history. The importance of her works lies in the depiction of a young nation made up of hard-working folks whose lives seem much simpler than ours today.

Above: In 1972, the Laura Ingalls Wilder Memorial Society of DeSmet, South Dakota, purchased the last home that the Ingalls family occupied. Today it is a museum. The society is headquartered next door to the Railroad Surveyors' Shanty, which was Wilder's first home during the winter of 1879–80.
Inset: The Wilder family in 1894. Laura is standing behind her father (center).

The frequent arrival of actors and musicians at the Republican Valley Railroad station south of town brought special delight into Willa's life, for Red Cloud was big enough to be a stop on the circuit of traveling theatrical companies. Willa and her friends would excitedly walk the mile to the station to watch and exclaim over the glamorous men and women alighting from the train. Then they would coax their parents to let them watch the performers at the Opera House over the hardware store on Main Street or in the hotel.

Older friends were important in Willa's life. She would ride with Dr. McKeeby in his buggy into the country and help him on his rounds. Once she even gave chloroform to a boy who had to have his leg amputated. That day she signed her name "Wm. Cather, M.D." and told everyone that she was going to become a doctor.

She learned from her neighbors, the Wieners, who spoke French and German. They had a large library, and Willa would lose all track of time as she read their books. William Ducker, a Latin and Greek literature scholar who clerked in his brother's store, introduced her to the classics and taught her Latin.

At the University of Nebraska, Willa's first essay was printed on the front page of the Nebraska *State Journal*. Seeing her name in print decided her career. She *had* to be a writer. She continued to write for the *Journal* all through college, then became the managing editor of *Home Monthly* magazine in Pennsylvania. She even taught high school in Pittsburgh. For six years, Cather was an editor at *McClure's Magazine* in New York City. During all that time, she was writing short stories and poetry. After her first book, *Alexander's Bridge,* was published in 1912, she was able to spend all her time writing.

Fame came with Cather's first prairie novel, *O Pioneers!* in 1913. She continued to live in New York but spent long periods of time in Nebraska, Colorado, New Mexico, and Arizona, writing about the experiences of pioneers and settlers on the Great Plains and in the Spanish Southwest. She wrote eighteen books in all, received honorary degrees from many universities, and won the Pulitzer Prize in 1922 for *One of Ours,* a story of a prairie boy in World War I.

Cather spent her last years in New York, with visits to New Hampshire and Nova Scotia in the summers. She died in 1947.

FREDERIC REMINGTON: HIS LIFE AND ART

What do you think of when you hear the word "art"? Do you think of something very old, such as the pyramids in Egypt? Or something very modern, such as colorful patterns created by a computer? Do you think of something lively and energetic — a sculpture of a bucking bronco? Or something quiet — a photograph of a sunset? Do you think of something very easy to understand, such as a portrait of a woman at a piano? Or something "abstract," such as splotches of paint on a wall?

Of course, all these things could be considered art. And it also is true that all art provides us with a kind of history. Each work of art we see tells us something about the world as it was at the time the work was created. Artwork also tells us something about the way a person or people living at a certain time saw their world.

His drawings, paintings, and sculptures capture some of the spirit and events of the Old West.

Marching in the Desert, 1888, from *A Scout With the Buffalo Soldiers.*

Frederic Remington created art that provides a clear and accurate record of a time in America's past. His drawings, paintings, and sculptures capture some of the spirit and events of the Old West, and they delighted people who lived the frontier life as well as those who only dreamed of it. We certainly would not consider Remington a historian; he was an artist. Yet his works teach us about the past just as old newspapers and artifacts do.

Remington, who grew up in New York, made his first trip to the West in 1881, when he was nineteen years old. By that time, many parts of the Wild West had long been tamed and settled. This came as a surprise to the young man whose images of the West included huge herds of buffalo on the open

TWO ARTISTS OF THE OLD WEST

by Elisabeth Godolphin

Frederic Remington   *Charles Russell*

In the days when much of America was still unsettled prairies and open plains, the American public was fascinated with the western frontier. Two artists — Frederic Remington and Charles Russell — were particularly enchanted by the West. Remington and Russell lived during the same time, saw similar sights, and often painted the same subjects. But the two men viewed the West, and painted it, very differently.

Remington, like many people of his day, believed that it was the United States' destiny to rule the lands once held by the American Indians. This attitude affected the way he portrayed the cowboys, Indians, and soldiers in his paintings. In addition, although Remington loved the West, he had grown up in the East. This made his view of western life different from that of a true westerner.

During his travels as a young man, Remington realized that the Old West would someday disappear, and he began to "record the facts." He journeyed all over the West with the U.S. Army, from Oregon to the dry Southwest. Along the way, he set up his easel and painted, hoping to preserve the Wild West in pictures that "civilized" society could understand and enjoy.

Russell was born into a Missouri farm family in 1864. A poor student but a good rider, he traveled to Montana when he was sixteen. Two years later, he found work as a cowboy, living the cowboy life for eleven years. He lodged with Indians for a time and painted or sketched whenever he could.

By the end of his career as a cowboy, Russell was well-known for his art, especially in Montana. He settled in Great Falls, where he spent most of the rest of his life painting, drawing, and writing stories. Russell painted from his experience as a cowboy and a resident of the frontier. His art revealed his love of the West.

Many people cannot tell a Remington painting from a Russell without looking at the signature. It is easy to understand why. Both men portrayed some of the same subjects, and both painted their subjects to look realistic. These two great painters also were alike in how hard they worked on their paintings. Each tried to make his paintings as accurate as possible, paying attention to details such as the color of the beads in an Indian's necklace.

But Remington and Russell differed from each other in important ways. Russell painted because he loved to paint and doing so was fun. In later years, he was able to make a living from painting. Remington loved painting, too, but he had a goal that Russell did not share: to make great art out of western subjects and, in the process, to record a way of life that he saw fading.

Many art critics think that Remington's paintings are clearer and less cluttered than Russell's. Remington's sculptures are considered more precise and artistic. A closer look at how the two artists treated one of their favorite subjects — cowboys — sheds light on their differences as painters and as observers of the Wild West.

In 1907, Russell did a painting he called *A Quiet Day in Utica*. The scene is anything but quiet. The canvas is full of action — a dog gallops, horses buck, chickens squawk, and cowpokes laugh. Dust covers much of the foreground.

Russell's cowboys are not noble heroes who demand our admiration. Instead, they are rowdy, slightly reckless, ordinary human beings. Russell took great pride in having been a cowboy and held that occupation and the old-time cowboy in high regard. He painted many of his cowboy friends into his works.

Remington's *The Cowboy* (1902) also shows action and drama, but all attention is focused on the rider and horse. The horse's muscles are precisely drawn and colored, as is the cowboy's balancing hand. Remington's rider is handsome and heroic. Even though the horse looks as if it might fall, the cowboy is relaxed and in control.

These two examples show how Russell and Remington achieved noticeably different results. Russell portrayed a lively, accurate scene of everyday life; Remington recorded for history a noble hero from the vanishing Old West.

plains and tribes of proud, free Indians. Remington's disappointment when he discovered that the frontier was vanishing led him to make a decision that influenced the rest of his life: He would attempt, through his art, to create a record of the way of life that was dying out in the Old West.

The fact that Remington was taking on such an important task did not make his work immediately successful. During the years that followed his first trip west, he often had to struggle to stay out of debt. He made money by selling drawings and articles about western life to magazines and newspapers. But he also lost money in several businesses, including a sheep ranch and a saloon.

By the late 1800s, Remington's drawings and articles were in demand. His work was popular because many people in the East were fascinated with the western frontier, and his work gave them a glimpse of it. By far, most of Remington's works show men of the Old West in action-packed situations. Some of his works feature women and quieter scenes, but his most famous works show rugged men during the liveliest and tensest moments of western life.

After the turn of the century, Remington could no longer go to the Old West to study his subjects. The Old West had vanished. Remington then began to paint from memory and experience. His paintings continued to be accurate in portraying scenes and events from the Old West, but they also began to take on a different look. Details of rugged frontier life appeared less often, and the men began to look somewhat mysterious and even more heroic than in earlier paintings. These changes indicated Remington's move toward a painting style known as impressionism.

Does such a change mean that Remington was tampering with history by no longer showing his subjects in a way that was truly accurate? Not necessarily. As time passes and the world changes, people tend to see things differently. This helps to explain why artists change the way they portray their subjects, and why people today might view certain historical events differently than people of the past.

Remington died in 1909 at the age of forty-eight, but his art, and the history it provides, lives on.

'THE WILD RIDERS AND THE VACANT LAND'

by Robert S. Fay

Frederic Remington was born on October 4, 1861, in upstate New York. As a boy, he developed a taste for travel and adventure and enjoyed activities such as hunting, fishing, swimming, and canoeing. His father, Seth, was an active person. Soon after Fred's birth, Seth volunteered for the Union army. When he returned home from the Civil War, he brought with him vivid accounts of the land to the west and tales of military adventure. These stories stirred young Fred's imagination and contributed to his lifelong interest in these topics. Seth also fostered in his son a fascination with horses.

Fred loved to draw. His favorite subjects were Indians, soldiers, and horses. When he was eight, he painted two watercolor scenes from the Civil War. Both seemed to reflect his father's storytelling.

In 1876, Fred's parents sent him to Highland Military Academy in Massachusetts. Two years later, he enrolled in the School of Fine Arts at Yale. His first published illustration appeared within three months of his arrival at Yale. In 1879, he decided to quit Yale, and less than two years later, he traveled to the land of his dreams — the American West. His first stop was Montana, where he met an old wagon driver. One evening, the driver explained how he had seen the western frontier growing smaller and smaller through the years. Remington later recalled his thoughts at that moment: "I knew the railroad was coming — I saw men already swarming into the land.... I knew the wild riders and the vacant land were about to vanish forever.... Without knowing exactly how to do it, I began to try to record some facts around me, and the more I looked the more the panorama unfolded."

Remington had a purpose in life: to record the Old West for future generations. The view that Americans today have of the Old West is largely a result of his work.

RESOURCES

These resources are geared to the eight- to fourteen-year-old unless otherwise indicated.

BOOKS

General

Archer, Jules. *A House Divided: The Lives of Ulysses S. Grant and Robert E. Lee.* Scholastic, 1995. This book documents the lives of the two Civil War generals who led opposing armies but showed respect and admiration for each other.

Batty, Peter, and Peter Parish. *The Divided Union: The Story of the Great American War, 1861–1865.* Salem House, 1987. The companion book to the Arts and Entertainment television series on the Civil War. Illustrated with more than two hundred color and black-and-white photographs. For older readers.

Bolotin, Norman, and Angela Herb. *For Home and Country: A Civil War Scrapbook.* Lodestar, 1995. An overview of the war.

Climo, Shirley. *A Month of Seven Days.* HarperCollins, 1987. A southern girl tries to save her family from a Yankee captain who uses their home for his headquarters.

Donahue, John. *An Island Far From Home.* Carolrhoda, 1994. The twelve-year-old son of a Union army doctor corresponds with a fourteen-year-old Confederate soldier imprisoned at George's Island, Massachusetts, and learns about the tragedies of war.

Donald, David Herbert. *Lincoln.* Simon & Schuster, 1995. This book traces Abraham Lincoln's career as a lawyer, politician, statesman, husband, father, and commander. For older readers.

Dorf, Philip. *Highlights and Sidelights of the Civil War.* Southfarm, 1994. A collection of stories, anecdotes, and incidents of the war.

Harwell, Richard B., ed. *The Confederate Reader: How the South Saw the War.* Dover, 1989. This anthology of documents offers a glimpse of life in the South from newspaper accounts of the initial attack on Fort Sumter to an address by Jefferson Davis in 1864. For older readers.

Hastings, William H., ed. *Letters From a Sharpshooter.* Historic Publications, 1993. A collection of letters written to and by seventeen-year-old private "Willie" Greene as he tries to get out of "the biggest mistake of his life" but ends up between the lines, in the very center of the Civil War.

Hunt, Irene. *Across Five Aprils.* Silver Burdett, 1984. The war tears a family and a community apart.

Kassem, Lou. *Listen for Rachel.* Avon, 1986. A young girl from Tennessee finds her life changed during the Civil War.

Kent, Zachary. *The Civil War: "A House Divided."* Enslow, 1994. This book discusses the war and Reconstruction.

Lyman, Darryl. *Civil War Quotations: Including Slogans, Battle Cries, and Speeches.* Combined Books, 1995. The Civil War's most memorable sayings are collected in this book.

Lyon, George Ella. *Cecil's Story.* Orchard, 1991. The story of a young boy left behind while his father serves as a soldier in the Civil War.

Marrin, Albert. *Unconditional Surrender: U.S. Grant and the Civil War.* Atheneum/Simon & Schuster, 1994. A portrait of the Union general who went on to become president.

Marrin, Albert. *Virginia's General: Robert E. Lee and the Civil War.* Atheneum/Simon & Schuster, 1994. A biography that presents the personal and wartime view of one of the important generals.

Meltzer, Milton. *Voices From the Civil War: A Documentary History of the Great American Conflict.* HarperCollins, 1989. Materials from primary and secondary sources are linked by the author's commentary.

Murphy, Jim. *The Boys' War: Confederate and Union Soldiers Talk About the Civil War.* Clarion, 1990. Using diaries, letters, journals, and photographs, this book explores the role of underage boys who fought in the war.

Nixon, Joan Lowery. *A Dangerous Promise.* Delacorte, 1994. Two orphans run away to become Union army drummer boys.

Nixon, Joan Lowery. *Keeping Secrets.* Delacorte, 1995. This book is part of the "Orphan Train Adventures" series about the Kelly family in the 1800s.

O'Dell, Scott. *The Two Hundred Ninety.* Houghton Mifflin, 1976. A young boy becomes a crewman aboard the Confederate ship *Alabama.*

Poe, Clarence, ed. *True Tales of the South at War: How Soldiers Fought and Families Lived, 1861–1865.* Dover, 1995. This anthology re-creates life in the South during the war with primary documents, including letters, diary entries, and commentaries by children. For older readers.

Ray, Delia. *Behind the Blue and Gray: The Soldier's Life in the Civil War.* Lodestar, 1991. This book portrays the everyday life of the common soldier with more than fifty early photographs of soldiers at work and play.

Ray, Delia. *A Nation Torn: The Story of How the Civil War Began.* Lodestar, 1990. Vintage photographs and prints enhance this account of the issues and events that led to the war.

Robertson, James I., Jr. *Civil War! America Becomes One Nation.* Knopf, 1992. An overview that explores the major battles, military leaders, and effects of the war on the country.

Sandler, Martin W. *Civil War.* HarperCollins, 1995. More than one hundred photographs and prints from the Library of Congress bring the Civil War to life.

Smith, Carter. *Prelude to War.* Millbrook, 1993. The events leading up to the Civil War are documented with reproductions of photographs and prints.

Wisler, G. Clifton. *Mr. Lincoln's Drummer.* Lodestar, 1994. The story of eleven-year-old Willie Johnston, who became a drummer boy and was the youngest person to receive the Medal of Honor.

Young, Robert. *The Emancipation Proclamation: Why Lincoln Really Freed the Slaves.* Dillon, 1995. This book suggests military, political, and moral reasons for Lincoln's Emancipation Proclamation.

Battles

Beatty, Patricia. *Charley Skedaddle.* Morrow, 1987. A Union drummer boy rethinks his ideas about the glory of war.

Beller, Susan Provost. *To Hold This Ground: A Desperate Battle at Gettysburg.* McElderry, 1995. The many smaller battles within the larger Battle of Gettysburg are explored.

Fleischman, Paul. *Bull Run.* HarperCollins, 1993. This historical novel consists of vignettes focusing on the lives and thoughts of sixteen people who participated in the Civil War.

Fleming, Thomas. *Band of Brothers: West Point in the Civil War.* Walker, 1988. A fictionalized portrait of several West Point graduates and their roles in the war.

Fritz, Jean. *Just a Few Words, Mr. Lincoln: The Story of the Gettysburg Address.* Putnam, 1993. A close-up study of Abraham Lincoln's Gettysburg Address and his family life. For younger readers.

Fritz, Jean. *Stonewall.* Putnam, 1979. This biography documents Thomas "Stonewall" Jackson's military career.

Gauch, Patricia Lee. *Thunder at Gettysburg.* Putnam, 1990. A fictionalized account of the battle through the eyes of a young girl who is inadvertently drawn into the war.

Haskins, Jim. *The Day Fort Sumter Was Fired On: A Photo History of the Civil War.* Scholastic, 1995. This book traces the course of the war from Bull Run to Robert E. Lee's eventual surrender at Appomattox Court House, Virginia.

Johnson, Neil. *The Battle of Gettysburg.* Four Winds, 1989. An account of the reenactment of the Battle of Gettysburg that brought together fourteen thousand people in 1988.

Keith, Harold. *Rifles for Watie.* HarperCollins, 1957. This Newbery Medal book tells the story of a young boy's wartime experiences.

Lincoln, Abraham. *The Gettysburg Address.* Houghton Mifflin, 1995. Lincoln's famous words are illustrated in black-and-white drawings by Michael McCurdy.

Murphy, Jim. *The Long Road to Gettysburg.* Clarion, 1992. The Battle of Gettysburg from the points of view of two young soldiers.

Perez, N.A. *The Slopes of War.* Houghton Mifflin, 1984. A young soldier from West Virginia fights against his relatives in the Battle of Gettysburg.

Tracey, Patrick Austin. *Military Leaders of the Civil War.* Facts On File, 1993. This collection recounts the lives and achievements of eight commanders from the Union and the Confederacy.

Reconstruction

Beatty, Patricia. *Be Ever Hopeful, Hannalee.* Morrow, 1988. A southern working-class family begins to rebuild after the war.

Calvert, Patricia. *Bigger.* Scribner, 1994. The story of a young boy's search for his father at the end of the war.

Cox, Clinton. *The Forgotten Heroes: The Story of the Buffalo Soldiers.* Scholastic, 1993. How these African Americans helped open the West.

Hakim, Joy. *A History of Us: Reconstruction and Reform.* Oxford University, 1994. One volume in a series that explores the history of America.

Lyons, Mary E. *Stitching Stars: The Story Quilts of Harriet Powers.* Scribner, 1993. A story quilt serves as a diary of the spiritual life of a former slave in 1886.

Mettger, Zak. *Reconstruction: America After the Civil War.* Lodestar, 1994. A chronicle of how the country began to rebuild.

Reeder, Carolyn. *Shades of Gray.* Macmillan, 1989. A young boy comes to terms with his uncle's choice to be a conscientious objector.

Stalcup, Brenda, ed. *Reconstruction.* Greenhaven, 1995. This volume in the "Opposing Viewpoints" series details Reconstruction and the growing power of African Americans.

Civil War Sites

Davis, William C. *Civil War Parks: The Story Behind the Scenery.* KC Publications, 1995. This book covers twenty-six Civil War–related sites of the National Park Service.

Davis, William. *Gettysburg: The Story Behind the Scenery.* KC Publications, 1995. Learn how Gettysburg National Military Park developed and the history behind the bloody battle there.

Waldron, Larry. *Lincoln Parks: The Story Behind the Scenery.* KC Publications, 1995. This book explores the seven National Park Service sites honoring Abraham Lincoln.

African Americans

Armstrong, Jennifer. *Steal Away.* Orchard, 1992. A novel about the friendship between a Vermont child and her slave.

Banim, Lisa. *A Thief on Morgan's Plantation.* Silver Moon, 1995. As the Civil War begins, young Constance Morgan is sent south from Philadelphia to live with relatives she has never met. Soon after she arrives, she finds herself embroiled in a conflict in which a young slave is accused of stealing a family heirloom.

Beatty, Patricia. *Who Comes With Cannons?* Morrow, 1992. Truth is orphaned and sent to live with her uncle's family, who are part of the Underground Railroad.

Berry, James. *Ajeemah and His Sons.* HarperCollins, 1992. A novel that portrays the early slave trade in Jamaica.

Bial, Raymond. *The Underground Railroad.* Houghton Mifflin, 1995. A historic look at the Underground Railroad and some of the stories of slaves who escaped to the North. A map of the railroad and an antislavery chronology are included.

Blos, Joan. *A Gathering of Days: A New England Girl's Journal, 1830–1832*. Scribner, 1979. The diary of a young girl who befriends a runaway slave and struggles with her conscience.

Chu, Daniel, and Bill Shaw. *Going Home to Nicodemus: The Story of an African American Frontier Town and the Pioneers Who Settled It*. Julian Messner, 1994. The story of the first all–African American town on the Great Plains.

Collier, James Lincoln, and Christopher Collier. *With Every Drop of Blood*. Delacorte, 1994. An adventure story of an unlikely friendship that develops when a white Confederate soldier is captured by a band of African American Union soldiers.

Cooper, Michael L. *From Slave to Civil War Hero: The Life and Times of Robert Smalls*. Lodestar, 1994. Smalls fought for the Union, campaigned for equal rights, and was elected to the U.S. Congress.

Cox, Clinton. *Undying Glory*. Scholastic, 1993. The history of the Fifty-fourth Massachusetts Colored Infantry.

Everett, Gwen. *John Brown: One Man Against Slavery*. Rizzoli, 1993. This story is told from the point of view of Brown's daughter Annie.

Forrester, Sandra. *Sound the Jubilee*. Lodestar, 1995. The story of three hundred freed slaves who lived on Roanoke Island, North Carolina, during the Civil War.

Fox, Paula. *The Slave Dancer*. Macmillan, 1973. A white cabin boy recounts the horrifying details of life aboard a slave ship.

Fritz, Jean. *Brady*. Peter Smith, 1960. A novel about the Underground Railroad told by a young white boy who helps African American slaves move from one station to the next.

Fritz, Jean. *Harriet Beecher Stowe and the Beecher Preachers*. Putnam, 1994. A biography of the famous author of *Uncle Tom's Cabin*.

Goldman, Martin. *Nat Turner and the Southampton Revolt of 1831*. Watts, 1992. Explores Turner's early years as a slave and the bloody events of his 1831 revolt.

Hamilton, Virginia. *Anthony Burns: The Defeat and Triumph of a Fugitive Slave*. Knopf, 1988. An account of a runaway slave in 1854 Boston.

Hamilton, Virginia. *Many Thousand Gone: African Americans From Slavery to Freedom*. Knopf, 1993. A collection of original slave narratives that recount a courageous struggle for freedom.

Hansen, Joyce. *The Captive*. Scholastic, 1994. This story follows young Kofi from his years as a slave in Massachusetts to his later life of freedom.

Hansen, Joyce. *Which Way Freedom?* Walker, 1986. This novel describes the contributions of African American soldiers to the Union cause.

Haskins, Jim. *Get on Board: The Story of the Underground Railroad*. Scholastic, 1993. A comprehensive look at the Underground Railroad and the stories behind many journeys.

Hurmence, Belinda. *A Girl Called Boy*. Houghton Mifflin, 1982. A young African American girl is mysteriously transported to the mid-1800s and finds out firsthand the tragedies of slavery.

Katz, William Loren. *Breaking the Chains: Afro-American Slave Resistance*. Atheneum, 1990. This book documents the heroism of slaves before and during the Civil War.

King, Wilma. *Toward the Promised Land: From Uncle Tom's Cabin to the Onset of the Civil War*. Chelsea House, 1995. This book is part of the "Milestones in Black American History" series.

Lester, Julius. *Long Journey Home: Stories From Black History*. Dial, 1993. A collection of stories about African American slaves.

Lyons, Mary E. *Letters From a Slave Girl: The Story of Harriet Jacobs*. Scribner, 1992. This novel is told through Jacobs's letters describing her life in slavery and her dreams of freedom.

McFeely, William S. *Sapelo's People: A Long Walk Into Freedom*. Norton, 1995. A sensitive portrait of the journey from slavery to freedom of the people of this island. For older readers.

Meltzer, Milton. *All Times, All Peoples: A World History of Slavery*. HarperCollins, 1980. A history of slavery and attempts to explain its cause.

Meltzer, Milton. *The Black Americans: A History in Their Own Words*. HarperCollins, 1984. This collection of primary source documents gives an overview of the African American struggle before and after the Civil War.

Meltzer, Milton, ed. *Frederick Douglass: In His Own Words*. Harcourt Brace & Co., 1995. The Civil War as seen in Douglass's writings and speeches. For older readers.

Mettger, Zak. *Till Victory Is Won: Black Soldiers in the Civil War*. Lodestar, 1994. The story of the Fifty-fourth Massachusetts Colored Infantry and other brave African American regiments and individuals.

Petry, Ann. *Harriet Tubman: Conductor on the Underground Railroad*. HarperCollins, 1996. A portrait of one of the pioneers of the Underground Railroad.

Piggins, Carol Ann. *A Multicultural Portrait of the Civil War*. Marshall Cavendish, 1993. African Americans, immigrants, and Native Americans discuss the causes of the war and their lives.

Polacco, Patricia. *Pink and Say*. Philomel, 1994. A heart-wrenching picture book for older readers about an African American Union soldier's rescue of a white comrade who was left for dead.

Robinet, Harriette Gillem. *If You Please, President Lincoln*. Atheneum, 1995. This historical novel documents a fourteen-year-old slave's journey to a small island off Haiti, where, instead of freedom, he finds he is part of a colonization project.

Rogers, James. *The Antislavery Movement*. Facts On File, 1994. A chronicle of the activism behind the antislavery and civil rights movements.

Schlissel, Lillian. *Black Frontiers: A History of African-American Heroes in the Old West*. Simon & Schuster, 1995. The story of African Americans who settled the West from 1865 to the early 1900s.

Washington, Booker T. *Up From Slavery: An Autobiography*. Airmont, 1965. The famous story of an eloquent former slave.

Yates, Elizabeth. *Amos Fortune, Free Man.* Dutton, 1967. A New-bery Medal book about a slave who was able to purchase his freedom and buy a small farm.

Native Americans

Cottrell, Steve. *Civil War in the Indian Territory.* Pelican, 1995. This book outlines the events that led to the involvement of Native Americans in the war and the effects of their participation.

Hauptman, Laurence M. *The Iroquois and the Civil War: From Battlefield to Reservation.* Syracuse University, 1992.

Women

Burchard, Peter. *Charlotte Forten: A Black Teacher in the Civil War.* Crown, 1995. This biography is based on the letters and diaries of Charlotte Forten, the daughter of prominent abolitionists.

Chang, Ina. *A Separate Battle: Women and the Civil War.* Lodestar, 1991. Brief biographies of Angelina Grimké, Sojourner Truth, Harriet Tubman, Louisa May Alcott, and Mary Chesnut, with a discussion of women's roles in the war.

Collins, David R. *Shattered Dreams: The Story of Mary Todd Lincoln.* Morgan Reynolds, 1994. The tragedies of Mary Lincoln's life unfold in this biography.

Colman, Penny. *Spies! Women in the Civil War.* Shoe Tree, 1992. A collection of brief sketches of Belle Boyd, Rose O'Neal Greenhow, and other women spies.

Hamilton, Leni. *Clara Barton.* Chelsea House, 1988. This biography documents Barton's early days setting up supply camps during the Civil War and her involvement in the American Red Cross.

Houston, Gloria. *Mountain Valor.* Philomel, 1994. This story is based on the life of Matilda Houston, one of the author's ancestors, who masqueraded as a boy to protect her family's farm in Appalachia.

Lyon, George Ella. *Here and Then.* Orchard/Jackson, 1994. A realistic novel about a girl who takes part in a Civil War reenactment and discovers the plight of Eliza Hoskins, a nurse during the war.

Ray, Delia. *A Separate Battle: Women in the Civil War.* Lodestar, 1991. Details women's experiences during the war as slaves, abolitionists, women's rights leaders, teachers, and refugees.

Reilly, Wayne E., ed. *Sarah Jane Foster: Teacher of the Freedmen. A Diary and Letters.* University Press of Virginia, 1990.

Reit, Seymour. *Behind Rebel Lines: The Incredible Story of Emma Edmonds, Civil War Spy.* Harcourt Brace & Co., 1988. The fictionalized biography of a feminist patriot who posed as a Confederate soldier to spy on the Union army.

Rutberg, Becky. *Mary Lincoln's Dressmaker.* Walker, 1995. This biography weaves together the life stories of Mary Todd Lincoln and Elizabeth Hobbs Keckley and their remarkable friendship. For older readers.

Shura, Mary Francis. *Gentle Annie: The True Story of a Civil War Nurse.* Scholastic, 1991. The fictionalized biography of a nurse on the front lines.

Zeinert, Karen. *Elizabeth Van Lew: Southern Belle, Union Spy.* Dillon, 1995. This biography is part of the "People in Focus" series.

The Arts

Alcott, Louisa May. *Little Women.* Little, Brown, 1968. This novel was originally published in 1868 and portrays the sacrifices a family made during the war.

Currie, Stephen. *Music in the Civil War.* Shoe Tree, 1992. A collection of sheet music, etchings, and historical references to composers, musicians, and drummers of the Civil War.

Reef, Catherine. *Walt Whitman.* Clarion, 1995. A biography of one of America's great poets. Whitman was an activist and nurse in the Civil War and wrote about the enormous suffering the war caused.

Stowe, Harriet Beecher. *Uncle Tom's Cabin.* Penguin Classics, 1981.

Photography

Barnard, George. *Photographic Views of Sherman's Campaign.* Dover, 1977.

Freedman, Russell. *Lincoln: A Photobiography.* Clarion, 1987. This photo history covers Abraham Lincoln from boyhood through the presidential years.

Gardner, Alexander. *Gardner's Photographic Sketch Book of the Civil War.* Dover, 1959.

Hamilton, Charles, and Lloyd Ostendorf. *Lincoln in Photographs: An Album of Every Known Pose.* Rev. ed. Morningside, 1996. The most complete collection of Abraham Lincoln's photos.

Russell, Andrew. *Russell's Civil War Photographs.* Dover, 1982.

Sullivan, George. *Matthew Brady, His Life and Photographs.* Cobblehill/Dutton, 1994. This biography of Civil War photographer Mathew Brady documents his technical skill alongside reproductions of his famous portraits of the war's leaders.

DISCOVERY ENTERPRISES

Discovery Enterprises, Ltd., publishes educational materials for students and teachers in grades 3 to 12. The "Perspectives on History Series" focuses on specific periods in American history and includes concise anthologies of primary source documents on each subject, with an overview of the period by the editor. Civil War era titles include *Women in the Civil War: Warriors, Patriots, Nurses, and Spies; Westward Expansion: Exploration and Settlement; The Underground Railroad: Life on the Road to Freedom; Forward Into Light: The Struggle for Woman's Suffrage; Iron Horses Across America: The Transcontinental Railroad; Reconstruction: Binding the Wounds.* These books, available singly or in sets, link American history with classic literature on the subject. Also popular from Discovery Enterprises are original plays for upper-elementary and middle school students, biographies, and curriculum materials for educators. For information or a catalog, contact Discovery Enterprises, Ltd., 31 Laurelwood Drive, Carlisle, MA 01741 (1-800-729-1720).

JOURNALS

The American History Herald. Steck-Vaughn Co., 8701 North MoPac, Austin, TX 78759.

America's Civil War. Cowles History Group, Inc., 741 Miller Drive SE, Suite D-2, Leesburg, VA 22075.

The Children's Chronicle. P.O. Box 1601, Plainville, MA 02762. A newsletter designed to help children understand American history during the 1860s.

The Civil War News. Route 1 Box 36, Tunbridge, VT 05077.

Civil War Times. P.O. Box 8200, Harrisburg, PA 17105-8200.

Prologue: Quarterly of the National Archives. National Archives, Washington, DC 20408. This magazine brings attention to the resources and programs of the National Archives, the regional archives, and the presidential libraries.

TEACHER RESOURCES

The Battle of First Manassas. Teaching With Historic Places. The Preservation Press, National Trust for Historic Preservation, 1785 Massachusetts Avenue NW, Washington, DC 20036. Study personal accounts of soldiers who fought in the first battle of the Civil War and discover how the day set the tone for the many bloody battles to come.

Civil War Cards. Atlas Editions, 33 Houston Drive, Durham, CT 06422. This collection of color-coded index cards documents the war from the beginning of the antislavery movement through Reconstruction.

The Civil War (Jackdaw No. 106) compiled by David Johnson. Jackdaw Publications/Golden Owl Publishing, P.O. Box A03, Amawalk, NY 10501. Replicas of primary source documents, including letters, recruiting notices, and newspaper articles, for classroom use.

The Civil War: Literature Units, Projects, and Activities by Janey Cassidy. Scholastic Professional Books, Scholastic Inc., 555 Broadway, New York, NY 10012-3999.

Civil War Teaching Resource Kit. Museum of American Financial History, 26 Broadway, New York, NY 10004. This multimedia kit focuses on the financial roots of the Civil War. It includes a syllabus of financial events following the conflict and twenty color slides featuring rare items from the original exhibit at the Museum of American Financial History.

Lincoln Life Lincoln-Douglas Debates. National Forensic League, P.O. Box 38, Ripon, WI 54971. High school students debate significant moral and value issues facing society.

Teaching Guide to TAD, Life in the White House During the Civil War. The Family Channel, CIC Dept., P.O. Box 2050, Virginia Beach, VA 23450-2050.

Woman Suffrage Illustrated Timeline. National Women's History Project, 7738 Bell Road, Windsor, CA 95492. The history of the woman suffrage movement is depicted in a dramatic and informative eight-panel display set.

CD-ROMs

The African American Experience CD-ROM. Primary Source Media, Woodbridge, CT 06525. Provides students with insight into the culture and history of African Americans from the beginning of the American slave trade to the Anita Hill hearings.

The Civil War. Primary Source Media, Woodbridge, CT 06525. Offers primary documents and images from 1820 to 1877, with a full examination of the war itself, its causes and repercussions, and Reconstruction.

Civil War: A Nation Divided. Softkey International, 1 Athenaeum Street, Cambridge, MA 02142. A reference tool with a multimedia time line from 1861 to 1866 that puts the war in perspective.

The Civil War: A Newspaper Perspective CD-ROM. Accessible Archives, Inc., 697 Sugartown Road, Malvern, PA 19355. This database contains the full text of major articles from more than twenty-five hundred issues of the *New York Herald, Charleston Mercury,* and *Richmond Enquirer* published between November 1, 1860, and April 30, 1865.

The Civil War CD-ROM. Empire Interactive, United CD-ROM, P.O. Box 159, Savoy, IL 61874. This CD-ROM allows you to plan and fight every major battle and campaign of the war.

Gettysburg Multimedia Battle Simulation. Swifte International, P.O. Box 144586, Coral Gables, FL 33114-4506. This simulation gives you a view of the action from the perspective of a field commander. Background on the battle is available, including clips from the documentary film and Lincoln's Gettysburg Address.

A House Divided: The Lincoln-Douglas Debates and Teacher's Guide. Grafica Multimedia, Inc., 940 Emmett Avenue, Suite 11, Belmont, CA 94002. Weaves together video reenactments, photos, music, illustrations, and political cartoons.

ON THE INTERNET

The Letters of Captain Richard W. Burt. http://www.infinet.com/~1stevens/burt/. This collection of letters presents a view of life in the field with Burt's patriotic war songs and poems

The National Civil War Association. http://ncwa.org/. A northern California nonprofit organization committed to educating the public about the Civil War. The group publishes a schedule of events around the country for the upcoming year.

The United States Civil War Center. http://www.cwc.lsu.edu. The center was created to facilitate the construction of archival databases of Civil War material and to promote the study of the war using a multiperspective approach. The web site currently receives four thousand "hits" a day (internationally) and is linked to more than eight hundred Civil War–related sites.

VIDEOS

Addresses for video sources are as follows: Acorn Media, 7910 Woodmont Avenue, Suite 350, Bethesda, MD 20814. Mastervision, 969 Park Avenue, New York, NY 10028. PBS Video, 1320 Braddock Place, Alexandria, VA 22314.

The Civil War. Florentine Films (see PBS), Walpole, New Hampshire, and WETA, Washington, D.C., 1990. This nine-part series by Ken Burns chronicles the war. Includes teacher's guide.

Civil War: The Fiery Trial. Acorn, 1988.

The Civil War Educator's Enhanced PBS Video Disc. PBS, 1994. A fully integrated teaching tool that includes a teacher's planning book, lesson plans, and a shortened version of Ken Burns's film *The Civil War* on videocassette.

Frederick Douglass: When the Lion Wrote History. PBS, 1994. An in-depth look at the life of one of America's most influential men.

Ironclads: The Monitor and the Merrimac. Acorn, 1988.

The Massachusetts 54th Colored Infantry. PBS, 1991. Relive the story of this African American regiment. Includes teacher's guide.

One Woman, One Vote. PBS, 1995. Follow the woman suffrage movement from the Seneca Falls convention in 1848 to the passage of the Nineteenth Amendment in 1920. Includes teacher's guide.

Robert E. Lee: Civil War Generals. Acorn, 1989.

Roots of Resistance — A Story of the Underground Railroad. PBS, 1989. Travel the secret Underground Railroad used by escaped slaves in the mid-1800s. Includes teacher's guide.

Smithsonian's Great Battles of the Civil War. Mastervision, 1994. This seven-volume video series puts you on the battlefield for a look at the military, political, and social history of the Civil War.

Ulysses S. Grant: Civil War Generals. Acorn, 1989.

PLACES TO VISIT

The Abraham Lincoln Museum, Lincoln Memorial University, Harrogate, Tennessee. This museum has one of the largest collections of Lincoln memorabilia, manuscripts, and books.

Appomattox Court House National Historical Park, Virginia. Restored village where Generals Lee and Grant met on April 9, 1865. Highlights include the reconstructed McLean House, where the generals signed the surrender papers, and Surrender Triangle, where the Confederates stacked their arms three days later.

Arlington House, The Robert E. Lee Memorial, Arlington National Cemetery, Arlington, Virginia. The home of General Robert E. Lee has been restored to its appearance in 1861.

Black History Museum and Cultural Center of Virginia, Richmond, Virginia. Virginia's African American history and culture are documented with artifacts, limited editions, prints, artwork, and photographs.

Chickamauga and Chattanooga National Military Park, Fort Oglethorpe, Georgia; *Lookout Mountain,* Lookout Mountain, Tennessee. The nation's first and largest national military park commemorates the Civil War battles that were fought in the Chattanooga area during the fall of 1863.

Confederate Museum, New Orleans, Louisiana. A military museum housed in Memorial Hall includes some of the personal effects of Jefferson Davis, Robert E. Lee, and other Civil War leaders.

Ford's Theatre, Washington, D.C. An extensive collection of items relating to Abraham Lincoln's life and death is on display.

Fort Sumter National Monument, Sullivan's Island, South Carolina. Visit the ruins of the fort and a museum that includes a model of the fort as it looked in 1861.

General Grant National Memorial, New York, New York. Also known as Grant's Tomb, this is the burial site of Ulysses and Julia Grant. The memorial houses Grant memorabilia, exhibit rooms, and a library.

Gettysburg National Military Park, Gettysburg, Pennsylvania. Preserved site of the war's most famous battle.

Harpers Ferry National Historic Park, Harpers Ferry, West Virginia. The park includes John Brown's "fort," a reconstructed village, and the Robert Harper home.

Hollywood Cemetery, Richmond, Virginia. Burial site of famous historical figures such as Presidents James Monroe and John Tyler, Jefferson Davis, and J.E.B. Stuart. Eighteen thousand Confederate soldiers are buried here.

Lee's Retreat: From Petersburg to Appomattox, The Final Days of the Civil War, Petersburg to Appomattox, Virginia. This twenty-stop driving tour through six counties follows the route of General Lee's retreat at the end of the Civil War.

Lincoln Home, Springfield, Illinois. The only home America's six-teenth president ever owned. Other Lincoln sites to visit in Springfield include *Lincoln Tomb,* Oak Ridge Cemetery; *Lincoln's New Salem,* a reconstructed historic village in the town where Lincoln lived from 1831 to 1837; and *Old State Capitol,* Downtown Mall, where an original copy of the Gettysburg Address is on display.

Lincoln Museum, Fort Wayne, Indiana. This museum displays one of the world's largest collections of Lincoln memorabilia, including thousands of books, documents, and photographs.

Museum of the Confederacy, Richmond, Virginia. An extensive collection of Confederate memorabilia, including the uniform and sword worn by Robert E. Lee for his surrender at Appomattox Court House. Contact the museum for information about Civil War Day Camps.

Petersburg National Battlefield, Petersburg, Virginia. Includes driving tours of the siege lines, walking tours at significant locations, and a visitors center.

Richmond National Battlefield Park, Richmond, Virginia. The National Park Service commemorates several Civil War battles of the 1862 Peninsular Campaign and the 1864 Richmond-Petersburg Campaign.

Shiloh National Military Park and Cemetery, Shiloh, Tennessee. The best-preserved Civil War battlefield includes a museum, two hundred artillery pieces, and one hundred fifty monuments of the Battle of Shiloh.

The United States Civil War Center, Louisiana State University, Baton Rouge, Louisiana. The center houses a number of original Edwin Forbes etchings from his *Life of the Great Army,* as well as a library focusing on unique works of the Civil War, including subjects such as medicine, sports, and religion explored through poetry, drama, children's fiction, and other sources.

U.S. Grant Home State Historic Site, Galena, Illinois. This memorial to Grant has been restored to its appearance in the 1870s.

Vicksburg National Military Park, Vicksburg, Mississippi. This park has a sixteen-mile tour road through Union and Confederate battle lines and the largest Civil War cemetery in existence.

Virginia Historical Society, Richmond, Virginia. Dramatic Civil War murals and a comprehensive collection of Virginia history.

The White House of the Confederacy, Richmond, Virginia. Home to Confederate president Jefferson Davis.

Index